Anthropology of Contemporary Issues

A SERIES EDITED BY

ROGER SANJEK

Renunciation and Reformulation

A STUDY OF CONVERSION IN AN AMERICAN SECT

Harriet Whitehead

Cornell University Press

Ithaca and London

First published 1987 by Cornell University Press.

International Standard Book Number 0-8014-1849-6
Library of Congress Catalog Card Number 86-16211
Printed in the United States of America
_Librarians: Library of Congress cataloging information
appears on the last page of the book._

_The paper in this book is acid-free and meets the guidelines
for permanence and durability of the Committee on Production
Guidelines for Book Longevity of the Council on Library Resources._

To my mother and father

Contents

Preface

This book examines the psychology of conversion from the perspective of symbolic anthropology. In it I attempt to integrate the insights of anthropologists who write about the psychological efficacy of ritual and religious symbolism with the insights of those, such as William James, who have given us our finest portraits of religious experience. As a bridge between the two discourses, I have relied upon Piaget's structuralist psychology. This theoretical integration of symbolic studies, structuralist psychology, and portraits of religious experience is the primary purpose of this book.

A secondary purpose cannot be entirely disentangled from the primary one. This is the drawing of an ethnographic portrait of the beliefs and conversionary techniques of the Church of Scientology, the sect I researched as my principal example. A few words on this example are in order. On January 22, 1986, just two days after I had sent the manuscript of this book to the publisher, I learned of the death of L. Ron Hubbard, the founder of Scientology. As is usually the case with the passing of founders, Hubbard's death will undoubtedly mark the end of an era for the sect he brought into being. It will also appear to give a certain timeliness to any book about the sect, and potential publications on the subject have probably been waiting in the wings for this occasion. This book is not one of them, however, and I wish to emphasize that Hubbard's death is entirely coincidental to the timing of its appearance. My research was conducted some fifteen years ago and the account of Scientology included here, although updated sometimes for clarity, cannot be taken overall to represent a portrait of contemporary Scientology belief or practice.

A fair amount of ethnographic detail is included, for two reasons. First, this material is both a context for and an illustration of the conversionary processes addressed in my theoretical argument. Indeed, the particular fusion of mystical and psychotherapeutic claims and the characteristic emphasis on spiritual "technology" found in Scientology were primary in leading me to some of the key theoretical integrations I have attempted here. Second, if unfamiliar cultural systems are not substantially portrayed, they are easily reduced to silly stereotypes from which no generalizations of real interest can derive. Ethnographic richness renders a system credible and fully imaginable to readers not personally acquainted with it, or acquainted with it primarily through trivializing media accounts. In turn, only a fair degree of credibility and imaginability enables us to perceive that the processes at work in the unfamiliar system might also be at work in familiar ones.

Yet this anthropological mandate to render credible and fully imaginable is not without its pitfalls. Those who are acquainted with the Church of Scientology, through whatever route, will know how controversial the sect has been throughout its history and will no doubt read the present account with an ear for my position in the debates the Church has stirred. They will probably be disappointed. Readers of earlier drafts who might be taken to stand for the interests of the Church and readers who might be taken to represent the views of the disillusioned have both expressed some dissatisfaction with the account—the one for my presuming to categorize Scientology and for inclusion of some less than flattering perspectives (or material conducive to such), the other for my taking the sect and its psychotherapeutic claims seriously. I would argue that it is the essence and the nature of an anthropological account of a subject to take that subject seriously, to convey various perspectives on it, and to attempt for the sake of theory to categorize it. That is what I have tried to do.

The research for this book was conducted in the United States and the United Kingdom primarily between 1969 and 1971 under an anthropological field-training grant from the National Institutes of Mental Health. I am indebted to many people for encouragement and intellectual assistance during that period and during the numerous write-ups and revisions that followed. Chief among these are David M. Schneider and Sherry B. Ortner, whose moral and intellectual support over the years has more than once helped to rescue this project from oblivion. Clifford Geertz and Walter Lippincott, Jr., are also greatly to be thanked for sustaining their enthusiasm for the manuscript through various publishing vicissitudes. I owe a special debt to Terence Turner, who introduced me to Piagetian psychology, and to Lynn Eden for a crucial round of editorial comments. Other colleagues who have given me useful readings include Jane Atkinson, Susan Harding, John Leavitt, Ellen Lewin, Bridget O'Laughlin, Lois Paul, Michelle Rosaldo, and Renato Rosaldo. For assistance in the understanding of the E-Meter, I am indebted to Michael Bazaral, William Rickles, Michael Cohen, and Karen Macintyre.

Finally, without the warmth, interest, and personal guidance of those persons pseudonymously disguised as "informants" in the text to follow, the elaboration of my central example, Scientology, would never have been possible. While expressing my sincere gratitude to them, I wish at the same time to dissociate them entirely from any errors I may have committed in the presentation of Scientology materials and from the interpretive framework into which I have cast Scientology practice.

HARRIET WHITEHEAD

Renunciation and Reformulation

Introduction

The present work is concerned with a problem that rose to the forefront of cultural anthropological interest sometime during the 1960s and has lingered there since. I will call it the problem of symbolic efficacy. Numerous writers who have dealt with the ritual and expressive dimension of culture, among them Clifford Geertz, Victor Turner, Terence Turner, Nancy Munn, and Godfrey Lienhardt, have stressed the idea that cultural complexes that appear to be primarily "symbolic" rather than utilitarian in their purpose—most notably myth, rites, and ceremonies—must be understood in terms of the psychological effects they are in some sense designed to produce. The effects that theorists ascribe to symbolic presentations and performances are various. The myth, rite, or magical manipulation may heighten social solidarity and reorient participants to the norms of the group; it may inspire or renew belief in a particular religious cosmology; it may help to resolve emotional and moral dilemmas; it may promote healing in the sick. Often it can be seen to accomplish several of these results simultaneously. Overall, those present or participating in such symbolic events emerge from them tuned up once again for the business of living, and living, of course, in a particular social and cultural universe.

The salient question is how are such effects achieved? In what way does a symbolic presentation work its psychological magic?

Claude Lévi-Strauss raised this question briefly, and supplied his own interesting answer, in an essay entitled "The Effectiveness of Symbols" (1963:186–205). He begins his discussion by singling out a South American Indian chant said to be used by the shaman to assist women experiencing difficult labor. Like many of the curing techniques of premodern medicine, this one is wholly magical. The shaman performs no manipulations of the patient's body; he dispenses no drug; he prescribes no regime for her to follow. He merely recites an incantation. Can such a procedure cure? Lévi-Strauss thinks that it can, given the nature of its imagery. The dramatis personae of the chant-narrative turn out to be thinly disguised representations of bodily parts, bodily processes, and sensations. These are first depicted in a state of disorder, matching the disorder within the woman's body; but as the chant unfolds, a reordering of the images slowly takes place until at the end a successful "symbolic" childbirth is portrayed. By capturing in concrete images the woman's previously inchoate experience, the chant gives her tools with which to reorganize this experience conceptually and thus to reorganize, indirectly, the somatic processes underlying it. So goes Lévi-Strauss's explanation of symbolic curing.

This sort of curing is not so out of fashion in the West as one might suppose, he points out to us. Something quite like it is to be found in psychoanalysis. The shaman's manipulation of bodily processes through the glossing of incoherent physical sensations is, he argues, paralleled in psychoanalysis by the patient's discovery of a vocabulary and imagery for his hitherto obscure emotions and impulses. In both cases, symbols provide access to inner states that may then be reordered by means of reordering the symbols. Even though at points Lévi-Strauss's structuralist language of oppositions and inversions puts a strain on the comparison, his basic line of thought is compelling, and it suggests that many of the familiar forms of modern psychotherapy might yield to the type of scrutiny that anthropologists have become used to directing at primitive rites and myths. I will return to this last point.

Overlapping Lévi-Strauss on certain points, but with no particular debt to him, Clifford Geertz placed the notion of symbolic efficacy in a much more ambitious context when in 1966 he published his seminal article on the anthropological study of religious systems, "Religion as a Cultural System." It is insufficient, Geertz argues, for anthropologists to continue "proving the indubitable"—that religious systems legitimate features of the social order, "reflect" dominant social forms, or facilitate life crises. Sooner or later we must come to grips with the question of how these legitimating, reflective, or facilitating symbolic

[16]

visions work their effects at the individual level. One aspect of this question is, quite simply, why is the religious vision *believed?*

> Just what does "belief" mean in a religious context? Of all the problems surrounding attempts to conduct anthropological analysis of religion this is the one that has perhaps been most troublesome and therefore the most often avoided, usually by relegating it to psychology, that raffish outcast discipline to which social anthropologists are forever consigning phenomena they are unable to deal with within the framework of a denatured Durkheimianism. But the problem will not go away, it is not "merely" psychological (nothing social is), and no anthropological theory of religion which fails to attack it is worthy of the name. We have been trying to stage Hamlet without the Prince quite long enough. [1972:109]

The question of belief can be approached in several ways, Geertz suggests. Belief is encouraged by the typical sources of religious authority: charismatic leadership, supersensible experience, and of course, tradition. But these can be seen largely as factors predisposing to belief rather than clinching it. A more critical factor, in Geertz's opinion, and the one that he is urging his readers to consider more seriously, is the way in which sacred symbols serve to knit together a normative with a metaphysical order so that each is sustained "with the borrowed authority of the other." The persuasiveness of religion is, in an important sense, a function of its powers of symbolic formulation.

This way of looking at the matter shifts the burden of analysis away from matching religion's message with society's requirements—an ingrained explanatory habit of the functionalist school—and onto demonstrating how a religion states its message effectively. Here we reach the point at which Geertz's line of thinking begins to overlap with that of Lévi-Strauss. Like symbolic curing (and often in fact empirically linked up with it), religion seems to work its psychological effect primarily through ritual or ceremonial action—that is, through deliberately invoked (or staged) symbolic presentations.

> . . . it is in ritual—that is, consecrated behavior—that this conviction that religious conceptions are veridical and that religious directives are sound is somehow generated. It is in some sort of ceremonial form— even if that form be hardly more than the recitation of a myth, the consultation of an oracle, or the decoration of a grave—that the moods

[17]

and motivations which sacred symbols induce in men and the general conceptions of the order of existence which they formulate for men meet and reinforce one another. In a ritual, the world as lived and the world as imagined, fused under the agency of a single set of symbolic forms, turn out to be the same world. [Geertz 1972:112]

For a decade or more the cultural anthropological analysis of value, myth, and magic has followed the trends that appear so well enunciated in Geertz's and Lévi-Strauss's essays. The writings of Nancy Munn, Terence Turner, Victor Turner, and Sherry Ortner all focus in various ways upon the reorganization of consciousness that takes place under the aegis of symbolic dramas. There is a continuity with past social science here. Durkheim and Freud both considered the power of religion to emanate from the psychological force of its symbolism, but their interest was limited to hypothesizing a grand and rather solitary referent to explain the symbol's psychological impact. For Freud this referent was (often as not) the father complex; for Durkheim, the social group. While holding the understanding of reference still indispensable to their analysis, our current theorists have shifted emphasis to contextual and presentational features of the symbolism. Symbolism as it unfolds in the ritual, ceremonial, or narrative context is taken as the object of analysis and the mode of its unfolding is thought to hold the key both to the referential meaning of any particular symbol and to the psychological effect of the whole. Myth, ritual, and ceremonial become, in this view, a style of argument, albeit not a rational one, in which images are the "terms" and dramatic sequences the "syllogisms." The changes of mind and heart brought about by the presentation of such symbolic arguments are, like the arguments themselves, of a subrational nature, but the more profound for being so.

As it happens, the anthropological theory of symbolic agency stands in problematic contrast to the more expressly psychological treatments of religious conversion, "faith healing," and psychic rejuvenation that also exist in the social science literature. The contrast is especially striking if among the profound effects anthropologists attribute to symbolic presentations we include the ecstatic and visionary states so often termed "religious experience." In the writings of such figures as William James, Gershom Scholem, Evelyn Underhill, even sociologist Max Weber, these peculiar states are taken more as the starting point than as the end product of religious symbolization. In their treatments, a far more dynamic religious psyche emerges. Rather than being merely acted upon, the religious mind appears as the active source of awarenesses in search of expression and of extraordinary perceptions that not infrequently burst through the established channels of religious imagery to carve out new ones. The ecstatic is, in Scholem's view, almost inevitably an innovator; in certain historical contexts, this may make him inevitably a heretic (Scholem 1965:22–29). In any event, he is hardly a figure upon whom traditional meanings may be ritually stamped.

It follows from the active and dynamic image of the visionary that these writers hold that they are cautious, not to say unconcerned, about singling out specifically cultural or social determinants of visionary experience. There are empirical grounds for their caution. Ecstatic and visionary states, which James regarded as a "well marked natural kind of fact," may occur spontaneously outside the context of ritual or religious activity and even among persons untutored in a sacred tradition. Efforts to correlate such experiences with special social circumstances have proved frustrating as well. Both Freud and Durkheim suggested (in addition to their symbolic hypotheses) that religious intensity is in some way a function of mob psychology (Freud 1960; Durkheim 1961:240–52). But pleasing as their speculations may be for explaining camp-meeting revivalism, mobs are not always in evidence when religious experiences are. The record of visionary ecstasy contains an abundance of lonely contexts as well—mountaintops, deserts, prison cells—where Durkheim would have been inclined rather to predict a suicide than an encounter with the sacred. It seems to be the consensus, at least among the writers just cited, that however much environmental factors may contribute to an individual's visionary career—motivating and educating, providing critical irritants and stresses—they do so only inasmuch as they fall upon the fertile soil of a special personality and temperament. Even though these writers cannot say with any assurance which people (or sort of people) *will* have religious experiences, they feel they can say, with reasonable assurance, that most people won't.

It is this sense of the relative rarity of intense religious states that leads to what at first may seem the solution to the divergent viewpoints on the psyche that appear in the writings of the cultural anthropologist and the religious psychologist respectively. Instead of there being a choice between two differing interpretations of religious psychology, it is possible that we are faced with evidence of two (or

[19]

more) different religious temperaments. Weber summarizes this perspective in his well-known passage:

> The empirical fact, important for us, that men are *differently qualified* in a religious way stands at the beginning of the history of religion. . . . The sacred values that have been most cherished, the ecstatic and visionary capacities of shamans, sorcerers, ascetics, and pneumatics of all sorts, could not be attained by everyone. The possession of such faculties is a "charisma," which, to be sure, might be awakened in some but not in all. It follows from this that all intensive religiosity has a tendency toward a sort of *status stratification*, in accordance with differences in the charismatic qualifications. "Heroic" or "virtuoso" religiosity is opposed to mass religiosity. By "mass" we understand those who are religiously 'unmusical'. [1958:287; his emphasis]

A cruder version of Weber's stratification theory appears in the idea frequently bruited in the Culture and Personality school of anthropology that shamans and other inspired religious figures—cult leaders, trance-dancers, and the like—are schizophrenic, pre-schizophrenic, "stabilized psychotic," or at the very least hysterical (Devereux 1956; Langness 1965). But whether we choose to plunge along with these anthropologists into the theoretical briarpatch that surrounds the relationship between religion and mental illness, or simply to invoke Weber's more discreet musical analogy, we wind up once again viewing the average person's belief as "evoked" by the compositions of the masters (the madmen, the virtuosi), and the average person's psyche as passively appreciative rather than actively constructive.

The trouble with the stratification solution is that now we have (at least) two psyches to explain instead of one, and neither appears any more comprehensible than previously.

The need to make clearer the psychology of religious/ritual transformation and to integrate, if possible, the two perspectives on religious activity just outlined began to urge itself upon me during the course of my research on the Church of Scientology. A word about the latter will help to show why this particular problem came so easily to the fore.

Scientology, now a recognized American religious sect, had its origins in the 1950s "Dianetics" movement, which began with the publication of founder L. Ron Hubbard's *Dianetics: The Modern Science of Mental Health.* Were it to appear today, Dianetics might pass scarcely noticed in the dense growth of popular psychotherapies on the American cultural landscape; but, appearing in 1950, it ranked among the earlier heralds of the popularizing trend that was to flourish so spectacularly in the decade of the 1960s. Dianetics (which means "through mind") was a theory of the mind combined with a method for bringing about psychic and psychosomatic changes. The method, called "auditing" (meaning "listening"), was modeled after secular psychotherapy. Through skillful use of questions and requests, the Dianetic "auditor" guided the subject through introspective forays into his or her feelings and previous experience, and it was expected that the resolution of the subject's current difficulties would eventuate once the problems of the past were sufficiently uncovered. I think it fair to say that what Hubbard had invented in Dianetics was a "symbolic curing" apparatus.

Through a series of steps that I will go into later, Dianetics evolved over the next four years from a rather cultic but secular self-improvement movement to a legally incorporated religious fellowship, re-named Scientology (meaning, "the science of knowledge"). In 1954 this fellowship became the Church of Scientology of California, a status it holds to this day. The doctrine, greatly elaborated from the Dianetics days, incorporates into its theory of the mind assumptions of a nonordinary reality; and auditing, still the dominant focus of movement participation and also greatly elaborated from its earlier forms, is now aimed not just at producing the conventional psychotherapeutic benefits but also at "freeing the spirit" from the conditions of the mundane world and fostering higher awarenesses. Scientology doctrine delineates a vision of reality that cannot be properly appreciated until one has experienced its varied dimensions. Auditing is the primary route to the appropriate experiences. Thus auditing performs the function Geertz ascribed to "consecrated behavior," that of generating a conviction of the truth and soundness of religious precepts. In effect, auditing, the "symbolic curing" apparatus, has become a method of religious conversion.

In turning to the question of what auditing does and how it does it, I found myself fortunate to have chosen an example of symbolic manipulation in which the researcher has reasonable access to the subjective dimension of participation. Scientology provides its practitioners with a rich and detailed vocabulary of inner activity and Scientologists relish discussions of their insights and experiences. I myself was permitted to receive some auditing and to undertake some of the training that goes into becoming an auditor. At points, I have drawn upon myself as an informant on the subjective repercussions of the practice. In the course of my research it became clear to me that the pattern of mental states that emerges in the accounts of Scientology practitioners (myself included) bore many resemblances to the experiential states achieved in other religious traditions as well as to various "altered states of consciousness" reported to occur outside of specifically religious contexts. It seemed that in the discipline of Scientology, each Scientologist becomes himself or herself the "religious virtuoso" of Weberian theory. And yet for the most part, Scientology practitioners do not conceive of themselves as inventing new spiritual or psychological categories but rather as discovering for themselves the categories of phenomena that are named and comprehended in Scientology doctrine. And though they often recognize in their experiences phenomena similar to those treated in other religious traditions or in depth psychotherapies, they feel that in comparison to the Scientology explanation of such matters, alternate formulations are crude and misstated. Their practice confers upon them not a polymorphous enlightenment but a specifically Scientological enlightenment. This is very much as would be indicated by the anthropological theories of ritual.

The task at hand, then, is one of bringing together the two understandings of psychological transformation, especially religiously relevant psychological transformation, that have been proposed in the anthropological discussions of ritual and the (primarily) psychological treatises on religious experience. The anthropological discussion directs attention to the way in which attitudes and ideas are tapped, articulated, and shaped by symbolically encoded messages expounded in culturally marked contexts such as ritual, ceremonial, myth recital. The writers in this tradition do not propose specifically that ritual etc. induces the classic visionary ecstasies of the psychological literature; indeed nothing in their theory predicates that any one class of subjective condition should arise in the ritual context, only that the participant be moved from one subjective condition to another. The religious psychology discussion, by contrast, begins with the recognition of a general class of extreme psychological states from which proceed, according to these writers, the sorts of insights and articulations that make their way into the vocabulary of a religious tradition. There may be special situations conducive to these states, but in the end individual temperament plays a decisive role; these states of mind are not accessible to everyone.

To get the two viewpoints together one needs to show that the experiences of the religiously inspired are to a meaningful degree available to the "masses," and that ritual and religious methods tend regularly to trigger the same broad class of experiences. Then it must be shown how such experiences are made relevant to *particular* religions and ideologies. Stating the project this way, one finds oneself confronted by a third body of opinion on the subject of transformation, one which, whatever its flaws and they are often serious, has the virtue of arguing the first part of the case—that ritual and religious methodologies, however inconsistently they may operate, do tend to induce special states of consciousness that may be ideologically exploited. I refer to the various studies of "brainwashing" and forcible conversion such as William Sargant's *Battle for the Mind* (1957), a classic in this field, or the recent popular work, *Snapping*, by Florence Conway and James Siegelman (1979). The significance of these writers' arguments to the present discussion is first that, contrary to the intuitions of the symbolic anthropologists cited earlier, it would appear the critical ingredient in psychologically transformative situations may not be so much the symbolism employed as the instrumental practice that accompanies it. Drug ingestion, sensory deprivation or bombardment, chanting, dancing, fasting, physical harassment and so on, are cited as examples of such practices. Second and more important, these authors suggest that, however varied the mind-altering mechanisms available and varied too the symbolic or ideological trappings under which these are exercised, there is a general similarity from instance to instance in the psychological syndrome that results. The cited components of this syndrome—distortions of reality and logic, heightened sense of meaning, loss of control, sudden reorganizations of perspective, increased suggestibility and dependency, and the sense of rejuvenation—harmonize well with descriptions of religious states found in the older literature on religious experience.

To be sure, "brainwashing" theorists cast these factors in a far more sinister light than the religious psychologists. Instead of seeing in the psychology of conversion, as James did, a unique capacity of the human spirit to transcend psychological adversity even in defiance of instituted expectations, these thinkers stand appalled at the power of instituted programs to crush the wills of their victims with an inexorable technology. Going along with this view of conversionary pro-

[23]

cedures as technological juggernauts are explanations of the psychology of conversion that too often leap over the symbolic significance of the experiences to arrive at the frailties of brain mechanics, physiology, or biochemistry that make such disastrous experiences possible. But as William Sargant puts it, in qualifying his own (stimulus-response) approach, "the eating of a large supper and the supine position in bed do not explain all that needs to be known about the subsequent nightmare" (1957:237). Just so, the invoking of stimulus-response patterns, biochemical factors, or even "holographic" models of the brain, notwithstanding the fact that intriguing correlates of experience can be found, still leaves the explanation many degrees removed from the specifics of how an experience acquires meaning for the experiencer. The second half of the needed demonstration, how special states of mind are made religiously or ideologically relevant, still presents a puzzle. It is not surprising that insofar as anthropologists have tried to work these conversion theories into their attempts at a more fine-grained analysis of the ritual process, they do little more than treat unusual states of consciousness as background facilitators of religious belief (as does Geertz, cited earlier), or mention that certain intoxicating techniques are used to heighten suggestibility (Wallace 1966:54ff.). The details of why an "intoxicated" mind is more likely than a sober one to embrace a new perspective are missing, because forcible conversion theorists have not been strong on supplying these details.

A notable exception to the theoretical thinness of the "brainwashing" literature is Robert J. Lifton's *Thought Reform and the Psychology of Totalism* (1961). Lifton's sensitive analysis of the way in which Chinese methods of indoctrination capitalized on latent guilt-provoking elements of the prisoners' identities helps to make apparent how important to the conversion process is the subjective contribution of the participant, whether this contribution is made willingly or not. His study also has the merit of downplaying the dramatic all-or-nothing image of thought reform, revealing as it does the inevitably complex and partial nature of both conversion and resistance to conversion.

Despite the importance of his salient points, however, Lifton does not explore the full range of subjective states that may be exploited in the conversion process, or attempt to unify these into a wide-ranging psychology. His generalizations, while always to some degree applicable to any psychologically transformative situation, have limitations imposed upon them by his key example—Chinese thought reform.

The latter in fact exploited certain dimensions of subjective sensibility far more than others, chiefly the guilt and doubts arising from the subjects' negative self-images. These factors are of course tapped in many religious and psychotherapeutic traditions. But the Chinese made little use of ecstatic and visionary materials so frequently enlarged upon in religion, and it is unclear how these are to be integrated into Lifton's concept of guilt-motivated identity alteration.

Fortunately some further promising leads as to the ideological and religious—or let us say broadly, "symbolic"—relevance of unusual experience have begun to come out of studies on drug-induced "altered states of consciousness" and the psychology of meditation. It only requires that these leads be worked through systematically in order to produce a model of religious psychology that puts into proper perspective the roles played respectively by psychological process and symbolic form in the context of religious or psychotherapeutic activity. This working through is what I have attempted in the pages that follow.

In brief outline I will argue that ritual and depth psychotherapeutic methodologies, when they truly take effect (which they do not invariably do), do so by activating and guiding a particular psychological process. The process has been recognized and partially comprehended under various theoretical rubrics: "regression" in psychoanalytic theory, "deautomatization" in recent cognitive psychological studies of meditation, "renunciation" in the older vocabulary of Western mysticism. Cognitively, the process takes the form of a (usually temporary) dedifferentiation of cognitive structures. It is this dimension of the experience that, manifested in its extreme forms, has won the label "altered states of consciousness." In terms of affect, the process consists of a withdrawal of emotional investment from its points of attachment and an inward migration of desire. This is the dimension recognized in the mystics' term "renunciation." In part because I feel the mystics have singled out a very significant feature of the process, in part because I prefer a term unencumbered by the implications of earlier psychological (chiefly psychoanalytical) theorizing, and lastly for the sake of brevity, I have adopted the term "process of renunciation" for the combined cognitive-affective syndrome.

The basic idea of this dual process has been succinctly sketched by psychologist Arthur Deikman in his article "Deautomatization and the Mystic Experience" (1969). Deikman's formulation has an implicit grounding in both Freudian theory and the structuralist psychology of

Jean Piaget. I have attempted to reconnect the idea to these foundations, incorporating as I do so Piaget's criticisms of certain misleading
portions of psychoanalytic theory.

The result of these theoretical refinements is an interpretation of
renunciation as a relatively common process, manifested nightly in
dreaming (as Freud pointed out to us) and daily in simple wool-
gathering, "daydreaming," and so on. It reaches extreme forms, however, under conditions of stress and privation or when it is deliberately cultivated, as it is, I argue, in religious and psychotherapeutic
activity.

In the context of these deliberate activities, the inducement of the
process of renunciation is not the function of the symbol system directly but of the accompanying practice. As Deikman's study suggests,
religious practice (in his study, meditation) triggers the renunciatory
mode through a straightforward attack on the structuring activity of
the mind. Besides the meditative disciplines and the dramatically
assaultive methods mentioned earlier—drug intoxication, physical
torture, and so on—renunciatory techniques include the more subtle
"free association" of psychoanalysis and the practices of guided fantasy
and introspection so salient in Scientology auditing. While varying in
severity and numerous peripheral qualities, all such techniques bring
about a disruption of the subject's ordinary reality and the correlative
driving inward of desire. The result is a welling up of unusual spontaneous restructurings of experience, of elusive but at the same time
deeply moving perceptions. It is here that an established symbol
system may begin to intervene—capturing, interpreting, and guiding
the wealth of autistic material set loose by renunciatory techniques.

From this perspective, the question of symbolic efficacy turns out to
be not so much how does symbolism produce profound perceptions,
but how does symbolism handle them? It is arguable that symbolic
forms serve to shape and orient feelings and perception wherever they
are utilized (which is everywhere), and that they do so in large part by
giving a name and a set of implications to the otherwise senseless
elements of experience. Religious and psychotherapeutic concep-
tualizations do not differ in this respect from mundane formulations.
But the experiences and perceptions that these systems address often
do differ from the mundane, and therein religious and psychotherapeutic formulations must differ too—not so as to be capable of induc-
ing or eliciting unusual perceptions but so as to be capable of "talking

[26]

about" them. The preference of religious culture for rich elemental images and paradoxical or circular constructs has its roots in the states of consciousness to which these images and constructs are addressed.

The main thrust of this book will be to explain the process of renunciation, clearing away some of the theoretical underbrush that impedes our understanding of it, and to show in detail how it is put to use in those typical culturally marked contexts such as ritual, religious worship, and psychotherapy. These clarifications and illustrations will, I think, resolve the problem of the disparate portrayals of the religious mind outlined at the start of this introduction, and provide what theorists of religious and ideological conversion have for the most part failed to provide: a psychology of conversion that is directly applicable to its symbolic meaning. Scientology practice and the doctrines supporting it serve as my principal example, but in a number of places I buttress my interpretations of the Scientology materials and simultaneously widen the analysis by bringing in comparisons to both psychoanalysis and the mystical traditions.

In the course of carrying out the major line of analysis, I hope to be able to clarify certain subsidiary issues that crop up in studies of psychological transformation and religious ideology. Chief among these subsidiary issues dealt with is the intimacy of the relationship between modern secular psychotherapies and religion. The reader will notice that I have been mentioning psychotherapeutic practices in the same breath as ritual, mysticism, symbolic curing, and religious activity generally. It would be superficial to say that I do so because Scientology methodology occupies a position midway between a psychotherapy and a religious discipline or because Scientology is a religious belief system that evolved from a secularly oriented psychology (Dianetics), although both these assertions are true. In fact what this "midway" and evolutionary situation suggests is a fundamental kinship between secular psychotherapeutic and religious procedures and doctrines, and it is this underlying kinship that will concern me in the early chapters of the book. Scientology is not the only religious or mystically tinged cosmology to have its origins in a secular psychotherapy, and I am not the first writer to notice similarities—doctrinal as well as methodological—between secular psychotherapies and religious traditions. I refer the reader not just to Lévi-Strauss's intuitions, already noted, but to the observations of David Bakan (1958) on Jewish mysticism and psychoanalysis, Alan Watts (1961) on "psycho-

[27]

therapy east and west," Herbert Fingarette (1963) on mysticism and psychoanalysis, and Thomas Szasz (1971) and Peter Berger (1965) on the similarities between religious and psychiatric ideologies.

Though none of these theorists has said so in so many words, I think a strong case can be made for including many modern secular therapies within a larger family of phenomena that includes the mystical disciplines and many forms of ritual, magical manipulation, and worship. This is not to say that important distinctions do not exist between the various family members. Nevertheless, their tendency to appear highly similar from diverse analytic perspectives as well as their tendency to blur together in concrete historical instances may be accounted for by the fact that numerous examples from all these categories operate on the same psychological and symbolic principles. All the mystical disciplines and many, though perhaps not all, rituals and psychotherapies make use of the process of renunciation as a means of dislodging individuals from their given perspectives and moving them toward new ones. There are implications to this commonality between religion and psychotherapy that deserve examination. These have to do with the psychological consequences and, linked with them, the cultural consequences of protracted use of renunciatory techniques. Unlike other more pedestrian methods of reeducation, reform through renunciation carries within it the tendency toward more and more transcendant, or in Weber's terms "other-worldly," perspectives. If this tendency, which is psychological in its roots, is pursued culturally to its logical conclusions, the cosmological system that surrounds a renunciatory discipline cannot for long remain "secular," that is, finite and this-worldly, in its orientation. This is one of the reasons, though by no means the only one, why secular therapeutic doctrines often develop a religious or mystical cast. It played an important role in the development of Scientology from Dianetics, and it has left a mark on other Western psychotherapies, even including psychoanalysis.

Another ramification of the protracted and systematic use of renunciation will concern me in the final section of the book when I turn to a phenomenon which frequently occurs in the careers of renouncers and which has received some cultural recognition in Scientology, in Western mysticism, and in psychoanalysis. This is the problem of spiritual collapse, disillusionment, and the inability to maintain either the beliefs or the practice of the system with which the practitioner is involved. I do not pretend to be able to explain this matter fully—

though I offer my own speculations and those of others—but I feel it is important to sketch its dimensions and make clear the part it has played in the elaboration of certain concepts that appear in the doctrines surrounding renunciation. "Negative transference" in psychoanalysis, "over-run" and "overwhelm" in Scientology, "spiritual aridity" and "the dark night of the soul" in Christian mysticism are all concepts pertaining to this phenomenon. It is another of the issues subsidiary to the understanding of conversion that requires greater scrutiny.

Finally, I have speculated briefly about what cultural and social factors tend to promote, within a religious or therapeutic movement, the extreme elaboration of renunciatory practice and its attendant other-worldly cosmologies. The lack of widespread social support for the doctrines of a movement, the absence of a workable program of worldly activity, and excessive commitment to utopian ideals of spiritual perfectibility (or mental health) are all cited as important factors. In the end I return to the cultural anthropologists' view of the psychology of ritual and suggest (to give these thinkers their due) that the degree to which a religion, psychotherapy, etc. relies upon renunciation and its psychological fireworks to validate their truths varies from case to case and is, in all probability, a function of the historical condition of the religious tradition in which we encounter the ritual in question.

There are certain things that I do not purport to do in the present work. One is to give a comprehensive and up-to-date description of the Scientology movement. My participation in and close observation of Scientology ceased in 1971. Since that time I have updated certain facts about the Church and its membership and policies from Church publications and academic accounts relating to Scientology (Wallis 1976; Wuthnow 1976), but this updating itself does not extend further than 1976. Thus the "ethnographic present" of this book is a slice of time from the early 1970s and should not be taken to be a precise account of current conditions. More recent developments in Scientology practice and belief may bear out what I say but knowledge of them is not essential to the concerns of this book.

I also make no pretense of calling this a sociological study in the usual sense of that term. I will paint Scientologists into the American social picture very briefly, in the first chapter. But I have not attempted to answer in any depth a number of the sociological questions common to studies of religious movements, such as why the move-

[29]

ment arose at a particular time, or why it attracts certain social categories and not others. A full account of religious conversion must ultimately address these issues because social affinities and pressures and the shape of the surrounding social order have as much to do with individual ideological alignment as do the nuances of experience that I will be discussing here. My neglect of this dimension does not arise out of any theoretical disdain for it, but rather out of an interest in devoting full attention to the special issues that I do address: the nature of religious experience and the problem of symbolic efficacy. The partial account of ideological reorientation that follows is so designed, in my opinion, as to nest comfortably within a wider sociological and historical analysis, but such analysis must await future effort.

The book is ordered as follows. The first chapter provides an overview of the early 1970s Church of Scientology and its membership and deals with the circumstances of my research. The second chapter traces the evolution of Scientology from the Dianetics movement of the early 1950s and raises the issue of the role of auditing as a visionary technique facilitating this evolution. In chapters 3 and 4, I turn to the theoretical understanding of religious and psychotherapeutic practice as renunciation. Having established a theoretical framework, I employ the remaining chapters to elaborate it, dealing in turn with auditing techniques, the belief system in which these techniques are situated, and the interaction between psychological process and belief as this is revealed in practitioners' experiences with auditing and auditor-training. In the final chapter I draw comparisons between the progress of personal enlightenment in the Scientology adherent, the mystic, and the psychoanalysand. I conclude with a return to the problem of symbolic efficacy in ritual.

[1]

The Face of Scientology

The typical Scientology "Mission" or "Church" consists of a complex of offices and classrooms and a reception area where literature is displayed and where one or two staff members are in attendance to answer questions, handle book sales, and route visitors to the appropriate departments. Furnishings, a mixture of the new and secondhand, are tasteful though not particularly noteworthy. At the busier centers Scientology training goes on day and night, and a glance into the classrooms will reveal students crammed together at tables, quietly questioning or reading to one another, adjusting or readjusting a meterlike instrument, making displays of modeling clay and paper, or simply sitting in pairs staring at each other for what seems to be an unnatural length of time. For the most part the students appear to be young adults, not unattractive, and dressed in the styles of the day. Staff members may be similarly dressed, but some of them—those who by special examination have qualified as ministers of the Church of Scientology—wear clerical black with reversed collars; and in the high-level establishments a navy blue military uniform is in evidence.

A brief glance through the colorful glossy brochures on the literature stands recapitulates, in rather more vivid form, these initial impressions. There are photographs of the premises of the "Advanced Orgs," where advanced Scientology training goes on. These look not unlike the premises upon which one is now standing; photographs of yet more classrooms with students crammed together at tables with their clay, meters, and bulletins, many of them endowed with smiles and eager expressions—and most centrally, photographs of two people (usually male and female, usually young and distinctly attractive) facing each other across an intervening "meter" and beaming ecstatically. With a few exceptions, the books on sale are all authored by the same person, L. Ron Hubbard, the founder of Scientology; and their titles make it obvious that a philosophy of life or self-improvement doctrine is to be found between the covers: *A New Slant on Life; The Science of Survival; How to Live Though an Executive; The Creation of Human Ability.* The blurb on the back of one explains:

> Scientology is an Applied Philosophy. The word Scientology comes from "Scio" (Latin) which means *knowing* in the fullest meaning of the word, and "Logos" (Greek) which means *to study.*
>
> Scientology was developed and completed after 35 years of research by L. Ron Hubbard, an American writer and philosopher. Probably no philosopher of modern times has had the popularity and appeal of Hubbard or such startling success within his own lifetime. And Mankind has no better friend.
>
> The goal of Scientology is total knowledge, which could also be defined as total freedom. As such, Scientology is a study of life, of science and of knowing. It includes a technology through which the individual can increase his ability, his awareness, his self-determination and attain increasingly higher states of existence not even dreamed of in the literature of Man.
>
> The adage, "The truth shall set you free," has been repeated through history from the earliest recording of philosophical thought on Earth. But until Scientology, the truth concerning man's relationship to the Universe had not been found and proven, though some truth had been guessed at. Scientology was born into an aberrated world of the "small wars" and the atomic bomb where Man is considered by some as only a creature of mud, without spirit. Without in any way condemning or scorning any man's beliefs, Scientology arose from the ashes of a spiritless science and again asked—and answered for the first time—the eternal questions: "Who am I?", "What is life?", "Where do I come from?", "What is death?"
>
> The book is a compact but broad survey of the subject of Scientology. No such knowledge has ever before existed and no such results have ever before been attainable by Man as those which can be reached by a study of this brief volume.
>
> This *is* how life works. This *is* how men and women and children can change for the better. [Hubbard 1956]

The cover art of this and other volumes conveys a more cultic flavor; it has something of the look of pulp magazine illustrations and features rather arcane symbols—a little dog, the face of a bearded sage, an erupting volcano, and, in one case, a woman dressed in a bear suit gnawing a chicken-leg. Inside the books a welter of unfamiliar words spring up, many of them acronyms (ARC, PTS), atypical abbreviations ("Org" for organization, "anaten" for analytical attenuation), or terms associated with physics or electronics ("charge," "mass," "flow," "static"). Each publication is provided with a glossary as well as a warning opposite the title page telling the reader not to "go past a word you do not fully understand" since the consequence of doing so is that you will soon tire of the subject and abandon it.

Scientologists proselytize on the streets by handing out tickets to introductory lectures or by inviting passersby to come in for a free personality assessment. The majority of potential converts who show up at the evening introductory lectures were not recruited on the streets, however. They are friends, relatives, or acquaintances of an already committed Scientologist, and the latter is usually there with them to help mediate their first experience with organized Scientology. He or she is also there to see Scientology friends, exchange gossip, and find out what exciting new bits of policy or "data" have come down from the higher levels. The atmosphere is chatty, quantities of coffee and cigarettes may be consumed, and Scientology jargon buzzes through the air. Some of this jargon will be elucidated in the lecture. Favorite topics for introductory lectures are the nature of the Reactive Mind—Scientology's version of the Unconscious—and how Scientology can help you overcome it; or the structure of Understanding: "ARC" (the initials stand for "affinity," "reality," and "communication," which together add up to "understanding"). The lecturer assumes a simple conversational tone, engages the audience with his or her eyes, and pauses frequently to let the uncomplicated points sink in. The effect is calming, if for some slightly boring, and the upshot of the message is that Scientology provides you with a scientifically valid theory of the mind and of life and a precise methodology for handling life's difficulties. The material chosen for illustration is usually undramatic. No cancer cures are mentioned; nor is there any raving about lives saved from suicide or drug addiction. Rather it is the nagging headache that begins whenever mother calls, or one's inability to convince the boss of one's full worth that is at issue. (Conversation after the lecture is more liberal. Like most other people, Scientologists have more to cope with than nagging headaches.) The point of the lecturer's manner is that Scientology is not for

the depraved or the desperate but rather for the reasonably able
individual who still encounters some difficulties in life and whose
intellect is not satisfied by the inconclusive answers handed out by the
supposed experts. Scientology's motto asserts modestly, "We make
the able more able." The first step toward this greater ability, after
one has attended a lecture or perused a book, is to purchase the first
levels of Scientology auditing or training.

The revenues of the Church of Scientology come principally from
the sale of these two services. One may begin with either. Both
auditing and training (which is billed as training for meeting life's
problems as well as the road to becoming an auditor) proceed by
graded steps, the completion of each step being marked by a certifi-
cate that entitles the practitioner to proceed to the next step, and in
the case of auditor-training to audit others up to a specified level (see
below, pp. 130–34). At the time of my research, the cost of being
audited by a licensed auditor averaged thirty-five dollars per hour;
training cost somewhere between five and ten dollars per hour depending on the speed of one's progress through the course. Since
students on an auditor-training course may be audited free of additional charge by fellow students practicing their skills, "going on
course" is a way to receive the benefits of both auditing and training
relatively cheaply. In addition to training and auditing, Scientology
establishments sell the books and materials required for the courses
and the small portable skin galvanometer, the "E-Meter," which is
used in most auditing. These meters are manufactured exclusively for
the Church of Scientology and in 1971 cost about 135 dollars.

Scientology establishments are to be found in all the English-speaking countries of the world, in most of Europe, and in some Latin
American countries. According to a listing published by a Scientology
organization in 1975, there are some 193 such establishments worldwide, with the greatest numerical concentration in the United States
(Hubbard 1975a). At the base of the organizational hierarchy is the
Scientology Mission (or Center), which is licensed as a franchise to
qualified Scientology practitioners. Missions are empowered to sell
auditing and training up to a certain level. The franchise returns 10
percent of its proceeds to the central coffers of the Church of Scientology. It allots the remaining amount to maintenance, staff salaries,
and owner income. As long as it is properly licensed, the Mission
receives the latest policies and "data" on belief and practice from
headquarters, and those receiving training or auditing at the Mission

[34]

are issued the appropriate certificates.[1] If these individuals then go on to the higher-level establishments for more advanced training, part of their payments there will be returned in the form of a commission to the franchise owner who routed them to the Advanced Organization.

Typically found in middle-to-large metropolitan areas, Missions range in size of operation from a one-person practice housed in a small office with a literature rack to a staff of twelve to fourteen occupying a large house or set of offices. The staff of a franchise may be hired or enlisted on any basis that the owner finds workable. They may be salaried, paid contingently according to the weekly take, commissioned, or enlisted on a purely volunteer basis.

The next level of Scientology establishment is the Org, or in more recent language, Church. Churches are limited to one per metropolitan area, and they deliver the same levels of service and training as Missions plus several more advanced levels.

Churches are owned by the larger Organization, managed by salaried executive directors, and return all their proceeds, after operating costs, to the central coffers. With the possible exception of the executive director's salary—which may be fixed—staff salaries fluctuate with the fluctuations of the Church's weekly income and are, in addition, subjected to a bonus and demerit system according to the staffer's productivity as measured by various Scientology indices. (Franchise owners may apply this system to staff salaries as well.) In Churches the element of voluntarism becomes more important, but strong additional incentive is given staff members by offering them heavily discounted auditing and training. Individuals may contract to work full-time or part-time for so many months or years for a Scientology Church on the understanding that they will receive, besides whatever rudimentary salary is involved, a certain level or number of levels of auditing and training at a reduced rate. Church staffs range in size from ten to fifty depending upon the prosperity of the Church.

The next highest units of the Organization are sometimes referred to collectively as the "Advanced Orgs." They occur in pairs of two types: the Saint Hill Organization, modeled after Saint Hill Manor in East Grinstead, Sussex—one of the founder's early headquarters—

1. Nothing debars a person from licensing more than one franchise if he or she can afford the initial investment in rent, salaries, and literature; and a franchise owner may sell his or her practice to another qualified Scientologist if he/she so desires. Pyramid franchising (selling the license to sell licenses) has never, to my knowledge, been permitted, however.

and the AO (Advanced Org). Saint Hill Organizations offer most of the advanced training, while AOs offer (and supervise) the higher levels of auditing.

Some of the lower-level courses and services associated with the Churches and Missions are available as well at the Advanced Orgs; but generally practitioners are encouraged to take these levels at their neighborhood Mission or Church. The main business of the Advanced Orgs is the delivery of the most advanced levels. Advanced Orgs (Saint Hills and AOs) are, so far, limited to one set per country; and, as yet, only the United States, the United Kingdom, and Denmark have these establishments—in Los Angeles, East Grinstead and Edinburgh, and Copenhagen. The lower ranks of the Advanced Org staff are usually filled according to the same arrangements as an ordinary Church but the higher positions—including that of executive director—are filled by members of the Sea Org, the inner core of Scientology.

The Sea Org is the overall controlling agency of the Church of Scientology. Its some 300 members,[2] which include persons at all levels of auditing and training, undergo a certain amount of screening before entry (outstanding debts, legal, medical, or familial problems, or a record of antagonism toward Scientology disqualify a candidate), and sign a "billion year contract" of service to Scientology. Sea Org enlistment is meant to be taken seriously. As long as they adhere to this contract, Sea Orgers receive bed and board, weekly spending money, and all levels of auditing and training free, but they must make good the cost of the latter should they decide to quit.

The Sea Org was started in 1966 when Scientology's founder L. Ron Hubbard, having received a frigid welcome for his organization in the United States, Southern Rhodesia, and the United Kingdom, decided to establish his headquarters at sea. He purchased a small sea-going vessel, the *Royal Scotman*, later renamed *Apollo* (sometimes described as a converted cattle boat), and made this the flagship of what eventually came to be a little navy of small craft manned by uniformed personnel. There were seven of these vessels at the time of my research. Most of them spent the greater part of their careers docked near one or another of the Advanced Orgs on land, and it was to these that new Sea Org recruits would report for Scientology training as well

2. Estimated for 1969–70. The number of Sea Org personnel increased during the 1970s, but I lack specific figures.

as lessons in seamanship and small craft maintenance. Stints of training on shipboard alternated with periods of service in the Advanced Orgs. The flagship *Apollo* customarily cruised the Mediterranean, but its exact course and location were kept secret. Those privileged to staff or make training visits to the *Apollo* participated in the development of Hubbard's latest innovations and were privy to the Organization's most guarded policies and plans. A continuous stream of bulletins on training and policy issued from "Flag" to the land Orgs; from there the relevant ones were dispatched to a vast network of Churches and Missions. Small teams of uniformed Sea Orgers were periodically sent out to check on the operations of Scientology Orgs, Churches, and Missions around the world, to introduce new programs, trouble-shoot areas of difficulty, and penalize personnel who had strayed from correct practice. On occasion, the Sea Org would also set up land Missions of its own for special purposes. An example is Celebrity Center in Los Angeles, which handles the lower-level training of "name" and "near name" Scientologists, such as Hollywood figures, published authors, and established artists. (Celebrity Center also provides promotional facilities for advancing the personal careers of its clientele.)

In 1975, Hubbard established a "Flag Land Base" at Clearwater, Florida, and this complex of offices, classrooms, and attractive hotel and motel facilities for visiting Scientologists absorbed many of the functions of the flagship. The inner core is still called "Sea Org," but its personnel now carry out most of their activities from the land establishments, and the little vessels are reportedly being sold.

The Church of Scientology has, in addition to the establishments just described, its own business offices and special departments in charge of publications, the production and distribution of the E-Meter, and legal defense. Ordinary staff, Sea Org staff, and even non-Scientology specialists—lawyers and accountants, for instance—are intertwined in these departments, branches of which are usually located near the Advanced Orgs.

Scientologists

According to differing reports of the Church of Scientology, five to fifteen million people worldwide have taken the "first step" toward Scientology participation, which is signing the membership card that entitles one to a discount on Scientology books. If involvement continues, the individual may in one or two years of virtually full-time study, or three to five years of part-time participation, attain the level of "Clear," Scientology's version of enlightenment. In 1966, the time at which the standardized Clearing Course was introduced, the Church began to keep a record of who reached "Clear." A 1975 issue of *The Auditor*, a church publication, lists 4884 Clear Scientologists, a yearly average of 543 new ones. Obviously not all of the five to fifteen million continue their involvement. The attrition rate is highest at the lowest levels. Unfortunately no published records appear showing how many graduate from these lower levels. My impression of the ratio of active senior Scientologists (Clear or above) to active junior ones was that it ran about 1 to 50. This would put the number of active Scientologists at any one year in the low hundreds of thousands rather than in the millions.

Yet if we are to speak of the cultural influence of Scientology, as opposed to its numerical strength, then it might not be misleading to say that several million have been, to some degree, touched by it. In support of this estimate of Scientology's visibility, let me cite a survey conducted by sociologist Robert Wuthnow and associates in five counties of the San Francisco Bay area in 1973. At that date, about a quarter of the Bay area population knew something about Scientology, though only 5 percent of those who knew something about it—thus 1.1 percent of the population as a whole—had participated in Scientology directly (Wuthnow 1976: 270–71). Were the counties of the San Francisco Bay area representative of the nation as a whole, we could project from such findings that some two million Americans had participated in Scientology, while over fifty million knew something about it. The Bay area cannot, of course, be taken as representative; by most reckonings, religious sectarianism and "personal growth" faddism are more prevalent in California, and especially in the urban areas of California, than in most other parts of the country. Nonetheless, any sect approaching these projected figures must be considered as having a noticeable claim upon the public consciousness.

Knowledge about Scientology, however, does not necessarily indicate an enthusiasm for it. Only 3 percent of those in Wuthnow's sample who knew something about it reported themselves strongly attracted to the sect (1976:270–71). Some of Scientology's unattractiveness to the general public, and, by extrapolation, some of the group's attrition rate, must be chalked up to the reputation Scientology has attained in the media of the English-speaking world. People usually hear about the sect when it is investigated by a parliament or when its offices are raided by a government agency. Then they have been likely to read that it is the money-making scheme of a former "science-fiction writer" who promoted mental-health quackery and ordered his zealous followers to treat Scientology's detractors as "fair game." Reports of skulduggery within the organization are highlighted, and Hubbard's wilder or more comical assertions are presented as representative of what Scientologists believe. Wuthnow's survey indicates that Scientology's public image in the Bay area is rather more negative than positive (270). Yet there are those who somehow filter through this negative screen. All my Scientology acquaintances were familiar with the "scandals of Scientology" most frequently retailed in the press because these are the stories frequently related among Scientology's inner circles as well. But while not ruling out these reports as untrue, my acquaintances did not take them as representative of the group experience. Similarly, they did not take Hubbard's wilder assertions as representative of what they believed. Still, the drop-out rate even among those who have passed the negative-image barrier is appreciable. The expense and rigor of training and auditing is a primary factor here. Of those whom one meets in Scientology social circles, a goodly percentage at any given moment are "on hold" in their progress through the levels. They haven't raised the money or found the time for their next step, or disturbances in their personal lives have temporarily destroyed the clarity of mind and purpose required to persevere in the auditing and training regime. Unless these obstacles are overcome, persons in this ambiguous status eventually fade from the scene. Scientology policy may also act in indirect ways to magnify the time and price barriers. Hubbard habitually inserted new steps into the auditing and training sequences, and, as such new steps have not always been announced far in advance, practitioners' plans have been disrupted. Efficiency crackdowns aimed at improving the flow of traffic through an Org or Center often have the contrary effect of alienating staff and frightening away tentative converts. While some who stray (or, as Scientologists put it, "blow") drift back again months or even years later, the internal pressures of Scientology participation take a significant toll.

Who are the people attracted to Scientology? Wuthnow's Bay area survey revealed that those attracted to the "self-help" or "personal growth" sects, Scientology included, were on the average younger and better educated than the population norm and more liberal in their social and political values. People attracted to Scientology in particular also ranked higher than the population norm on experience with drug "highs," experimenting with meditation, and valuing "getting to know one's inner self." On all of these scales, however, Scientology's audience was closer to the norm than was the audience for the Eastern sects—Hare Krishna, TM, Zen (Wuthnow 1976:276–88). According to my own and others' impressions (cf. Wallis 1976:163–67; Wilson 1970:141–42, 163–66), Scientologists come predominantly from the secularized urban stratum of the middle class. It is this stratum that, according to Wilson, has furnished recruits to all of what he calls the twentieth-century "manipulationist" sects, and Scientology does indeed fit Wilson's characterization of such sects:

> Sects emphasizing special knowledge, . . . a *gnosis* that gives the diligent believer mastery to manipulate the world, arise only in particular historical periods and social circumstances. They are most evident in metropolitan centres, where relationships are impersonal and dominated by role-performance. The people who belong to the manipulationist sects regard themselves as sophisticates. . . . They are acquainted, usually, with other systems of religious belief and worship, and they know that there is a baffling variety of cults: what they accept, they justify intellectually and pragmatically. The manipulationist sect tends to present its message in abstract terms, in literature rather than by means of emotional expression, and its adherents are those who can be reached through literary channels. [1970:141–42]

Scientology establishments appear more like schools or special training institutes than like churches, and Scientology argues that its doctrines are scientific and its methods of proven practical benefit. A certain percentage of Scientologists feel that they are in the sect not simply to "get their heads mended," as is the attitude of many who turn to psychotherapy, or solely to learn skills that will help them in life—though the last is a significant motivation. More than this, they feel they are becoming part of a highly trained professional corps whose worth will one day be recognized and whose expertise will be in wide social demand, as is that of licensed mental health professionals. (Scientology literature portrays Scientology as in direct competition with the psychiatric establishment for legitimacy and ideological allegiance.) Those who become full-time staffers and auditors—in their terms "professional" Scientologists—do so under the sway of this attitude.

The majority of Scientologists are nonprofessional, however, and their interests are in learning how better to cope with the world. No systematic data exist on the occupations of Scientologists and those attracted to Scientology, but occupations cannot be without significance, since the abilities that Scientology promises to develop in its adherents are primarily those having to do with work performance and achievement, with communication and self-presentation. If there is a "need" to which Scientology constitutes a response, it would seem to pertain more to the world of work than to the sexual and familial relationships that are the focus of so much of conventional psychotherapeutic interest.

Among the Scientologists whom I encountered in the course of my research, there was a heavy representation of persons in the entertainment world, the business services (personnel, management consultancy, computer services), sales, and petty enterprise, especially crafts. Not only were significant numbers recruited from these areas, but persons entering Scientology from other backgrounds (housewives, students, clerical workers) often began to consider careers in such fields. This was in part a function of their new social contacts, but in part too a function of their desire to put their new Scientology skills to work in areas where they could see immediate results: persons won over, new projects launched, salesmanship, self-promotion, and interpersonal dexterity applauded.

Over and above emphasizing personality skills that are important to a range of contemporary middle-class occupations, Scientology places these abilities within a system of belief that, however alien-seeming on the surface, is subtly continuous with the deeply ingrained free-enterprise mystiques of Western culture. As we shall see below, Scientologists learn to view themselves as "free spirits" who use their native powers to create their "own universe" while the unenlightened world remains bogged in an oppressive web of material and social considerations. In this respect, Scientology speaks to the frustrated entrepreneur locked in the breast of many a middle-class dependent employee. It does not necessarily do so, however, in such a way as to transform him/her into a real entrepreneur; real entrepreneurship for the most part requires a larger capital than the average middle-class "worker" possesses. Instead Scientologists gravitate toward positions in which there is opportunity to gain recognition through inspired people-handling, self-promotion, and organizational creativity, and where one is not apt to get tied down for too long on a single project.

[41]

We need only look at some of the benefits promised the practitioner to sense the flavor of Scientology aspirations: "moving out of fixed conditions . . . "; "freedom from inability to handle power"; "freedom from inability to project intention"; "freedom from uncertainty of self"; "return of full self-determinism" (Scientology Classification, Gradation and Awareness Chart).

My Research

In 1969, two Scientologists whom I had met socially began to explain their beliefs to me and invited me to attend lectures at a Scientology Center located not far from where I was then living. Intrigued, I decided to do an anthropological study of the Scientology movement with a view toward understanding how a novel belief system is developed and maintained. Trying to allay the anxieties of certain informants, I wrote to L. Ron Hubbard explaining my interests and asking for his reaction. A letter came back over his signature that took the form of a cleverly hedged "permission." If my study was all right with those to whom I spoke and with the executives of the establishments I visited, then it was all right with him.

In fact, the Church of Scientology has a policy (promulgated by Hubbard) to grant no particular hospitality to "outside investigators." Journalists, government agents, and social scientists are usually met with guarded, sanitized responses; some are turned away entirely. But for a variety of reasons, the Church policy did not weigh too heavily upon me during the first year of my research. Lay Scientologists (those who have no position in Church organization), and "field" Scientologists (the personnel of local Missions) tend to exercise their own judgment in the matter of whom they will talk to. Scientologists of advanced training or long experience are usually confident enough to take on outsiders' questions and sincerely interested in promoting better understanding of the movement. A certain endemic intellectualism among Scientologists, a fondness for endlessly analyzing their experiences in Scientology terms, acted in my favor as well.

A more crucial fact was that I presented myself as someone informed by a different ethic from that of the typical outside investigator. I was an anthropologist, a researcher who participates as well as observes, someone who seeks to learn the culture as the "natives" perceive it, without imposing preconceptions. Sporting neither notebooks nor tape recorder,[3] I enrolled in the introductory Scientology courses, attended Scientology parties and get-togethers regularly, and eventually began to receive auditing. Rather than pursuing a select sample of respondents to subject to standard interviews, I let the vagaries of personal affinity connect me to a circle of Scientology friends with whom and in whose larger milieu of acquaintances I made my life for over a year. My profession had already established for me the idea that participant-observation was an indispensable method for understanding meaning-systems in action, and in this respect I was not disappointed. At the same time it so happened that participant-observation was about the only method open to me for studying the movement at all.

This apparent harmony between social necessity and academic virtue began eventually to show its morally murky side. Scientology does not demand immediate commitment from newcomers, but expects rather that increased knowledge of Scientology "data" will lead ineluctably to faith in it. It was not surprising, then, that some of my informants felt there wasn't much difference between the method of cultural learning that I planned to undertake and gradual conversion (nor were they far wrong). Although I continued to explain my status to those with whom I spoke, my research style was sufficiently unfamiliar and my profile sufficiently low to be easily ignored by those who saw me struggling through the materials with the rest of the students, or, like them, demanding explanations that would be relevant to daily life. New acquaintances, after minor hesitation or none at all, took me into their confidence; some told me things that an "outsider" had no business hearing. Having checked upon completion of the current manuscript, I note with some relief that I have not needed to rely upon any such questionable confidences for the documentation of the points addressed here.

My participation in Scientology at the formal level ended as the outcome of a review auditing session in which I admitted to enrolling on a course at the Los Angeles Org without having notified the Org executives that I was conducting research. Thus brought into the matter, these executives asked me to leave. Individual friendships

3. I preferred to write up fieldnotes in private and had considerable practice, from past research, in verbatim recall. One Scientologist did volunteer to sit for a series of taped interviews; his words, where they appear in the text, are indicated as taped. The quotations of all other Scientologists are from fieldnotes that were written up shortly after the occasion.

survived this rupture for some time, but knowing that I would eventually publish my research and that my viewpoint would inevitably disagree with that of my friends if only by virtue of being that of an academic and not a committed practitioner, I took my departure from the Org as occasion to diminish and soon cease my inquiries.

[2]

The Origins of Scientology

The technique of Scientology auditing and the concepts surrounding it were preceded by Dianetic auditing and the Dianetic theory of the mind. Both are the invention of Lafayette Ronald Hubbard, an American fiction writer who, until recently, controlled the operation of the movement that grew up around his ideas. When he presented his first theory—Dianetics—to the world in 1950, he made no argument that it was a religion. He claimed rather to have empirically discovered the psychological source of human "aberration" and to have worked out a valid therapy for its cure. Some of his Dianetic theories were implausible in the light of contemporary science, but he couched them in a finite, materialistic framework. Somehow in the course of the two years after Dianetics became popular, this materialistic framework dropped away, and both Hubbard's doctrine and the movement based upon it took on the clothing of a religion. The doctrine, greatly elaborated from its early days, was renamed Scientology, and the movement supporting it was incorporated, in 1954, as a "church." The roots of this transition from secular psychotherapy to religion—from Dianetics to Scientology—lie, in part, in Hubbard's style and background; in part, in the misfortunes that befell the early Dianetics movement. Yet there is a way in which we can see the psychotherapeutic effort itself as a significant factor in the evolution of a religious system. Let me deal with each of these elements in turn in order to put the last—the linkage between psychotherapy and religion—in proper perspective.

L. Ron Hubbard

Much of what has been reported about the career of L. Ron Hubbard before he launched Dianetics in 1950 comes from biographical sketches put out by the Church of Scientology, sketches written either by Hubbard or under his guidance. Outside investigations of these accounts over the years have added little of great substance, but have subtracted Hubbard's pretensions to any advanced education in some of the fields in which he claimed expertise such as civil engineering, nuclear physics, philosophy, and psychology (Malko 1970:31; Hopkins 1969:110; Wallis 1976:21). While I suspect that further biographical embellishments or omissions may one day come to light, the larger outlines of the official sketch seem too unremarkable to arouse serious questions. Thus this authorized background on Hubbard, coupled with whatever of his interests, character, or experience may be deduced from his writings, furnishes us with some broad boundaries within which to contextualize his Dianetics and Scientology creations.

Born in 1911 in Tilden, Nebraska, the son of U.S. Navy Commander H. R. Hubbard and Dora May Waterbury Hubbard, young Ron spent much of his childhood on the Montana cattle ranch of his maternal grandfather. According to him, his family moved to Washington, D.C., when he was twelve, although there is a record of his having attended Helena (Montana) High School for a time (Malko 1970:31). In the D.C. area, he attended Swavley Preparatory School for Boys in Manassas, Virginia, and Washington's Woodward Prep School, graduating from the latter in 1930.

During this same period, between his fourteenth and eighteenth years approximately, he traveled, he claimed, with his naval officer father in the Far East and in the course of these travels learned from the "holy men" of India and northern China. Likewise during this period, he said, he received an education in Freudian theory at the hands of a Commander Thompson of the U.S. Navy Medical Corps, a friend of his father. Both these elements appear in his biography in support of the assertion that from early on he manifested an interest in the mysteries of the human mind and human existence. It would seem that the Far Eastern journeys must have been confined to periods of summer vacation, for, as George Malko points out, they did not interfere with his high school attendance in the United States (1970:31).

As far as investigators have been able to determine, Hubbard did not complete college, although he spent two years at George Washington University beginning in 1930. Rather than scholarship, this period witnessed the blossoming of what was to be an eighteen-year career as a writer-adventurer. During what must have been a fairly hectic six years, Hubbard is reported to have acquired experience as a Marine Corps reservist, a barnstorming aviator, and a neophyte explorer. In 1931, according to his own report, he led a "Caribbean Motion Picture Expedition for Submarine Movies," and the following year the "West Indies Mineral Survey" expedition to Puerto Rico. (He was eventually to receive the honor of election, in 1940, to the Explorers' Club of New York, and subsequently led three expeditions flying the Explorers' Club flag [Malko 1970:33–34].) He also began submitting articles and stories to aviation and sports magazines and by 1936 was a prolific contributor to *Argosy* magazine. At about the same point he first tried his hand at Hollywood scriptwriting, the adventure tale again being his medium.

The genre to which Hubbard gravitated favors certain themes that he was capable of endlessly exploring: masculine heroism in some skilled technical occupation (flyer, engineer, explosives expert, diver); male rivalry; the attaining of manhood (or the redeeming of it) by meeting some formidable challenge, often as not in some skilled occupation and in competition with an opponent. The areas of his fictional characters' expertise and the exotic lands through which they travel are in most cases not so convincingly portrayed as to encourage our seeing in these stories veiled autobiography (Hubbard was adroit at making some small tidbit of knowledge go a long way in a tale); nevertheless, there is sufficient richness of context and detail in a number of the stories to suggest that Hubbard had at some point spent time around the construction camps of Latin America (and possibly the Philippines) picking up a rudimentary knowledge of Spanish, roadbuilding, and mining, and acquiring an admiration for the rootless and often eccentric contract engineers who blasted their roads and tunnels through the jungles of the Third World. That he had come to know his way around ships and aircraft is even more apparent.

There is a snappy ease and lightness to these early adventure stories. Many of Hubbard's creations have about them the humor and hyperbole of the barracks (or hangar) "tall tale." The typical hero is characterized by some humanizing foible—superstitiousness, procrastination, hard-drinking foolhardiness—that makes his comrades skeptical and repeatedly undermines his advancement; but in the end, usually through technical expertise and stubborn insouciance, the son-of-a-gun prevails. Villains are frequently absent altogether or when present limited to the most widely accepted stereotypes: bullies, sneak-thieves, business sharpsters. In a couple of stories, we find a gruff, awe-inspiring father taking in hand his soft, eastern-educated son and tricking the boy into manhood by foisting him into a challenging job ("River Driver," "A Lesson in Lightning").

The early adventure stories do not reveal any particular penchant for seeking after meaning, but then the genre does not demand—in fact it rather discourages—excursions into the deeper side of things. It was not until Hubbard entered the science fiction and fantasy genre, which in the late 1930s had begun to welcome psychological and metaphysical imaginings in addition to technological ones, that his writing showed elements of this sort of interest. As he began to supply such magazines as *Astounding Science Fiction* and *Galaxy*, starting around 1938, Hubbard came to make effective use of what some have called the "psychological thriller." In stories such as "Slaves of Sleep," "Fear," "The Ultimate Adventure," "Triton," and "Typewriter in the Sky," a hidden reality subjacent to the apparent one opens up to the hero through some trick of magical or mental manipulation: a dream, a sensory-deprivation experiment, an encounter with a djinn, and the like. In many ways, it is the old adventure story transposed: the new reality furnishes another arena wherein the hero may achieve the glamorous manhood that has eluded him in the ordinary world. At the same time, however, a greater sense of the tragic possibilities of fantasy adventure began to appear in Hubbard's fiction; in some stories, the new magical reality meshes disastrously with the hero's inner failings and obsessions. In "Fear," a demonologist becomes demon-possessed and murders his wife and best friend in a jealous rage. The aviator hero of "Death's Deputy," embittered when an injury terminates his flying career, lapses unwittingly into a pact with "death" that leaves him a veritable jinx. Those around him die in mysterious accidents and he flees his new wife, fearful that his deadliness will claim her too. In these tales, the timid young greenhorn of the earlier adventure stories seems to have grown to a maturity haunted by disappointment and hidden angers.

At the same time, the eccentric but lovable so-and-so's of the earlier tales give way to a hero who is, in some sense, their derivative but cut on a far grander scale. The "Lieutenant" of *Final Blackout* (1940), and Ole Doc Methuselah, central character in a series of "space opera" adventures, retain certain endearing foibles but shed the underdog status of the earlier type. Instead, the new hero is a natural aristocrat: aloof, visionary, a born leader of men. Doc Methuselah is a member of a governing elite, the Lieutenant the shaper of one; each seems to have his warmest relations with a doting subordinate, each knows how to put sharply in his place any outsider guilty of lèse majesté. One senses from the loving care that went into their portrayal that both represented to a great degree Hubbard's personal ideal of leadership and manliness.

The continuities between Hubbard's fiction writing and his later career, though hardly extensive, are nevertheless more evident during this period—1938–41—than during the preceding phase. Hubbard himself was later at pains to assert that his first breakthrough in the understanding of human existence occurred in 1938 when he composed a lengthy philosophical treatise entitled "Excalibur," which he never published. According to him this treatise contained most of the ideas that are now Scientology. It must be said, however, that despite themes here and there taken from occult lore (mainly magic and demonology) and the appearance of a term or two that now occupies a marginal position in Scientology, Hubbard's writings of this period give little indication that their author was in the grip of any overarching philosophical or occult system. The tales are varied in their premises and decidedly undidactic. Foreshadowings of things to come are of a more general and characterological sort: the vision of a dedicated elite with its charismatic leader; absorption with hidden realities that may be partly tricks of the mind; a still guarded but rather more intense interest in the darker side of human nature.[1]

Yet the late 1930s were probably a time of considerable intellectual ferment for Hubbard, as he had then begun to take his place as a charter member of science fiction's first really outstanding generation of writers, a generation that reached its literary maturity the year the United States was drawn into World War II (Moskowitz 1966:218). This exciting new milieu and the war itself were apparently to have appreciable impact on Hubbard's destiny. But for a while it seemed that what the science fiction world had given him by way of intellec-

1. This generalization might be subject to modification were we to have all of Hubbard's writings in our view. He claimed to have written under as many as twenty pen names and published in some ninety publications. He did not reveal his pseudonyms, however. Only one or two are known. The Ole Doc Methuselah stories were first published under the pseudonym of Renée Lafayette. Malko guesses that Kurt von Rachne was another Hubbard nom de plume (Hubbard 1970c; Malko 1970:94–95, 34).

tual stimulation and literary inspiration, the war very nearly took away. Sam Moskowitz, science fiction chronicler, writes:

> One author who today might be rated with the giants of modern science fiction—with Heinlein, Sturgeon, Van Vogt, and Asimov—if only he had continued to write, is L. Ron Hubbard. Recruited from the adventure pulps where he had been a superior stylist capable of touches of human interest that evoked comparison with the great pulp air story writer George Bruce, he ably carried his talent into science fiction when recruited by John W. Campbell. His three-part novel, *Final Blackout* . . . was a stunning achievement. . . . The readers waited for Hubbard to come back from the war. When he did his red hair had become pure white from suffering caused by injuries. . . . It was years more before his writing seemed to assume its old magic. For a flash, in *To the Stars* (*Astounding Science Fiction*, March-April 1950) . . . he came near to writing the most effective human drama based upon the time dilitation effect. One month later, *Astounding Science Fiction*, May 1950, published his article, *Dianetics, The Evolution of a Science*, and L. Ron Hubbard was launched on a new career which marked a point of no return as far as his science fiction writing was concerned. [1966:414–15]

Shortly after creating his fine portrait of "the Lieutenant" of *Final Blackout*, Hubbard himself was commissioned a lieutenant in the U.S. Navy. He was assigned to corvettes doing convoy escort and antisubmarine duty primarily (perhaps his previous experience with small craft had something to do with this assignment), and before World War II was over he had seen action in both the Pacific and the Atlantic. Toward the end of the war he sustained massive injuries, he later claimed. He gave no details of these, only the dramatic upshot: "In 1944 he was severely wounded and taken crippled and blinded to Oak Knoll Naval Hospital." He maintained that he had been twice pronounced dead (*Scientology* 1[1]:7). The Navy would confirm only that he spent time in a naval hospital (Malko 1970:37).

Whatever the nature and severity of his injuries, they were by his own account the critical impetus for his development of a science of mental healing. By drawing upon varied sources of inspiration, including Freudian theory, Eastern mysticism, and nuclear physics, Hubbard said later, he gained enough insight to patch himself up again in a couple of years. By 1949 he was reclassified as fully fit for military duty (*The Auditor* 63:7; *Scientology* 1[1]:7).

A source of inspiration that may have been most crucial to his development of Dianetics was the psychotherapeutic methodology developed during the war for use on cases of combat fatigue and traumatic neuroses. The primary technique is described by William Sargant as a type of abreaction therapy facilitated by drugs.

> A drug would be administered to a carefully chosen patient . . . and as it started to take effect, an endeavor would be made to make him re-live the episode that had caused his breakdown. Sometimes the episode, or episodes, had been mentally suppressed, and the memory would have to be brought to the surface again. At other times it was fully remembered, but the strong emotions originally attached to it had since been suppressed. The marked improvement in the patient's nervous condition was attributed to the releasing of these original emotions. It was also found that the emotions which were most profitably released—or "abreacted," as the psychiatric term is—were those of fear or anger. [1957:xxiv]

Dispense with the use of drugs and the qualification concerning which emotions are most profitably abreacted, and you have the basic principle of Dianetic therapy. Military psychiatrists also discovered that abreaction of traumatic episodes need not be restricted to real episodes; often imaginary situations suggested to the patient worked as well or better as long as they could be utilized to bring the patient's fears and angers to a crescendo (Sargant 1957:xxv). In Dianetics, as we shall see, this principle is operative but it is interpreted quite differently.

It need not be surmised that Hubbard himself received abreaction treatments while hospitalized at Oak Knoll, only that he may well have had opportunity to become acquainted with such a method there and that he had a compelling personal reason to take an interest. Certainly by the time he announced Dianetics, he admitted a familiarity with the method and its original context (the treatment of "war neurosis"). In *Dianetics: The Evolution of a Science*, he claimed to have worked with the technique but to have found it—like all other methods besides his own—wanting (Hubbard 1966:24–25).

His own allusions and statements of early followers suggest that from the time of his hospitalization Hubbard began to experiment with psychotherapeutic ideas and to play amateur therapist to friends and acquaintances. His new avocation apparently met with success (Winter 1951:5). Thus it may well have been primarily after the war rather than earlier that he was galvanized to work with and further explore the various theories of "the human mind" and "human existence"—occult, psychiatric, and philosophical—to which his early works on Dianetics make allusion. He would then have come into contact, either directly through available sources or indirectly through friends, with more of the mixture of Freudian- and Pavlovian-inspired therapeutic theories which circulated at that time and to which Dianetics bears resemblances: ideas concerning conditioning, birth and prenatal traumas, the uses of hypnotic age-regression, and so on (see Wallis 1976: Part I, ch. 2).

In trying to extract from the personal style on view in Hubbard's pre-Dianetic background and his later public behavior some sense of what motivated the creation of Dianetics and Scientology, one must bear in mind that a process of discrediting inevitably overtakes all attempts to mass market religious or therapeutic solutions in our culture as well as all attempts to gain a following for scientific claims outside the established channels of credentialing and peer review. In an important sense, the actual personality of the religious entrepreneur or deviant scientist is irrelevant to the operation of this process. The activities themselves invite suspicion of quackery or megalomania (or both). It is little surprise then that when the press examines a figure such as Hubbard who, as it happens, was both selling hope and pressing questionable scientific claims, the interpretive problem (if any is perceived) typically revolves around which of two stereotypes is most fitting: the con man or the crank (see for example, Gardner 1957:263–80).

The structure of this situation duly noted, it must be said that Hubbard's style of presenting and promoting his inventions furnished his critics with material for either form of damnation. Affectations of historical grandeur ("Mankind has no greater friend"), the announcement of his Dianetics breakthroughs as "comparable to [man's] discovery of fire and superior to his invention of the wheel and arch," the advertising of a secret early work as so powerful that "four of the first fifteen people who read it went insane," his practice of writing encomniums to himself under pseudonyms (Gardner 1957:263), are just a few of the many reported examples of a promotional approach that seems to dovetail all too nicely with the story that Hubbard once declared to his fiction-writing friends, "If a man really wanted to make a million dollars, the best way would be to start his own religion" (*New York Times* July 28, 1977).

Elements of hype and razzle-dazzle, however, do not necessarily a

con artist make. Taken in the context of Hubbard's long-term commitment to the elaboration, promulgation, and defense of his idea system, even during financially unrewarding years, and also in light of
the barricades of secrecy, conspiracy theory, and defensive litigation
with which he surrounded his embattled organization (see Wallis
1976:190–241), these traits seem less indicative of greed for gain than
part of an egoistic complex that often characterizes visionaries, cranky
or not. If Hubbard had trouble appearing fully sincere about his ideas
when broadcasting them to the general public, this is arguably the
result of a deep unwillingness to reveal his real vulnerability in regard
to them. Knowing that his ideas were apt to take a critical pounding in
the press, he hid behind flamboyant overstatement and commer-
cialism. He preferred, it may well be, to appear a cynic rather than a
fool.

A somewhat different form of self-distancing can be discerned in his
taped lectures to Scientology audiences. Here, instead of a pitchman,
we hear a genial pedagogue, expounding his theories in a way best
described as affectionate and playful. His more stupefying assertions,
sliding by almost parenthetically, seem to bemuse him and are often
followed by some mood-lightening irreverance, as if to proclaim, "The
truth is whacky, isn't it, but what can I say?" Here Hubbard models
the stance of the pragmatic intellectualist who, upon finding that it
somehow "works" to subscribe to certain ideas his critical faculty may
have difficulty accepting, surrenders his resistance but not his sense of
humor, the latter remaining to attest to his fundamental good sense. I
observed this stance in a number of his followers too.

The traits we are inclined to read into Hubbard's style and his
productions—a drive to impress and provoke wonderment, the dis-
guising of vulnerability with flippancy and cynicism, the fantasy of
leading a dedicated elite—must of course remain speculative. Moreover, even if the speculations are on target, the traits that emerge are
quite general in nature and have relatively little bearing on the content and specific character of the doctrines Hubbard came to promote.
In many ways the governing impulses of Dianetics and Scientology are
clearest when seen against the background not of a personality but of a
particular cultural milieu. Let us turn now to this side of the problem.

The Cultural Context of Hubbard's Ideas

Hubbard's Dianetics and Scientology writings evidence a vast but
superficial erudition in all those areas in which he has sought to bol-

ster his image as expert: Eastern and other exotic religions, physics and engineering, psychoanalysis, philosophy. He lavished credit for his inspiration on, among others, Buddha, Freud, Confucius, Count Alfred Korzybski (inventor of "general semantics"), Clerk Maxwell, Henri Poincaré, and Will Durant—a heterogeneous assembly. This sort of intellectual background, as well as his invention ultimately of a "scientific religion," is best explained by Hubbard's involvement in occult and science fiction circles.

Both science fiction and occultism are favorite haunts of America's fringe intelligentsia, and there has been much cross-fertilization between the visions of science fiction writers and occult/metaphysical enthusiams (Whitehead 1974). The importance of this milieu for understanding Hubbard lies less in the existence of specific doctrines that he may have appropriated than in the general intellectual orientation that characterizes it. Chiefly there is the urge, usually latent in or ironically handled by the science fiction writer but more explicit in the case of the sci-fi "buff" and his occultist cousin, to combine systems of worldly manipulation—such as science—with a salvational meaning that exalts such systems to near-religious status, or conversely (but with equivalent logic) to seek in the mysteries of religion a pragmatic truth that can be applied directly to the material of the mundane world. The occultist would in one stroke make science magical and magic scientific. "Manipulationist" sects in Western culture—Christian Science, New Thought, Rosicrucianism, and others—exemplify this posture, and Hubbard's ultimate creation, Scientology, is of this type (see Wilson 1970: ch. 8). The occult and positivist blurring of epistemological boundaries between knowing in the sense of grasping a deeper relevance and knowing in the sense of possessing empirically useful abstractions supports a wide-ranging religious and scientific eclecticism, a homogenization of great thinkers with small (Freud and Alfred Korzybski; Buddha and Will Durant), and the promulgation of eccentric philosophic and scientific theories. "No one has a monopoly on the truth," averred the occultists interviewed by H. T. Dohrmann in the middle 1950s (Dorhmann 1958:98). Although he was later to castigate such an attitude when the orthodoxy of his own theories was at issue, Hubbard's early account of how he developed his theories of the mind offers a good illustration of this free-market approach to knowledge:

> In a lifetime of wandering around many strange things had been observed. The medicine man of the Goldi people of Manchuria, the

shamans of North Borneo, Sioux medicine men, the cults of Los Angeles, and modern psychology. Amongst the people questioned about
existence were a magician whose ancestors served in the court of Kublai
Khan and a Hindu who could hypnotize cats. Dabbles had been made in
mysticism, data had been studied from mythology to spiritualism. Odds
and ends like these, countless odds and ends. [Hubbard 1966:14–15]

Roy Wallis's research linked Hubbard, for the period just after the
war, with a man named Jack Parsons, then a research chemist at the
California Institute of Technology and a follower of magician Aliester
Crowley (Wallis 1976:22, 111). Science fiction acquaintances may
have been a greater influence. Hubbard came to be identified with a
literary cohort that dominated the science fiction publications of the
1940s and 1950s and included such luminaries as Robert Heinlein
who—according to Scientologists—was once Hubbard's roommate,
A. E. Van Vogt, who was to become a convert to Dianetics in the first
year, and John Campbell, Jr., editor of the popular magazine *Astounding Science Fiction*. Of these individuals, the most influential in
the development of Hubbard's thinking appears to have been Campbell. Campbell began touting Hubbard's ideas privately in 1948 or
1949, then publicly in the pages of *Astounding Science Fiction* in 1949
and 1950. He and a Dr. Joseph A. Winter (a science fiction fan) were
Hubbard's closest collaborators in the setting up of the first Dianetics
foundation. Campbell's intellectual influence may well have begun
long before this.

The two men began their professional acquaintance and most likely
their personal acquaintance in the late 1930s when, according to
Moskowitz, Campbell, who had recently assumed the editorship of
Astounding, "recruited" Hubbard to the science fiction genre. Campbell was only a year older than Hubbard and, like Hubbard, had
begun his writing career in college, making quite a name for himself
among science fiction readers with his gigantic space epics. Like Hubbard he had had to drop out of college—in this case MIT—as a result
of neglecting his studies (German, specifically), though he later obtained a degree in science from Duke University (Moskowitz 1966:36).
His record as a scientist, however, was a good deal more developed
than Hubbard's. He consistently attracted the attention of his science
professors, some of whom were disappointed that he did not choose to
make a career in their fields. Nuclear physics, chemistry, and mathe-
matics were all strong subjects for Campbell, and for a time he enjoyed the friendship of Norbert Weiner, whose pioneering work in
cybernetics, Moskowitz suggests, may have inspired Campbell's re-

peated use of computer themes in his stories (Moskowitz 1966:34). Both nuclear physics imagery and to an even greater degree computer and communications terminology were to surface in Hubbard's Dianetics and Scientology writings. If we are to see this tendency as the result of Campbell's influence, and put it together with the fact that the two got to know each other in the late 1930s, we may have located the kernel of truth in Hubbard's claim to have laid the theoretical groundwork for Scientology as early as 1938.

Campbell had his occultist leanings as well, though he did not reveal the full extent of these until his enthusiasm for Dianetics had passed. In 1952 we find him endorsing "the search for Bridey Murphy," and in 1956 he promoted a "psionics" machine that purportedly revealed auras and radiations of some mysterious sort. He wrote at the time, "There is a reality-field other than, and different from, what we know as science" (Gardner 1957:316–17, 346–47). But this sort of flagrant excursion into the magical lay in Campbell's future. In 1948–49, when he became openly involved with Hubbard's new mental theory, Campbell was at the height of his brilliant editorial career at *Astounding.* He had succeeded in moving science fiction away from the "space opera stuff" full of "gee whiz, double-talk science" (which he himself had indulged in as a young writer) and toward more sophisticated and reflective works in which literary merit and moral concern achieved a balance with intelligent technological speculation (Canary 1977:166). His attraction to Hubbard as a writer, like his attraction to the others he encouraged—among them, Robert Heinlein, Ray Bradbury, Isaac Asimov, and Frederick Pohl—can be seen as arising from his regard for literary values and psychological sophistication in science fiction writing.

Yet Campbell's stewardship of science fiction during this period, while radical in the respects just cited, was at a deeper level impeccably conservative. His editorial purging of science fiction's social and psychological naivety, its unadulterated positivism and gadgetry, did not extinguish but rather seems to have brought to mature expression the technocratic elitist vision that motivated the genre. Campbell himself exalted reason as man's highest function, and the fiction which he encouraged promulgated, according to one critic, "a conception of the human condition as merely a set of problems which some theoretical or technological breakthrough will 'solve.'" (Wymer 1977).

This technocratic vision, conjoined with a preference (common among social scientists of the time) for explaining social phenomena in terms of individual psychology, helped to make the Cold War situation that obtained during the years that Hubbard and Campbell began their collaboration resolvable into a set of specifically psychological problems, the solution to which could be provided by a "breakthrough" in mental technology. The train of reasoning I am talking about was by no means limited to science fiction circles. If we follow popular arguments (that persist even to this day), it seems that public anxiety over the possibility that "reasons of state" might, through their own internal logic, set off nuclear holocaust had a way of boiling down to the more specialized and improbable fear that someone who fingered the buttons of war might one day take leave of his senses. It followed that more adequate controls over individual irrationality were very much in order. So too, the ideological competition—the "battle for the mind," as it has been called—between "free world" and communist world that thrived during the Cold War years underwent a similar specializing interpretation. In 1950, following the Moscow "show trials" and the trial of Joseph Cardinal Mindszenty, the term "brainwashing" first surfaced in the media. The appeal of this concept revealed more than just the common assumption that doctrines unacceptable to oneself can be embraced by others only under duress; it indicated a fundamentally mechanistic understanding of the relationship between mind and idea. Brains could be cleansed of their present contents, then filled up again with something new. Speculation abounded that with the aid of sufficiently sophisticated devices, an "idea" could be implanted in or extracted from the mind as if it were a splinter (Brown 1963:285, 291). Experiments then current in Pavlovian conditioning, "truth" drugs, and hypnotic suggestion seemed to reinforce, at the same time as they were guided by, this model. According to John Marks's recent study, the CIA's dalliance with "mind-control" research, initiated in 1951, exemplified an attempt to follow out the mechanistic model to its logical conclusion—the construction of a "brainwashing machine."[2]

The assumptions that shaped CIA and popular thinking in response

2. The CIA, upon investigating Russian and Chinese techniques of forcible persuasion, were satisfied that these represented no new scientific achievements, but they were not satisfied that such achievements were impossible. Says Marks, "If such a machine were even remotely feasible, one had to assume the communists might discover it. And in that case, national security required that the United States invent the machine first. Therefore, the CIA built up its own elaborate brainwashing program. . . . It was a tiny replica of the Manhattan Project, grounded in the conviction that the keys to brainwashing lay in technology" (Marks 1979:131).

to the Cold War did not fail to undergo related evolutions in the science fiction world, where these assumptions were so deeply cherished. In collaboration with Campbell, Hubbard presented his new therapy, Dianetics, as a technological "fix" for the mind that worked by removing all sorts of forcibly implanted suggestions and had the effect of wiping "clear" the entire irrational component of a person's nature, leaving only the rational. The implications of his theory for the times were quite clear to Hubbard.

> A science of mind is a goal which has engrossed thousands of generations of Man. Armies, dynasties and whole civilizations have perished for lack of it. Rome went to dust for the want of it. China swims in blood for the need of it; and down in the arsenal is an atom bomb, its hopeful nose full-armed in ignorance of it. . . . In the larger sphere of societies and nations, the lack of such a science of mind was never more evident; for the physical sciences, advancing thoughtlessly far in advance of man's ability to understand man, have armed him with terrible and thorough weapons which await only another outburst of the social insanity of war. [Hubbard 1950:26, 27]

When we examine the "countless odds and ends" that appear to have actually gone into Hubbard's Dianetic discoveries, we find, as Wallis points out, that all were present in the orthodox or fringe psychological literature of the day. The abreaction approach and the idea of a hidden realm of mental content (both suggested in Freud's early writings), concepts of post-hypnotic suggestion and hypnotic age-regression, the idea of conditioned reflexes, theories of the neurosis-engendering potential of birth and prenatal trauma and, last but no means least, the generally held psychotherapeutic principle that cure proceeds from the airing of things past—all of these components Hubbard wrapped in a bundle and persuasively tied together with the imagery of the mind as computer.

His personal fascinations and ambitions given due credit, it must be borne in mind that Hubbard developed his magically charged "science of mind," Dianetics, within an intellectual milieu that strongly supported just the sort of positivist enthusiasms and speculative "bricolage" that his theory so abundantly manifests. Moreover, it was a milieu that was seized, in its own extravagant way, with the same concerns that animated the respectable sciences of the day and that set about its work with the aid of many of the same intellectual tools.

[58]

When Dianetics made its debut in 1950, then, it had a certain familiarity and plausibility about it. In the contemporary mind, it must have had the appearance of the kind of "breakthrough" one would expect from the nature of the questions then being asked and the lines of speculation then being offered.

Dianetics and the Dianetics Movement

In *Dianetics: The Modern Science of Mental Health*, Hubbard argued that much of human ills, psychological and psychosomatic, stems from unremembered past incidents, the contents of which are deeply programmed into the sufferer through pain and unconsciousness. These "occluded" incidents act much like implanted hypnotic suggestions after the hypnotic trance has passed; they dictate inappropriate behavior and feelings, the nature of which the subject cannot explain. It is as if the mind were a programmable computer with two entirely separate sets of memory banks, each feeding into the computer's solutions but neither coordinated with the other. The two different "banks" Hubbard chose to speak of as two different "minds," the Analytical Mind and the Reactive Mind.

The Analytical Mind is operative in a person's usual, wakeful, fully conscious, "rational" state, and it contains information and memories that are, if not always in awareness, at least readily available to awareness. The only reason, Dianetically speaking, for the Analytical Mind to mislead an individual or cause him or her to act in an inappropriate manner would be if the individual had acquired misinformation or false data. Inappropriateness or "mistakes" of an Analytical nature are thus easily corrected by proper education. The Analytical Mind is a storehouse for consciously acquired and accessible information, and it operates upon this information by what is usually called the "reasoning process": it discriminates, sorts, assesses, and explores, and—within the limits of the data provided—delivers up judgments, interpretations, and responses appropriate to the situation at hand. Thereby it serves in a sophisticated and flexible manner to aid the survival of the individual.

The other mind, the Reactive Mind, which later came to be termed simply "the Bank," is also geared to survival adaptation, but it works on a primitive stimulus-response or reflex level. It takes in and records any information that comes to the individual during states of

[59]

pain and partial or total loss of consciousness, or during states in which earlier such states have been "keyed-in," that is, restimulated. On this information it performs only one operation: equation. Thus, all bits of stimulus information present during the critical incident become inextricably associated with pain or painful emotion and with each other. Hubbard explained, somewhat malapropishly: "[It's] so beautifully, wonderfully simple that it can be stated, in operation, to have just one equation: $A=A=A=A=A$" (1950:80). What he meant really is $A=B=C=D$ and so on, but the point is clear. Critical incidents, recorded by the Reactive Mind, are under ordinary circumstances unavailable to the Analytical Mind, but they influence the latter's computations through the mechanism of association. Stimuli coming to the individual in an ordinary Analytic state may, through similarity or identity to an item recorded in a forgotten traumatic incident, "key-in" the entire incident, thus causing the person to act in a manner appropriate to the original incident but irrational in terms of the present occasion. This reflex "reactive" activity goes on outside the control of the individual will or rational judgment.

Incidents of pain and unconsciousness recorded in the Reactive Mind, Hubbard termed "engrams"—that is, "traces." (This term was in use in biology and psychology before Hubbard adopted it. In psychology it was used to mean very much what Hubbard meant by it, but in a more general sense: "a permanent effect produced in the psyche as a result of stimulation"—see *Webster's New World Dictionary*.) One simple illustration of the workings of an engram is Hubbard's "fish" story:

> Let us now take an example of the reactive mind's processes in a lower echelon of life: a fish swims into the shallows where the water is brackish, yellow and tastes of iron. He has just taken a mouthful of shrimp when a bigger fish rushes at him and knocks against his tail.
> The small fish manages to get away but he has been physically hurt. Having negligible analytic powers, the small fish depends upon reaction for much of his choice of activity. . . .
> The computation of the fish reactive level was: shallows equals brackish equals yellow equals iron taste equals pain in tail equals shrimp in mouth, and any one of these equals any other. . . .
> The small fish, after this, swims into brackish water. This makes him slightly "nervous". But he goes on swimming and finds himself in yellow and brackish water. And still he does not turn back. He begins to get a small pain in his tail. But he keeps on swimming. Suddenly he gets a

taste of iron and the pain in his tail turns on heavily. And away he goes like a flash. No fish was after him. There were shrimp to be had there. But away he went anyway. Dangerous place! And if he had not turned away, he would have really gotten himself a pain in the tail. [1950:81]

A good deal more elaboration upon this simple principle is necessary before one can fully appreciate the impact of the Reactive Mind on everyday life. Engrams, as hinted above, are not the sole occupants of the Reactive Mind. Incidents of loss or painful emotion ("misemotion"), because they invariably link to an engram or engrams, also come to be stored in the Reactive Mind. These are called secondary engrams, or "secondaries." Additionally, any incident which "keys-in" an engram or a secondary—even though the incident in question is itself devoid of pain, misemotion, or loss of consciousness—gets recorded in the Reactive Mind. These are called "locks." Engrams, secondaries, and locks not only intervene in the affairs of Analytic life through the mechanism of association, but also, through the same mechanism, chain up within the Reactive Mind, so that any stimulus which keys-in one incident may equally well key-in a whole chain of them—all linked by an identity or similarity of an item or items of their content. Furthermore, the Reactive response of the individual to a key-in or restimulation may vary tremendously. The response may be relatively mild—an inexplicable feeling of discomfort or a fleeting twinge of the old pain; or it may be a severe influx of distress, painful emotion, or bodily malaise. Psychosomatic illnesses are the result of restimulated engrams. Enduring illnesses bespeak a continuous restimulation. Some key-ins take the form of a "redramatization" of an entire incident, with the further complication that the keyed-in individual may assume the role of actors in the original situation other than himself or herself. A dramatization may manifest itself in psychotic, hysterical, or dissociated states, or it may take the far more insidious—but far more common—form of an apparently rational act, overlaid with Analytic justifications and explanations while being all the while Reactive, and thus at some root level inappropriate.

Words spoken during engrammic incidents become part of the engram—whether or not they were comprehensible to the subject at the time of the incident—and may set up "aberrations" in later life based upon puns or double-entendres on the engrammic phrases. Since many of the most "aberrative" engrams are acquired prenatally, according to Hubbard, a person's pet generalizations and argumentative gambits may be based on words muttered during an attempted abortion or a brutal act of parental coitus (an interesting light in which to view the arguments of an opponent or the demands of a dependent). In short, the concept of the engram, sufficiently compounded and modified, becomes flexible enough to handle the whole varied spectrum of human behavior.

> The engram can dictate all the various processes incident to living; it can dictate beliefs, opinions, thought processes or lack of them and actions of all kinds, and can establish conditions remarkable for their complexity as well as their stupidity. An engram can dictate anything it contains and engrams can contain all the combinations of words in the entire language. And the analytical mind is forced, in the light of irrational behavior or conviction, to *justify* the acts and conditions of the organism, as well as its own strange blunders. [Hubbard 1950:95]

The purpose of Dianetic auditing was to make sick people well, unhappy people happy, failing people successful, and those otherwise discontented with themselves content. Hubbard decided this could be done by emptying the Reactive Mind of its stored contents, in essence "clearing" the human computer of its hidden irrational data so that proper computation could proceed thenceforth. A completely "clear" individual would behave with total rationality, even superior rationality. A person who had not yet reached this posited state was spoken of, in the context of auditing, as a "pre-clear," or, abbreviatedly, a "p-c." The elimination of even one engram was a step in the right direction and was spoken of as a "release." In *Dianetics: The Modern Science of Mental Health*, Hubbard made no claims to being himself "clear" or even extensively "released." Though it was perhaps desirable, he did not hold it necessary that a person be cleared or released in order to audit another. Auditing was an impersonal technique that could be applied to anyone by anyone with good results providing the basic rules were followed. Perusing the book, however, one finds that the basic rules squirm beneath one's grasp. Like the concept of the engram, the concept of auditing has a simple skeletal form that comes fleshed out with numerous modifications, additions, and elaborations until its complexity matches that of the corresponding psychological theory.

Skeletally, Dianetic auditing goes as follows: one person, the auditor ("listener"), sits down with another, the pre-clear, gets the pre-clear into a receptive and relaxed state of mind, then guides him or her into reexperiencing painful past incidents. A good deal of attention is devoted to getting the subject to "contact" the past incident fully, so that rather than relaying it to the auditor in the form of an abstract memory, the p-c relives the incident—"runs" it, in Hubbard's words—with almost hallucinatory realness. Ideally, all the forgotten details of the incident should come to light, the emotion experienced in the past should be reexperienced in the auditing session, and its force fully discharged. Once this has occurred, the incident is "erased" from the Reactive Mind and can no longer affect the pre-clear's life. Symptoms and behavior connected with the incident will disappear; vital energy—"life units"—trapped in the engram will return to the rational self, causing in the pre-clear a feeling of invigoration and optimism. After full discharge of an incident, the pre-clear will find himself/herself unable to "run" it again. If it is remembered at all, it will be recalled in an abstract schematic fashion, that is, in the fashion of the Analytical Mind. If the running of an incident falls short of full erasure, the "charge" on it may nevertheless be somewhat reduced; one can audit it again in a later session. It is forbidden, however, to interrupt a session while the pre-clear is in the middle of an incident.

The function of the auditor is to guide and to listen. He or she must not interpret the pre-clear's productions nor evaluate them. If the incident being run appears logically impossible, inconsistent with what the auditor knows of the pre-clear, radically different from the way it was represented in an earlier session, or even, for that matter, if it appears to be a scene from a book or movie—so be it. The auditor concentrates only on the characteristics of contact and discharge, not on the content of the incident *per se*. After all, the Reactive Mind contains "aberration"; it does not contain logic. In other words, maximum permission is given for a free flow of spontaneous fantasy. Guidance is addressed to this end and to the discouragement of any attempt on the part of the pre-clear to evade, resist, excuse self, chit-chat, or in any way avoid it. As one may have surmised from the description of the Reactive Mind above, resistances and evasions are quite easily handled by treating them not as objective discourse but as manifestations of Reactive Mind. One method that Hubbard strongly recommends in *Dianetics: The Modern Science of Mental Health* is the "repeater" technique. The auditor seizes upon whatever phrase the p-c is using to protest or evade the auditing process and makes the p-c repeat it over and over until an "incident" begins to blossom around it. The auditor then has the pre-clear run this incident. Hubbard explains: "The rule in diagnosis is that whatever the individual offers the auditor as a detrimental reaction to therapy is engrammic and will prove so in the process. Whatever impedes the auditor in his work is identical to whatever is impeding the patient in his thinking and living" (1950:192). He then illustrates the "repeater" remedy:

> (In reverie—the pre-natal basic area)
> PRECLEAR: (Believing he means Dianetics). I don't know. I don't know. I just can't remember. It won't work. I know it won't work.
> AUDITOR: (repeater technique, described later). Go over that. Say, "It won't work."
> PRECLEAR: "It won't work. It won't work. It won't work. . . ." etc., etc. Ouch, my stomach hurts! "It won't work. It won't work. It won't work . . . " (Laughter of relief.) That's my mother. Talking to herself.
> AUDITOR: All right, let's pick up the entire engram. Begin at the beginning.
> PRECLEAR: (Quoting recall with somatics [pains]). "I don't know how to do it. I just can't remember what Becky told me. I just can't remember it. Oh, I'm so discouraged. It won't work this way. It just won't work. I wish I knew what Becky told me but I can't remember. Oh I wish . . . " Hey, what's she got in here? Why, God damn her, that's beginning to burn! It's a douche. Say! Let me out of here! [1950:192–93]

Another technique that serves to mark off a piece of discourse as engrammic is the "flash answer" technique. The auditor demands that on the count of three, or at the snap of his fingers, the pre-clear is to blurt out whatever comes to mind. The marked item then becomes a gateway into the Reactive Mind. (This is similar to the "head-press" technique Freud used in some of his earlier cases. See Breuer and Freud 1964:79.)

Since in the auditing session the pre-clear's productions are denied the status of anything other than manifestations of Reactive Mind— even attempting to leave the session or falling asleep is treated as a dramatization of one sort or another—there is no way in which he or she can fail to conform to the pattern anticipated by Dianetic theory and, in practice, usually little he or she can do to avoid coming up with and running incidents. Dianetics as a therapy, however, may come to have its validity questioned if the pre-clear fails to improve or benefit from the running of incidents. As his system developed, Hubbard learned to forestall this potential invalidation by pointing to auditor error and by elaborating more and more nuanced rules for correct auditing. In this way, auditing failure like "ritual failure" could be ascribed to the violation of some minutia of the rules. Such a strategy, like the clever turning of the pre-clear's objections into engrammic phrases, would help to make the particular construction of reality out of which the therapy proceeded proof against any puncture.

This, in brief, was the new therapy that infatuated a good portion of the American public in 1950, when Hubbard's book hit the stands. *Astounding Science Fiction* readers were already primed for its appearance in 1949, when Campbell published Hubbard's account of how he had developed the new science.[3] Even before that, Campbell had been touting Dianetics to his friends and to some of the contributors to *Astounding*, including Dr. Joseph A. Winter, who later published an account of early Dianetics. In his letter to Winter, Campbell claimed that Hubbard had audited nearly a thousand cases ranging in severity from the psychosomatically ill to the totally schizophrenic, and had cured every case he worked on (Winter 1951:5). (Hubbard's auditing had relieved Campbell himself of chronic sinusitis—a condition into which he relapsed two years later, after becoming disillusioned with Hubbard.)

Like Campbell, Hubbard had been busy before publication, calling upon friends and acquaintances to come to New Jersey and join him in his experiments with Dianetics. Thus a small core of interested people had formed around him before the appearance of "Evolution of a Science" in *Astounding*. After publication, when interest began to increase, Hubbard went into business in the small town of Bay Head and shortly thereafter in Elizabeth, lecturing, training, auditing, passing out certificates and in general exercising his remarkable talent for promotion. A. E. Van Vogt, one of those Hubbard had been urging to join him, recalled how he was eventually recruited to the cause.

> Early in 1950, I began to receive phone calls from Mr. L. Ron Hubbard, whom I had met in 1945. He would call me long distance [Van Vogt was in California] from New Jersey, every morning, and talk to me for an hour trying to get me interested in dianetics.
>
> I said, "No, I'm a writer. I'm not interested in anything but being a writer."

3. This account now appears in the Scientology publication *Dianetics: The Evolution of a Science.*

Now, surprisingly enough, I don't know how this happened. People began to send me money. I can imagine that Hubbard actually wrote inquirers and told them to contact me. Anyway, I would receive checks in the mail for a hundred dollars, or more, for the course in dianetics that was not yet in sight. I received, altogether, about five thousand dollars in the mail, and I was receiving these calls from Hubbard at the same time.

Then I got a complimentary copy of the book on dianetics from Hubbard when it came out. . . .

Anyway, I read the book. My wife had had a migraine headache for thirteen years for four days at a time each month.

After reading the book, I said, "All right, lie down. We'll see what can be done."

We cleared up her headache! She's never had it since! . . . I said, "This guy's got something." Meanwhile these phone calls continued.

The phone would ring at seven o'clock in the morning and I would know who it was. At about ten after eight I'd be off the phone, and he would have talked for that whole hour and ten minutes from New York or New Jersey.

He'd finally say, "Well, I've got to go. I'm teaching a class."

This shocked me. Finally around the seventeenth or eighteenth day, my stubbornness was shattered. That kind of phone calling, long distance, was completely out of my reality. It was beyond my conception that anybody was phoning that often and talking that long at those rates. I had to put a stop to that, so I made an agreement, and I was in dianetics.

People who were associated with Hubbard told me later on that his phone bills were six thousand dollars a month. I don't doubt it, because he wasn't only calling me; he was calling dozens of other people over in Europe and elsewhere. [1964:237–39]

The main book, *Dianetics: The Modern Science of Mental Health,* provoked a vogue around the country for what George Malko calls coffee-klatch auditing (1970:54). Upon one reading, or even one-half reading, people would sit down and blithely audit their friends and relatives through war injuries, birth traumas, and back into the hubbub of the uterus where introduced objects, pressures of constipation, ill-advised medication, and the blows of angry or passionate mates seemed to provide a never-ending source of engrammic misery. For many, Dianetic experimentation went no further than an afternoon's or a week's infatuation. Sizable crowds, however, began to flock to the Hubbard Dianetic Research Foundation, Inc., in Elizabeth. Among the followers there was always a core of the most loyal and the most

[66]

persistent who joined the staff of whatever organizations Hubbard set up and even trailed him around the country, working long hours for little or no pay just to be close to the center of action. A more common pattern was for enthusiasts to attend mass training sessions wherever those happened to be taking place, then to return to their home towns in certified possession of the latest techniques with which to audit and train the locals.

Having set things going in New Jersey, Hubbard expanded the operation almost immediately by setting up another foundation in Los Angeles and branch organizations in Chicago, New York, Washington, D.C., and Honolulu (Wallis 1976:43). The two foundations handled the majority of traffic in the first two years. Van Vogt estimates that the Los Angeles foundation had taken in between two and three hundred thousand dollars by January 1951. But by that spring, its bankruptcy was imminent.

Several things had gone wrong, not the least of which was financial and organizational mismanagement and Hubbard's penchant for over-extension. The foundations apparently teemed with "staffers" expecting weekly paychecks. No one had any idea of where many of them came from, but all claimed that Hubbard had hired them. The telephone company began demanding the not inconsiderable sums he owed it, and publicity brought down boards of medical examiners on Hubbard's head. To worsen the public image of Dianetics, Hubbard's then wife, Sarah Northrup Hubbard, whom at one point he pronounced "clear"—that is, a totally rational being—had him pronounced insane by some doctors she consulted and sued for divorce.[4] In early 1951 his attempt to present Dianetics to a large gathering at Los Angeles' Shrine Auditorium failed disastrously. What was left of the Los Angeles foundation broke away from Hubbard, and he fled in temporary despair to Cuba. He returned in a couple of months, however, for another attempt, this time in Wichita. Once the Wichita foundation seemed established, Hubbard branched out to Phoenix. But shortly thereafter the Wichita foundation was forced into bankruptcy, owing, again, to overextension and the debts inherited from the previous foundation. A legal battle erupted between Hubbard and his financial backer, Wichita businessman D. G. Purcell, who had acquired Hubbard's rights to the foundation and the copyright of

4. Hubbard eventually won a countersuit against his ex-wife, and she signed a statement retracting her allegations (Wallis 1976:49–50).

Dianetics in exchange for rescuing him from the first round of debts. The conflict was not resolved until 1954, when Purcell, quitting Dianetics altogether, sold the copyright and the foundation's mailing list back to Hubbard (Wallis 1976:95). The Phoenix organization, which Hubbard had already renamed the Hubbard Association of Scientologists (H.A.S.) was, in 1954, incorporated as the Hubbard Association of Scientologists International (H.A.S.I.) Inc. of Arizona. Up until 1966, this corporate entity served as the chief legal and financial organ through which Hubbard directed Scientology affairs, foreign and domestic (Foster 1971:26–29; for a detailed account of the crisis period, see Wallis 1976: chs. 2 & 3).

The Emergence of Scientology

The turbulent first two years of Dianetics were also the period of Scientology's equally turbulent beginnings. The new term first appeared publicly in 1952, when *Time* magazine announced "Hubbard's latest 'ology" (Malko 1970:60). Shortly before that Hubbard had told Van Vogt that a significant change was taking place in his thinking: "He said that Dianetics was only an atomic bomb, and he had something that would be a hydrogen bomb" (Van Vogt 1964:252). The new doctrine retained most features of Dianetics: the engram theory, the auditing procedures, the goal of "clear." The practice was still billed as "scientific." But what had vanished was secularism. Scientology, the new creed, contained previously inadmissable supernaturalist ideas. In Wichita, Hubbard had begun to speak of a distinction between the material universe, governed by the laws of "matter, energy, space, and time" (acronymed MEST in Scientology usage), and the source of human sentience and vitality—"theta" (from the Greek letter theta, often used according to Hubbard to stand for "thought"). It would not be long before Scientologists were enjoined to conceive of themselves as "thetans," that is, spiritual beings capable of transcending material laws. In Phoenix, Hubbard gave lectures stating that the earliest glimmerings of Scientology wisdom lay in the Vedic hymns and the teachings of the Buddha (Hubbard 1968d). Instead of birth traumas and prenatal engrams, the focus of the past-incident search in auditing shifted to engrams received in previous incarnations. There appeared as well an assortment of auditing exercises aimed at producing the experience of being out of one's body. Hubbard's theories of

[68]

the mind thus took on the appearance of a theology, and his therapeutic methods began to resemble, in intention as well effect, mystical exercises. The question here is why this shift toward the mystical and supernatural took place.

In the search for an answer to this question, one set of factors cannot be ignored: Hubbard had been finding it increasingly difficult to maintain control of the Dianetics movement, and Dianetics itself, like any other unorthodox healing procedure thrown upon the market, occupied a precarious legal position. Taking up the first point primarily, Roy Wallis has argued that the transition from Dianetics to Scientology represented a consolidation of a distinctive authority structure and orthodoxy in the face of the usual tendency for faddish new philosophies to fade and dissolve into the jumbled repertory of the occult world. Early Dianeticists, like "manipulationists" in general, had greatly valued their intellectual independence and their right to use Hubbard's work as a basis for innovation or to combine it with bits and pieces of other practices and doctrines, a fact that Hubbard resented from the start. These early followers were not particularly inclined toward centralized organizational structure either. The announcement of new theoretical breakthroughs and a new name for the doctrine (Scientology) enabled Hubbard to shed fractious followers, gather the reins of authority back into his own hands, and begin to enforce the distinction between orthodoxy, which meant "created by Hubbard," and heresy, which meant "created by someone else" (Wallis 1976:16–18, 77–100). In this respect, a religious revelation, by dint of its nonempirical character, has a virtue missing in a science. Wallis writes: "With the promulgation of Scientology, Hubbard was able to claim the new gnosis as a revelation into which he had privileged insight, heightening his authority over the movement, and inhibiting competing claims to revelation" (1976:125). A new label also represented a way for Hubbard to distance himself from the public discrediting to which Dianetics had been subjected by the medical and psychiatric establishment. Finally, the emergence of Scientology marked a recourse to the legal status of "church" for Hubbard's organization, with all ensuant protections and immunities. In 1954, when Hubbard incorporated H.A.S.I. of Arizona, he made it a nonprofit "religious fellowship." In the same year, the Church of Scientology was incorporated in California.[5]

5. The name of the latter was changed in 1956 to the Church of Scientology of California (Foster 1971:29). Scientology was not, however, given full recognition as a

All in all, then, it is tempting to see these quite worldly considerations of protection and consolidation of authority as the primary impulses behind the rise of the new faith. That they were important impulses cannot be denied. The record of his activities during the first years of Dianetics and the recollections of early followers testify that Hubbard jealously guarded his discoveries. Labeling the innovations of others "black Dianetics," he responded to this threat with a battery of defensive maneuvers that included decertifying offenders, encouraging followers to harass splinter groups, instigating law suits, and hiring private detectives to dig up scandal about his opponents (Wallis 1976:88–93). (In later years he fell back on the same responses when he perceived threats to Scientology.) It is not difficult to see the move to churchly status as simply one more defensive maneuver, especially when Hubbard is quoted as slyly remarking, "Of course anything is a religion that treats of the spirit. And also, parliaments don't attack religions" (Foster 1971:29).

To rest the case here, however, as Wallis is inclined to do, is to overlook other important factors that, during its early days, caused Dianetics to veer in a religious direction, and that did so in a way that was often contradictory to the impulses exerted by pragmatic and defensive considerations.

The first of these factors was the epistemological slipperiness of the occult orientation that Hubbard and his early followers to varying degrees shared. To be sure, Hubbard himself, as well as other key figures in Dianetics like Dr. Winter and John Campbell, Jr., maintained a distinction between "science" and "religion," a distinction centered on the idea that science is empirically based while religion is not. In terms of truth value, this thinking gave an ostensible superiority to science. At the same time, it was felt that religion had truth value too. The historical importance of the great religions, their enduring appeal, their reputed understanding of the "mysteries of life," were evidence of some veridical grounding; and if science proved unable to account for this religious dimension of truth, this could mean that science itself was too limited in its purview. It could mean in Campbell's words, that "there is a reality-field other than, and different from, what we know as science." Or—a more daring pos-

---

religion in this country until 1969, following a successful defense of its religious status against charges made by the Federal Drug Administration that Scientologists practiced unlicensed medicine.

sibility—it could mean that the perceived but unexplained truth value of religion issued from a heretofore undiscovered empirical ground.

Hubbard proved adept at pursuing both lines of possibility. Having noted, after what one suspects was a fairly casual perusal of Vedic and Buddhist philosophy, some striking similarities between these bodies of knowledge and his own ideas, he felt safe in saying that Scientology and the traditions of the East dealt in the same subject, a subject he decided to call "wisdom." The trouble was explaining this concept to the Western mind. As he remarked in his Phoenix lectures, "You have just not communicated in the west when you have said, 'we study wisdom.' You see, if you just said that, they would say, Oh yes, that's all very well, I did that in third grade. . . . [Therefore] it is necessary to resort to various shifts in trying to describe what you are doing" (1968d:3). One "shift" was to emphasize the great practical and even scientific orientation of the ancient thinkers. "They also are tremendously practical. Their practicality is such as to stagger a westerner" (1968d:5). And "I think, by the way, that Gautama Sakyamuni probably had a better command of scientific methodology than any of your Chairs of Science in western universities" (1968d:11). When the religion of the ancients is thus made rather more scientific than the Westerner is accustomed to believe, one can comfortably view Scientology, with its similarities to Vedic and Buddhist philosophy, as rather more ancient and religious than heretofore acknowledged.

> . . . we do know as we sit here in the western world, that man has a tradition of wisdom which goes back about 10,000 years, which is very positively traceable. And we find Scientology's earliest certainly known ancestor in the Veda. . . . It [the Veda] is a religion. It should not be confused with anything *but* a religion. [1968d:10]

> Scientology, then, today, could not possibly be characterized as a science the way the western world understands science. Scientology carries forward a tradition of wisdom which concerns itself about the soul and the solution of mysteries of life. It has not deviated. [1968d:34]

If this reasoning seemed to tilt Scientology too far in the direction of religion, as conventionally understood, Hubbard could slide it back along the truth scale in the direction of science by emphasizing its empirical results. He repeatedly argued, first in regard to Dianetics, then in regard to Scientology, that, call it what you will, "it works," it

[71]

"gets results." By implication of course, something that works and that "tests out" cannot simply be called what you will, but has something of the standing of an empirical science. In fact Hubbard's empirical argument is even more specific than this. Consider the following assertion from his treatise *The Fundamentals of Thought:*

> Probably the greatest discovery of Scientology and its most forceful contribution to the knowledge of mankind has been the isolation, description and handling of the human spirit. Accomplished in July 1951, in Phoenix, Arizona, I established along scientific rather than religious or humanitarian lines that that thing which is the person, the personality, is separable from the body and the mind at will and without causing bodily death or mental derangement. [1956:58]

In statements such as this there is no apparent appeal to a privileged religious gnosis. Rather, here Hubbard is erecting a commemorative plaque to his discovery comparable to the one found on the University of Chicago football stadium marking the Manhattan Project's splitting of the atom. From this perspective, Scientology was "religion" only inasmuch as religions of the past (which Scientology resembles) bear murky testimony to the empirical truth of certain principles that Hubbard's new scientific methodology had now validated. Others before him had stumbled upon past incarnations and the separability of spirit from body, but they had failed to comprehend fully and to master these phenomena. It took Hubbard's little "Manhattan Project" to split this spiritual atom.

> . . . to reach salvation in one lifetime—that was the hope of Buddhism. That hope, by various practices, was now and then, here and there, attained. But no set of precise practices ever came forward, which immediately, predictably, produced a result. . . . The material which was released in that [ancient] time is cluttered with irrelevancies. A great deal of it is buried. You have to be very selective, and you have to know Scientology, actually, to plot it out, get it into the clear. [1968d:22]

What exactly was this empirical base that Hubbard detected in religion?

We are led here to a second factor that, independently of external pressures on his movement, operated to bring about a "supernaturalizing" of Hubbard's doctrine. This factor was auditing's potential to open up and make experientially convincing to practitioners a reality beyond the mundane. Already working on questionable assumptions with prenatal engrams, Dianetic auditors and their pre-clears had, within the first six months of the movement, pushed their search for "basic" engrams beyond the boundaries of the womb and into prior existences. The recollection of past lives, which amounted in essence to the recollection of incidents that could not plausibly have occurred in the subject's current life, did not, for many, differ in subjective quality from the elusive but often quite vivid recollections of early childhood experiences. Moreover, therapeutic insight and the dissipation of symptoms proved to be as attainable through this new route as through the old—sometimes more attainable. Adding to the possibilities raised by past-life memory was another peculiar phenomenon that not infrequently arose in auditing sessions, the sensation of being outside of one's body. Hubbard had noted this phenomenon, which he dubbed "exteriorization," in *Dianetics*, but he made little of it in that publication. During that monumental month of July 1951, however, he concluded that various auditing procedures produced the experience regularly. "Exteriorization" seemed to furnish even more persuasive evidence of what past-life recollections had suggested: the existence of an immortal consciousness that transcended the laws of the material universe. In other words, auditing was Hubbard's laboratory apparatus; its mental results, his empirical findings; his conclusions from these findings, Scientology.

Not everyone in the Dianetics movement was as convinced by the new discoveries as Hubbard. It is said that the emerging tendency toward supernaturalism, in particular the pursuit of past-life memories, was one of the factors that lost him the support of Campbell and Winter, though disagreements over the general conduct of business and disillusionment with Hubbard's increasing authoritarianism also have been cited as reasons for their decision to exit (Wallis 1976:78; Winter 1951:30). But that Hubbard's commitment to his new "empiricism" was quite genuine is indicated by the literal-mindedness with which he pursued the Scientological investigation of the "human spirit." Throughout most of the 1950s he had his followers plot out their past-life recollections in an effort to reconstruct an actual history of our existence as immortal beings. He also tried to devise exercises that would enable practitioners to experience their "exteriorized" state in a convincing fashion and purposefully direct their out-of-body activities.

[73]

It is important to see then that while the organization of Hubbard's movement was taking on the legal status of a religious fellowship owing to a set of pragmatic considerations, the doctrine of the movement was evolving what would appear in the eyes of outsiders to be "religious" characteristics from a quite different source. The psychodynamics of auditing were, if followed to their conclusions, sufficient to bring the new practice and the insights gleaned from it into a rather remarkable alignment with already existing mystical traditions, and to give the resulting formulations a "supernaturalistic" cast. But there was a double paradox involved in this supernaturalizing trend. Insiders and, most important, Hubbard himself seem to have viewed what was going on not as the eruption of supernatural beliefs within a secular framework, but quite the reverse: a secularization, or demystification, of matters previously thought to be religious. No piece of mumbo-jumbo after all, the immortal spirit began to look to Scientologists as respectably concrete as a microbe. But of course their interest in such a phenomenon could only give them the appearance of having become "religious." This appearance would naturally be fortified by Hubbard's decision to present the Scientology movement to the outside world as a religion. It would be fortified, that is, unless his motives appeared to be "ulterior." And for a while the latter was the appearance that he actually achieved. To retain the enthusiasm of those followers who, in good occultist fashion, demanded a truth comparable in authority to the findings of science and not, as the term "religion" connotes to the modern mind, just another set of arbitrary beliefs, Hubbard could do worse than hint that the move to present Scientology as a religion was every bit as cynical as outside critics were suggesting. There is an almost detectable wink to the insider in statements such as "Of course parliaments don't attack religions," and in the carelessly ad hoc rituals (for example, marriage and christening ceremonies) he devised to adorn the "Founding Church of Scientology" that he established in 1955 in Washington, D.C. But except for intermittent uses of the term "church," the Scientology organization tended for years to keep its religious image in the background. It was not until the late 1960s, coincident with press attacks and government investigations in both Australia and the United Kingdom, that Scientology "Orgs" and "Centers" (or "Franchises") were officially retitled "Churches" and "Missions," and a serious effort was made to have certain of the staff of these establishments wear clerical garb.

By the early 1970s, Scientologists seem to have become reconciled to the religious character of their doctrine. (The increased legitimacy of religious perspectives, especially those associated with Eastern religions, that came about with the 1960s countercultural wave and the proddings of sophisticated legal counsel have undoubtedly played a part in this reconciliation.) But this acceptance does not erase the evidence of a much more ambivalent posture during the earlier years of the Scientology movement. In fact Scientology's move toward religious institutional status was at the outset at significant odds with the interpretation Hubbard and his followers were placing upon their emergent revelation. The result was, for many years, a hedged and imperfect commitment to a religious identity.

But let us look more closely at Hubbard's empirical findings of a supernatural truth. I said at the beginning of this chapter that there is a way in which the psychotherapeutic effort itself contributed to the evolution of a religious system from a secular one. True, we perceived in Hubbard, the founder of the system, a person predisposed to weave marvels into the fabric of ordinary reality, and we found him operating within a subcultural milieu that was in many ways dedicated to the synthesis of religious with secular perspectives. True too, there were legal and social incentives for the Dianetics/Scientology movement to affect a religious posture quite apart from any theoretical considerations. This overdetermination of Dianetics' drift toward religiosity might obscure for us that component of the change that was specific to depth psychotherapy as a mental and symbolic activity. What singles this component out, however, and allows us to isolate it from the other regroupings and reformulations to which Hubbard subjected his new movement, is the fact that it has appeared in other, more soberly directed, psychotherapeutic movements. Peculiar "revelations" of a similar sort to those of past lives and out-of-body states bedeviled Freudian theory and became an important factor in the drift of Carl Jung's Analytic Psychology toward mysticism—a drift that markedly parallels the evolution of Scientology from Dianetics. In Freudian theory, the most central of these peculiar revelations was the scene of parental intercourse witnessed in the patients' childhood—called by Freud the "primal scene." In the Jungian framework, a vast array of patients' fantasy and visionary productions, by virtue of their resemblance to mythic themes of ancient or exotic cultures, came to be considered "archetypes of the Collective Unconscious," that is, elements of a transpersonal symbolic arsenal passed down through the generations. While the Freudian "primal" and the Jungian "archetyp-

[75]

al" were not assimilated by their authors quite so straightforwardly to familiar religious conceptions as were the past lives and out-of-body states of Dianetics, nevertheless they bore the same relationship to prevailing scientific understandings of reality, which is to say that they fell outside the established paradigms. Also, much in the manner of Hubbard deciding that his pre-clear's memories and bizarre experiences illuminated the empirical basis of religious ideas, Freud and Jung felt that the concepts of the "primal" and "archetypal" and the notion of the Unconscious which encompassed them provided the basis for a secular explanation of the repertory of cultural notions usually labeled "supernatural."

The contrary was more nearly the case, for rather than explaining the supernatural, these depth psychotherapeutic concepts permitted Jung and Freud, like Hubbard, to embrace it. To judge from Freud's case, even a strong commitment to secular modes of explanation is not necessarily sufficient to prevent such "proto-"supernaturalistic notions from becoming the springboard for quasi-religious or certainly overly ambitious cosmologizing. It would thus be facile to dismiss the promulgation of a quasi-empirical supernaturalism in the Dianetics movement as simply the product of amateur theorizing by a spinner of tales, when Hubbard's predecessors who established the framework within which psychotherapy, amateur and otherwise, would subsequently develop, did hardly any better.

A good deal of the problem, if one wants to call understanding depth psychology in quasi-mystical terms a problem, resides in the theoretical framework of modern psychotherapy, the framework inherited from Freud. It may be the case, and I will argue it is the case, that psychotherapeutic and religious activities utilize the same psychological and symbolic processes, and that this is one of the reasons for the affinity of the one type of tradition to the other, but this state of affairs in itself does not necessarily mean that theoretical interpretations of these processes must inevitably fall back upon supernatural or "proto-"supernatural constructs. The fact that such interpretations have tended to do so is as much a function of starting assumptions as it is of the nature of the activity being explained. Here it is of particular importance to consider Freud's writings on the subject of peculiar revelations—in his scheme, "primal" events—because in his attempts to grapple with this phenomenon we see the impediments to his understanding thrown up by assumptions regarding psychotherapeutic change and the nature of the Unconscious. It is only by threading our way through these impediments, to which depth psychological theory is still hostage, that we may begin to rephrase Freud's questions and arrive at a more accurate appraisal of the common psychological underpinning of psychotherapeutic and religious activity. The two chapters following are devoted to this project. I will first consider why psychotherapeutic revelations have eluded adequate interpretation, and go on from there to propose a different and I think more adequate interpretation. After this theoretical excursion, we will move to an illustration of the psychodynamics of religious and psychotherapeutic activity, using Scientology examples.

[3]

The Puzzle of Religious and Psychotherapeutic Revelation

In developing his own mental theories and therapeutic methods, Hubbard worked on the basis of assumptions that have been part of depth psychotherapy since Freud. One assumption is that given incentive and the right sort of probing, the patient can be made to reveal critical experiences of the past which have helped to bring about the unhappy condition of the present. Probing is directed toward the past and even when direct recollection is absent, other materials of the patient's mind such as recent dream images, current trains of thought, spontaneous associations, and so on will be interpreted as possible derivatives of things that the patient has felt, thought, done, or experienced at a stage when his or her personality was still in the process of development. Further, it is assumed that certain thoughts and memories, being in conflict with other areas of the personality, will be dynamically barred from consciousness and that it is the retrieval of these particular items and the integration into the conscious personality of the emotions and attitudes associated with them that bring about beneficial psychic reorganization. Some have gone so far as to insist upon the reliving, or "abreaction," of previous hidden experiences, but Freud himself placed greatest emphasis on the accurate designation and removal of the attitudes that have kept the hidden material hidden. (These latter attitudes he speaks of as the "resistances.")

The idea that personality develops out of experience is not controversial, and the idea that neuroses may spring up as the result of defects in this development, while perhaps still controversial, is entirely plausible. It is a good deal more theoretically mysterious why the working through in later life of past experiences and the conflicts surrounding them brings about alleviation of dysfunctional traits or a transformed outlook on the world, yet clinical experience shows this to be the case. In particular, reduction of tensions and symptoms may follow the recovery of aspects of the past (with accompanying feeling) that fit the character of something the patient would rather forget and seems to have—until therapy—succeeded in forgetting, or the making of connections that the patient would rather not make and has so far managed to avoid. Of the sorts of experiences thus beneficially "retrieved," a certain percentage fit convincingly into the patient's known (unrepressed) past, and their appearance adds strength to the hypothesis that it is the reworking of an actual history that is at issue.

Since a developmental theory of personality would hold that the earlier a shock to development, the more general and important its consequences for the personality, the therapist is theoretically enjoined to push the patient's reminiscences as far back as they will go. But it is here that the puzzling phenomena of which I have spoken arise. Freud writes:

> You know that from analysis of symptoms we arrive at the knowledge of the infantile experiences to which the libido is fixated and out of which the symptoms are made up. Now the astonishing thing is that these scenes of infancy are not always true. . . . what we find is that the childhood-experiences reconstructed or recollected in analysis are on some occasions undeniably false, while others are just as certainly quite true, and that in most cases truth and falsehood are mixed up. So the symptoms are thus at one minute reproductions of experiences which actually took place and which one can credit with an influence on the fixation of the libido; and at the next a reproduction of phantasies of the patient's to which, of course, it is difficult to ascribe any aetiological significance. [Freud 1958:376]

The "phantastic" occurrences which Freud himself most frequently encountered in the childhood of neurotics were observations, at an inordinately young age, of parental intercourse (the "primal scene"), seduction of the child by an adult, and the threat of castration. He adds, "The greatest feat achieved by this kind of phantasy is that of observing parental intercourse while still unborn in the mother's womb" (Freud 1958:378, 379).[1]

To generalize from the experience of Freud and his colleagues and from later experiments in hypnotic age-regression, the further one pushes the subject back into the past, the more apt one is to provoke confabulation. It is hardly surprising that almost every implausible construct of the sort provoked—unlikely infantile scenes, birth traumas, prenatal traumas, sperm-dreams, inherited racial memories and past-life events—are extrapolations on the idea of a prior history. Prior history is, after all, what the therapy is trying to elicit. It would seem fairly evident that the patient simply accepts the frame of reference handed him and "cooperates"—wittingly or unwittingly. The prior history aspect of these fabulous constructions thus need not puzzle us further. So too, the type of event, incident, or theme recovered, whether it be a prehistoric family episode or a mother goddess motif from the ancient Near East, can be understood in terms of the indirect suggestive thrust of the tradition in which therapist and client are operating. Suggestion, indirect or direct, is inescapable in the psychotherapeutic situation. But the mere fact that it operates is not sufficient to clear up all that is mysterious about the appearance and effect of the suggested forms.

One of the striking and still perplexing characteristics of these psychotherapeutic fictions is that they are for many patients vividly convincing, and—just like recollections or reconstructions of "real" events—therapeutically valuable. Freud found that the analysis could proceed in the same way regardless of whether recovered infantile scenes were plausible or implausible, for in either case the analyst's task is to unravel the feelings and motivations surrounding the scene (1958:367–85; 1963:237). Jung argued that the movement of the patient's psyche beyond the purely personal into archetypes of the Collective Unconscious was in his experience of *greater* therapeutic value than a perseveration upon mundane infantile themes (1973:280). And

1. Primal scenes, when encountered—and they were more often arrived at by inference than by direct recall—always took the same form: the child, still an infant, sleeping in the same room as the parents, awoke one afternoon or morning to witness them in the act of intercourse. It had to be afternoon or morning, otherwise he would have been unable to see them. Furthermore, in order for the scene to produce the ideas about sexuality and anatomy that it did produce, the parental act was always intercourse *a tergo* so that the genital organs were visible. Lastly, the intercourse was always interrupted by the child's passing a stool, thus providing itself with an excuse for screaming (Freud 1963:247–48).

Hubbard justified the auditing of everything from birth traumas to past-life incidents on the grounds of efficacy, strictly forbidding auditors to impose a standard of verisimilitude upon the pre-clear's recollections.

The problem then is not what to do with an implausible past in practice, but what to do with it in theory. Freud's answer to this problem was, as he realized, a bit of a surprise to his audience:

> Whence comes the necessity for these phantasies, and the material for them? There can be no doubt about the instinctual sources; but how is it to be explained that the same phantasies are always formed with the same content? I have an answer to this which I know will seem to you very daring. I believe that these *primal phantasies* (as I should like to name these, and certainly some others also) are a phylogenetic possession. . . . It seems to me quite possible that all that to-day is narrated in analysis in the form of phantasy . . . was in prehistoric periods of the human family a reality; and that the child in its phantasy simply fills out the gaps in its true individual experience with true prehistoric experiences. [1958:380]

In this conclusion, which was to inform many of his subsequent explorations of culture history, Freud appears to have been unduly beguiled by the quality of conviction, the sense of overwhelming significance that so often accompanied the emergence of such "primal" material in the psychoanalytic session. In his report of the case of "Wolf Man," Freud's most probing engagement with the problem of plausibility in psychoanalytic revelations, his bottom line of defense in regard to the "primal scene" was that "the patients themselves gradually acquire a profound conviction of the reality of these primal scenes, a conviction which is in no respect inferior to one based on [actual] recollection" (1963:239).

Jung, as we know, rarefied the idea of phylogenetic memory so that his Collective Unconscious, a panhuman mental repository of powerful images, was no longer particularly anchored in hypothesized past events; rather, these images revealed their antiquity by their likeness to the imagery of ancient cultures. The function of Jung's concept was the same, however. The patient's productions were anchored, if not in specific past events, at least in a type of reality beyond the merely imaginary. And this of course provided a way to account for the reality value that these images assumed in the patient's mind. Jung held that

[81]

a compelling sense of significance was one of the diagnostic features of an archetypal form (1973:128).

But falling back on the sense of deeper reality or significance that surrounds these constructs in no way salvages their reality status, historical, phylogenetic, or other. As it happens, sensations of profound reality have throughout history authorized religious revelations and illuminations of every sort. Religious revelations are often spoken of as "self-validating" or "apodictic," both expressions summarizing the idea that their appeal circumvents logic (and plausibility) and secures for the believer a certainty that cannot be debated. William James observed:

> It is if there were in the human consciousness a *sense of reality, a feeling of objective presence, a perception* of what we may call "something there," more deep and more general than any of the special and particular "senses" by which the current psychology supposes existent realities to be originally revealed. . . . So far as religious conceptions were able to touch this reality-feeling, they would be believed in spite of criticism, even though they might be so vague and so remote as to be almost unimaginable. [James 1967:62–63, his emphasis]

James's argument is that religious conceptions are indeed addressed to this deeper reality feeling and that this is indeed one important reason they are believed.[2] A comparable deeper reality sense attaches to the realm of the "primal," for Freud, and the "archetypal," for Jung, and the feature serves these theorists as a justification for treating the posited realms and their content as fundamental presences in the psyche. Paradoxically, religious belief is dismissed—at least by Freud—as a form of illusion, a thing less fundamentally real than the "primal." Jung, not sensing his tautology, felt he had a way around this dilemma.

If religious motifs have throughout history been felt to be charged with an aura of the deeply significant and portentous, he reasoned, this is because they spring from the Collective Unconscious, the archetypes of which (surprise!) they so closely resemble. Here we have thinking comparable to Hubbard's empirical explanation for the wisdom of the ancients. Freud's solution was less sophistical, but the

---

2. Roy Rappaport has argued (1971) that religion's self-certifying quality makes it possible for religious and ritual appeals to guarantee (that is, certify in turn) social commitments; hence ritual processes often serve as regulators of social processes.

dilemma shows up just as sharply. Rather than make virtually every item of human culture's repertory of religious and magical beliefs reappear in the Unconscious in the form of an archetype, Freud chose to install in the Unconscious only a few choice primal items—the "scene," for instance, and the story of the primal horde with its various component elements, the primal sire, the slaying and eating, and so on (see Freud 1950). Mankind's collection of mythic and religious forms were then considered "derivatives" of this primal material, disguised and transfigured by repressive countertendencies. In effect, he exalted his theoretical favorites while relegating the rest of the competition to a derivative status. It is obvious that competing theories with different "favorites" can play the same game. Thus the acceptability of any particular depth psychological theory is not advanced by this exercise.

The same difficulties arise if, instead of a sense of deeper reality, the therapist invokes "cure" or psychological transformation as his test of the reality of the strange things discovered in the patient's mind. Hubbard, we recall, found that the auditing of past lives "worked." Jung apparently had good success with archetypes. And there is the statement cited earlier of the wartime abreaction therapists who suggested actually supplying the patient with a suitable traumatic "memory" if the patient's own recollections weren't moving the case along. Perhaps with fewer, or simply different, theoretical axes to grind, the abreaction therapists were able to accept matter-of-factly what the early depth psychotherapists could not, which was that fictional scenes and borrowed imagery might serve the cause of psychological transformation as effectively as material from the patient's own real experience.

Why was this possibility never fully confronted by Freud and Jung? One rather obvious reason springs to mind. Certainly if the core findings of the new science of psychoanalysis were admitted to be no different in epistemological status from religious revelations, the scientific credibility of the new doctrines would suffer. But it must be conceded that Jungian Analytic Psychology borders on making just this sort of admission; Jung was in fact willing to sacrifice scientific pretensions for the sake of getting on with his therapizing (or, one could argue, satisfying his private religious preconceptions). Freud too was willing to be, as he put it, "daring." Though the need to maintain a scientifically credible surface to the enterprise clearly exerted an influence, it was hardly the only factor inhibiting the sober assessment of implausible revelations.

[83]

The deeper problem posed by these implausible findings was that it was not possible simply to isolate and extrude them, to cut off the offending part, as it were. Appreciation of their nature fed back upon the theoretical understanding of the entire psychotherapeutic endeavor. If fictional memories produced therapeutic results, then the status of any of the patient's productions, plausible or implausible, became empirically inscrutable, and the idea that psychotherapy must entail a working out of developmental damage incurred in the past was thrown into limbo. Suppose the patient's plausible-seeming childhood memories were fictions as well, simply plausible-seeming ones? What then?

Obviously some new theoretical entry must be made into this situation if we are to understand therapeutic efficacy and with it the relationship between psychotherapeutic and religious revelation. The place to start is where Freud left off, asking what it was that derailed his explanation, for in determining the impasse to which one theory is brought one is often able to construct a bridge to the next.

Up until the point where he presents us with his hypothesis about phylogenetic traces, there is nothing soft-headed about the way Freud interpreted his patients' more bizarre recollections. His "economic" explanation of what these productions represent is unimpeachable. Like the elements of dreams, the improbable childhood scenes express an amalgamation of psychic forces: on the one hand the plea-sure-directed energies of the instincts, on the other, the counter-cathexes (counterenergies) of ego and superego which hold instinctual impulses in check. If their reality is, in this respect, dreamlike, why not conclude that they have the same relationship to real events as do the component elements of dreams? These reduce upon analysis to a pastiche of actual events, perceptions, and vicarious experiences (some quite trivial) which have been, through association to a wish, caught up in the service of expressing or countermanding it.

This was, in fact, one of Freud's conclusions. At points he argued that implausible past events, even if they are fantasies having no actual reality, have a "psychic reality" and must therefore be accorded a causative status in the aetiology of neuroses (1964:368–70). But the phrase "psychic reality" only brackets the problem, so to speak. Without further explanation, which Freud did not furnish, "psychic real-ity" can mean only "a type of reality we do not understand."

Two things deterred Freud from pursuing the dream analogy further. First there was the fact that certain fantasies, the ones to which he was to give the name "primal," held convincing sway over patient after patient. ("How is it to be explained that the same phantasies are

[84]

always formed with the same contents?") Of course this is precisely the part of the problem that lends itself to being explained as the product of suggestion on the part of the analyst, the analytic tradition, or even the larger cultural tradition of which analyst and patient are part. Freud was understandably ill at ease on the point. The second deterrent was that the analogy to dreaming in the end only begs the question, for there comes a point where one must account for what it is that the elements of a dream are linking up with such that they become subject to the forces of repression. Sequences from the patient's "real" past, as well as sequences confabulated from diverse elements of the patient's past, enter into the Unconscious only by virtue of their association to an instinctual drive. But the difficulty is this: that between the instincts and their ever-accumulating retinue of "representatives," something must intervene to explain how a formless drive can find its home in structured form. As Paul Ricoeur states it, Freud's problem was one of making sense of "the idea of an energy that is transformed into meaning" (1972:395).

Experience encountered in the course of development was one of the most likely candidates for the role of shaper of the instincts. Under this line of reasoning, one would have to posit "real," rather than purely imaginary experience, for how could the latter, as Freud rightly observed, be of "aetiological significance"? The other possibility, a more refractory one, was that of some sort of genetically preformed instinctual organ. Freud manages to touch both bases with his suggestion of Lamarckian traces. But in either choice of candidate for this theoretically essential role, the present-day extrusions of the Unconscious must be seen as leading back ultimately to specifiable experiential happenings (individual or phylogenetic) which constitute the fixation points of libidinal energy and make up the core of the Unconscious. These are the privileged incidents which account for the content of what will later, through association to them, be attracted to and drawn into the Unconscious. The drives of the instincts thus take on form by becoming entrapped in critical scenarios.[3]

The force of theoretical necessity behind this hypothesis, the way in

3. It is important to distinguish doctrines of hidden scenarios from simply poor theories of memory, although a notion of memory as veridical record is not incompatible with a hidden-scenario concept of the Unconscious. Freud in fact recognized the interpretive character of stored impressions. His quest for what Laplanche and Pontalis call "the bedrock of event" (1973:332) was motivated not by conviction that an accurate record of critical experiences lay buried in the Unconscious, but by the conviction that what did lie buried in the Unconscious took its form from a limited number of critical experiences.

which it satisfied so many trains of psychoanalytic reasoning, seems, if anything, to have increased Freud's imperviousness to the factor of "suggestion." While one may infer from his asides about patients who remembered witnessing parental intercourse while still unborn in the womb, that some of his (or his colleagues') patients produced the "primal scene" as a reminiscence, in the main it was Freud himself who imputed the experience to the patient on the basis of the latter's symptomatology, associations, dreams, and sexual dispositions. He confessed that in many cases, the "scene" itself was irretrievable and had to be reconstructed from its derivatives (1963:238). So saying, he came full circle from needing an explanation for the commonality of certain bizarre constructions to supplying that commonality when it was not furnished to him by the patient. In this way he brought to light an Unconscious that imposed its order on the data of individual experience even when these data were insufficient in themselves to constitute such an order.

The theoretical impasse here seems to be the inseparability in psychoanalytic theory of "structure" and "event." Event is seen as producing structure, but only in its own image. The primal forms embedded in the Unconscious are indistinguishable from events, they are the trace-patterns of real happenings. Further, not every "event" counts equally. Those that make up the core of the Unconscious do so, we can only surmise, either because they impinged upon the individual at a critical stage of development, or because they are somehow more dramatic or traumatic, or because they are prefitted in some sense to instinctual responses. Any of these solutions hovers very close to a doctrine of "imprinting."

The need to rescue structure from a concretistic reduction to event has provoked Lévi-Strauss and, following him, structuralist psychoanalyst Jacques Lacan to speak of the Unconscious as not a realm of "content," but a realm of special structuring processes or structuring rules (like a grammar) to which "content" (for Lévi-Strauss) or "desire" (for Lacan) is subjected (Lévi-Strauss 1963:186–205; Lacan 1968). While we do not learn from these theorists quite how the "rules" are acquired, and the retention of the concept of a special "realm" poses problems further down the line, their notion of "structures" as not static forms, but rather form-generating activities or operations that are theoretically separable from the forms they generate, is an essential instrument for working our way out of Freud's dilemma.

[86]

The most parsimonious and useful contemporary structuralist formulation of what it is that is revealed in the productions of the analysand is Jean Piaget's concept of mental schemata. Although in Piaget's system, actual experience is essential to the emergence of a mental schema, the latter is not reducible to stored impressions, but exists at a more general level. One might speak of a schema as "organized dispositions" or as an organized set of mental activities abstracted from myriad similar experiences and in turn generating out behavioral and ideational sequences that share a formal similarity. Since Piaget embeds his definitions in lengthy illustration, I will cite here the summarizations of John Flavell (Piaget's principal interpreter) concerning schemata:

A *schema* is a cognitive structure which has reference to a class of similar action sequences. [Flavell 1963:53]

Schemas are "mobile frames" successively applied to various contents. . . . They may be envisaged as the structural precipitates of a recurrent assimilatory activity. [55]

If schemas are named [by Piaget] by their referent action sequences, it is not completely accurate to say that they *are* these sequences and nothing more. To be sure, Piaget would certainly say that an infant who performs an organized sequence of grasping behaviors is in fact applying a grasping schema to reality. . . . However, and the point is a rather subtle one, to say that a grasping sequence forms a schema is to imply more than the simple fact that the infant shows organized grasping behavior. It implies that assimilatory functioning has generated a specific cognitive *structure*, an organized *disposition* to grasp objects on repeated occasions. . . . It implies that a psychological "organ" has been created, *functionally* (but, of course, not *structurally*) equivalent to a physiological digestive organ in that it constitutes an organ for incorporating reality "aliments." [53; his emphasis]

The notion of the schema, which can be applied, Piaget argues, to the organization of affect as well as to that of cognition, is situated within a significantly different understanding of "experience" from that utilized by Freud. To be relevant to the development of mental organization, an experience must engage the active functioning of the subject, for it is only from the subject's own activity that schematic organization is precipitated. Information not actively received is simply not

[87]

received. Further, the way in which information is received, and thus the impact of any "event" on the subject's development, are functions of the level of activity the subject is able to bring to bear upon it. The infant who is as yet capable of interacting with grasped objects only to the extent of bringing them to its mouth, for instance, does not learn to stack blocks even though its hand may on occasion accidentally stack them. Greater elaboration, differentiation, and coordination of its mental schemata will be necessary before the activity of "stacking" falls into place.[4]

Over the course of development, mental/affective schemata grow increasingly complex and differentiated through the joint operation of three functions. The first is *assimilation*—the appropriation by a schema of fresh information that can be made to "fit" its preexisting shape. The second function, *accommodation*, is the reciprocal of the first; it consists of the gradual alteration (and concomittant splitting into subtypes) of a schema so as to conform to fresh information. Finally there is *organization:* the coordination of schemata with each other and the abstraction therefrom of general operational principles. The constant tendency of these functions is toward the production of a state of systemic equilibrium. The three "functional invariants," as Piaget terms them, and their equilibrating tendency are characteristic of all living systems, and "mind" is but one example of a living system (Piaget 1963:1–20).

When one reviews Freud's "primal scene" from this perspective, it seems highly unlikely that a child observing parental intercourse at age eighteen months to two years, as the Wolf Man supposedly did, could grasp from this observation the various ideas about anatomy to which Freud attributed his patient's adult symptomatology. The child's schematic organization is not sufficiently developed to think in terms of who does or does not possess a penis, whether intercourse is taking place rectally or in some other fashion, and so on. This is not to say that nothing of the observed scene would register on the mind at that age, but only that, as Freud correctly and uncomfortably admitted, the ideas supposedly generated by the primal scene seemed far more appropriate to the concerns of a five- or six-year-old than to those of a barely verbal infant. We do not fare much better with

4. The infant's activity and hence all subsequent development are set in motion by a collection of simple hereditary reflexes—sucking, grasping, kicking and broad arm movements, head-turning, etc.—to mention only those most frequently followed by Piaget.

Freud's proposal that the "scene" might be recorded uncomprehendingly at an early age and then simply lie dormant in the memory until maturation made possible its comprehension. True, this sort of re-analysis of the remembered takes place constantly in developed minds, but then developed minds have many different systems under which to grasp and thus record information, guaranteeing thereby a "store" of impressions to reanalyze subsequently. The smaller the arsenal of thinking tools, however, the less likely is there to be memory storage of any kind.

In contrast to a "stored scenario" argument, it would be altogether appropriate to argue, in Piagetian terms, that over the course of a person's emotional and sexual development, general affective/erotic schemata form which, depending on how the individual adapted to those factors in the environment relevant to this development, would predispose him or her to respond *as if* he or she were in possession of certain unspoken irrational notions of the sort that Freud regularly detected in the dreams, associations, and symptomatology of his patients. It would not be necessary for the specific notions articulated by the analyst (or images embodying these notions), ever to have formed in the patient's mind for the patient nonetheless to "appropriate" them, that is, find them subjectively fitting, when he or she encounters them in psychotherapy, or for that matter in some other suitable context. What we have here is merely a matter of schemata appropriating, that is, assimilating, fitting ideas and images. There is no theoretical need to reduce the images appropriated by schemata in the therapeutic session to a specific past experience, or to reduce the images appropriated in any later context to those appropriated in an earlier one. Piaget's own commentary on psychoanalytic reasoning states the case in its strictest form:

> There is no need to ascribe a representative memory to this unconscious in order to explain the continuity between past and present, since the schemas insure the motor and dynamic aspect of this continuity. [Piaget 1962:208]

> When an individual has rebelled inwardly against excessive paternal authority, and subsequently adopts a similar attitude to his teachers or to any constraint, it does not follow that he is unconsciously identifying each of these persons with the image of his father. What has happened is merely that in his relations with his father he has acquired a mode of

feeling and reacting (an affective schema) which he generalizes in situations that are subjectively analogous. Similarly, though he may have acquired the schema of free fall by dropping a ball from his cot, it does not follow that he subsequently identifies all falling bodies with that ball. [189]

In the therapeutic session, as in life, the images that memory provides the patient, the images provided by spontaneous fantasy, or even those images spontaneously selected from a book, a movie, or from the analyst's latest theory of mythopoeic thought, all may reveal the outlines of the patient's acquired modes of feeling and thinking—his or her schemata—without of course being the same thing as the schemata. Fictive memories or mythic imagery give access to and enable the therapist to manipulate the patient's mental structures as readily as do real memories. Viewed in this light, the analyst's theory of what is in the mind, no matter how well rationalized this theory in terms of the scientific plausibility systems of the day, is, in the therapeutic session, acting essentially as a projective format. The sexual dramas of childhood, mythic motifs, past lives—all may be, in this regard, equally revelatory.

To illustrate how this principle operates in the psychotherapeutic context, let me turn to an example of a Scientologist's recollection of past lives taken from my early field notes. The subject, Miriam, was one of the people who first introduced me to Scientology. She was being audited on chains of engrams, in this case engrams she had caused in others (this was a novel type of incident auditing that had just come into use at the time of my research).

[The question of whether or not I should do an anthropological study of Scientology had been the subject of much discussion between Miriam and me. We had become close friends. I suspected that her primary interest was in seeing me convert to Scientology. She meanwhile feared that I would write an "exposé" of the movement. At the time of this session, I had not yet managed to win her trust. A day after the session she gave the following account.]

There were three incidents on the chain, she told me. The first took place in an Arab setting which she dated 1784. She was a young Arab boy, in his teens, a member of an Arab tribe. People were in bedouin garb, there were tents, desert, etc. A spy had been caught by the tribe's people. He had been judged guilty of spying and condemned to punishment. The punishment for spies in this particular tribe was to cut off their eyelids. [Miriam] was assigned the task. It was the first time she'd ever had to do anything like that. Under the supervision of an older man, she took a knife and managed to cut off one eyelid before the whole thing made her sick and she had to abandon the task. She doesn't know what happened to the spy subsequently—that was the end of the incident.

The second incident on the chain she dated 343 A.D. It took place in a dungeon torture chamber, she thinks somewhere in Italy, but the place isn't certain. She was one of the staff of torturers and was called in on a case where they were torturing a young blond girl, a member of some powerful family, from whom they expected to get some sort of information. Her job was to gouge out the girl's eyes with a hot poker. She did one eye (the left eye; in the previous incident it was the right eye), then in the course of her activity she had the realization that the girl genuinely didn't have the information sought—was "innocent"—and that the whole thing was quite pointless. She felt bad about it and again abandoned the task.

The last and "basic" incident on the chain found her an African tribesman, 440 B.C. She had been acclaimed "warrior of the day" or something honorary like that, and a big dance and festivity were under way. As part of the celebration, they had an enemy from another tribe tied up and were dancing around him. Part of the duty of the "warrior of the day" was to kill the enemy by throwing a short wooden spear into his right eye. This was both a test of the warrior's skill and an omen, since if the man screamed out on being speared, this was considered a propitious sign for the tribe; if he didn't, it was unpropitious. She carried out the assignment beautifully—"Spot on." The guy screamed, too.

I asked Miriam, after she'd told me the chain, whether she had any "locks" in this lifetime on the chain. She said she hadn't thought of any, she'd just gone straight "into the pictures." I said they all seemed to deal with doing in treacherous outsiders, and was I to find myself with a stake through the eye one day? She laughed knowingly, but refused to comment further.

This is an unusually neat incident chain, since the same invariants show up all the way down it, and the isomorphic relationship of each incident to the circumstances of the subject's life is fairly evident. Both the idea of engrams-given-others and that of past lives provide the "format" for her spontaneous constructions; in addition, preconceptions about typical anthropological subjects provide useful motifs. What is actually revealed, it seems safe to assert, is not a series of real past experiences, but the organization of feelings and impulses that Miriam was then experiencing vis-á-vis her anthropology friend and

[91]

her "tribe." It is this schematic organization of feeling that accounts for the relative constancy of thematic relationships within the incidents.

We do not have knowledge of the "real" history of the particular arrangement of feeling shown here. Presumably had Miriam directed her attention to "this lifetime" recollections alone, some remembered experiences might have come to light that (along with other similar experiences) played a part in the shaping of those dispositions now revealed. But equally well, other "real" memories that were not of actual aetiological significance, to borrow Freud's phrase, could be seized upon by currently stimulated schemata simply by virtue of analogies now present that previously did not obtain. Just as a book read in the past may, on our rereading, take on new meaning because in the interval we have developed and encountered conditions of life that altered the arrangement of our feelings, so too the remembered text of our lives is continually seized upon and reanalyzed by our changing dispositions. In this way, "real" personal history itself becomes something of a projective format.

The Piagetian clarification, as clarifications are wont to do, brings us to the next set of problems. If the real history of an individual's inner organization holds no privileged position in the production of therapeutic (as opposed to scientific) insights into this organization, being on an equal footing with fictive or borrowed imagery in this regard, it remains to be seen quite how any of these revelatory phenomena serve to bring about psychological transformation.

The problems in this regard are several. One has to do—again—with the profundity of some of the revelations that we are concerned with, a profundity that in itself seems somehow to bring about radical psychological transformation. Yet the appropriation of imagery and idea by mental schemata is an everyday and ongoing activity of the mind. Why then does its intensity vary so widely? Obviously some account of this variation in intensity must be given if we are to understand the role of these radical experiences in the engenderment of belief.

A second problem, one that may or may not be related to the first, has to do with what sorts of manipulations of the subject's schemata are being conducted in the psychotherapeutic session. The use of projective formats to illuminate inner states certainly makes possible catharsis and increased insight into self, but any psychoanalyst can remind us that these are not the only processes involved in bringing about the sorts of psychological changes sought within the psychoanalytic tradition, and one might suspect they are not the only processes involved in other traditions either. In psychoanalysis, the handling of the so-called transference relationship that arises between patient and therapist is given signal importance in the reduction of neurosis. This is a subject we have not as yet begun to approach.

Lastly, we have to deal with the question of what relationship obtains between visionary processes that are (or seem to be) induced and manipulated within culturally defined contexts such as psychotherapy, ritual action, and religious worship, and spontaneously occurring ecstatic and visionary states. The existence of these "wild" experiences is a reminder that whatever goes on in ritual and therapeutic contexts cannot be entirely special but must be to a great extent continuous with processes that occur in ordinary life.

On all of these questions we are not much further along than we were before. However, the structuralist solution to Freud's dilemma does help us to avoid what might be termed the "true revelation" answer to them. If the notion is embraced that the mind is a repository of hidden scenarios or quasi-religious images, and that these are both the generators of other "derivative" ideas and at the same time the storehouses of tremendous psychic (or instinctual) energies, then it becomes all too easy to rationalize the profundity of any apprehension in terms of how close it comes to a revelation of this energy-charged hidden core, and to see the psychotherapeutic process as little more than a peeling away of the veils and disguises that hide the core from view. Once, however, we eliminate the theoretical need for real hidden content, these lines of reasoning dry up, and it becomes clear that many further factors must be unraveled before we can understand either the sorts of radical psychological transformations that often occur in conjunction with compelling visions or even the more gradual and long-range alterations that tend to occur over the course of repeated psychotherapeutic and ritual occasions.

In the next chapter I will take up these issues, particularly the question of profundity and therapeutic manipulation, extending the structuralist perspective to cover these phenomena. This accomplished, it will be possible to interpret in detail the action of Scientology auditing and its role in the generation of the Scientology worldview—the subject of succeeding chapters. Finally, against this background of theoretical and ethnographic illustration, we will take up the question of "transference" and the long-range effects of psychotherapeutic and religious activity.

[4]

The Dynamics of Revelation

We want to know why some visions are profound and compelling, for these are the sorts of visions that seem most often to act as switch-points in the psychological career of the experiencer, setting in motion a thoroughgoing reformulation of his or her view of the world. One obvious place to look for answers to the question of profundity is in the content of the vision itself. In my concern in the previous chapter to overcome the idea that powerful ideas or images refer to a preexisting set of ideas and images stored somewhere in the mind, I have made it seem as though any ideational complex might be forcefully apprehended as long as it fits some mental/affective schema. But this ignores the fact that imagery and symbolism carry external ("real world") implications and are linked up to collective public meaning systems in addition to being reflectors of private inner states. Personally relevant symbolizations may thus differ drastically in their power to situate the individual within a wider external order and in their portrayal of what this order is. No doubt Rorschach blots serve quite admirably as projective devices that facilitate insight into a subject's inner moti-vational organization, but they are unlikely triggers of a compelling vision of the world for the obvious reason that they "say" nothing about the world. Indeed, the blots were specifically chosen for their relative paucity of external reference. A cycle of deaths and rebirths, on the other hand, or the idea of a divine savior is rich with cos-mological and social implications above and beyond its applicability to the apprehender's inarticulate personal materials. So we are invited to consider whether visionary profundity and therapeutic efficacy are not related to the ideological potential of the projective format being employed.

Herbert Fingarette in his book *The Self in Transformation* has proposed an explanation of therapeutic efficacy very much along these lines. Rejecting, as I did above, the Freudian concept of "hidden content"—but also begging the question of underlying psychic structures—Fingarette argues that the therapeutic effects of a psychotherapy are a function of its capacity to formulate existentially meaningful assertions. The complaint of the client is a complaint about meaning—or the absence thereof—and the neurosis a symbolic, not a neurophysiological disorder. More specifically, the neurosis can be seen as a botched attempt at meaning, an isolated, fragmentary construct. It falls to the therapist to reweave the broken threads of meaning into a system that is humanly livable, using the materials of the patient's life. Therapeutic breakthroughs occur at those points where the multifarious elements of dream, association, behavior, and affect can be shown to knit together into an interpretation that orients understanding and orients commitment.

> We are faced with patches of the meaningless. From this standpoint, it is easy to see that the therapist's effective introduction of a different meaning-scheme from that formerly used by the patient is a way of *directly* acting upon, a way of reorganizing the current experience rather than a way of revealing the truth about a hidden past. . . . In psychotherapy, we must assume that the patient's former meaning-scheme did not work; it did not tie together enough of experience. The therapist's interventions aim at suggesting schemes which do work; everything "fits" and takes on a new value when cast into this mold. [Fingarette 1963:23; his emphasis]

While he is uncomfortable about saying that the therapist is actually constructing ideology, as this is commonly understood, Fingarette does insist that a *scientifically* satisfying meaning-scheme may not be an *existentially* satisfying one—that is, a therapeutically effective one. In seeking therapeutic impact, the therapist is inevitably drawn away from the impersonal and morally neutral languages of science and into the language of choice and commitment.

Fingarette's viewpoint gives us a way to think about why some of the wilder and more implausible constructions placed upon the patient's mental materials are found to be so therapeutically beneficial—

even superior, Jung would argue, to the more mundanely plausible interpretations. It must be that such concepts offer a greater yield of "meaning"; they connect the individual to a more existentially satisfying view of the world.

Of course we have a way to go—as does Fingarette—in explaining what is meant by "existentially satisfying." Without attempting to work out a comprehensive statement on the subject, but merely to suggest the fruitfulness of this line of reasoning, we might concentrate on one feature of ideological systems and world-views that is usually recognized as important to their emotional appeal: their capacity to make us see the particulars of personal experience in terms of the general and the shared. Arthur Koestler has observed: "Even painful experiences are tempered with relief once they are recognized as particular instances of a general law. . . . The only effective consolation in the face of death is that it is part of the cosmic order; if chimneysweepers were exempted from it, we should resent it very much indeed" (1964:327).

This collectivizing and universalizing function appears very clearly in the fabulous constructs of the depth psychologists. In psychoanalysis, the sexual life of the patient ceases to be a collection of shabby personal secrets and becomes his or her link to an ancient ancestral order; in Jungian analysis, every dream can be made to offer up a nugget of our shared heritage; in Scientology auditing, the recollection of past-life experiences projects the pre-clear's identity throughout all of history. Linking up this way of viewing the fables of depth psychology to our preceding discussion of mental schemata, we may say that not only do these telling constructs display for analytic scrutiny the patient's fundamental motivational patterns, thereby facilitating therapeutic insight; they also simultaneously serve to situate these patterns, and thus the patient's most intimate self, within a larger cosmological and collective order, thereby ennobling his suffering and sparking within him a sense of higher purpose. Nancy Munn, a cultural anthropologist, has observed about ritual that in it, "symbols of collectivity are constantly recharged with intimations of self" (1970:152). This is an apt description of what happens at the "primal" level of psychotherapy. Or, one can state Munn's observation in reverse; that in ritual or psychotherapy, intimations of self are constantly assigned their place within a collective symbolic order.

Munn's statement, distilled as it is from the anthropological study of ritual, alerts us to the fact that Fingarette's "meaning-reorganization" explanation of psychoanalysis has much in common with the explanations that cultural anthropologists offer for the psychological effectiveness of ritual and religious worship. These anthropologists—among them Geertz, Terence Turner, Victor Turner, Ortner, Lienhardt, and of course Munn—see ritual activity as restructuring the participant's subjective orientation by symbolically reordering the meanings of problematic situations typically encountered within the participant's society and culture. Ortner summarizes:

> The reshaping of consciousness or experience that takes place in ritual is by definition a reorganization of the *relationship* between the subject and what may for convenience be called reality. Ritual symbolism always operates on both elements, reorganizing (representations of) "reality," and at the same time reorganizing (representations of) self. The experience of each dimension depends upon the experience of the other: A certain view of reality emerges from a certain experience of self; a certain sense of self emerges from a certain experience of reality. [1978:9; her emphasis]

The point is elegantly simple but easily overlooked in the depth psychologists' narrow vision of psychotherapy as solely concerned with revelations of self. Unless, and this is seldom the case, self-revelation is mediated only through the most referentially stripped-down forms (such as inkblots), then inevitably a statement about the world is made each time a statement about the self is made, and the two axes of statement dialectically interact with each other.[1]

The theoretical model before us now unfolds as follows: in therapy, as in ritual, a process is engendered whereby the structures of feeling and cognition are linked up to a wider, and publicly sharable, vision of reality that is existentially satisfying—and, as a subspecies of this, ideologically appealing—through the medium of symbolic formula-

---

1. One of the larger implications of this twofold process is that not only is the therapist drawn, as Fingarette points out, into value-relevant formulations of reality (for these are essential to therapeutic efficacy), but conversely, theories about the self, once these are believed to be therapeutically valuable, will tend to assume a halo of cosmic importance. Jung comments with exaggerated irony on what he believes happened to Freudian doctrine as a result of its curative reputation: "Freud himself, the founder of psychoanalysis, has taken the greatest pains to throw as glaring a light as possible on the dirt and darkness and evil of the psychic background, and to interpret it in such a way as to make us lose all desire to look for anything behind it except refuse and smut. He did not succeed, and his attempt at deterrence has even brought about the exact opposite—an admiration for all this filth" (1973:469).

tions that "fit" the deeper structures of the self while simultaneously making assertions about the world. The intensity with which this symbolic connection is made, the profundity in other words, of visionary apprehension, is not a function just of the "inner fit" of the symbolism but, perhaps more important, of the view of reality being articulated by it.

Thus an argument can be made that connects intensity of visionary experience with the content of the vision. Meaning of vision affects quality of experience, plain and simple. This sort of equation is implicit (when it is not explicit) in much of cultural anthropology's treatment of the ritual process. To the extent that a ritual, or more accurately, a ritually mediated view of the world, reshapes consciousness and reorients feeling, to the extent, that is, that it has psychologically transformative effects; to that extent, we are driven to explore the symbolic manipulations of the ritual for ever more subtle, clever, and far-reaching reorganizations of meaning.

But is this formulation adequate? In the final analysis, I think not. Although every step of the argument is useful, and its usefulness will be demonstrated in the later chapters of this work, when compared against accounts of visionary and religious experience, one senses that it closes the theoretical circle too abruptly. Something has been left out.

Let me start with the first type of perturbing evidence: spontaneous visionary experiences that occur outside of any apparent ritual or therapeutic context and remote from religious training or teaching. These may indeed seize upon purely idiosyncratic ideas and images. Here is one of the more striking such experiences from James's collection:

Whilst in this state of philosophic pessimism and general depression of spirits about my prospects [we are not told the source of these feelings], I went one evening into a dressing-room in the twilight to procure some article that was there; when suddenly there fell upon me without any warning, just as if it came out of the darkness, a horrible fear of my own existence. Simultaneously there arose in my mind the image of an epileptic patient whom I had seen in the asylum, a black-haired youth with greenish skin, entirely idiotic, who used to sit all day on one of the benches . . . with his knees drawn up against his chin. . . . He sat there like a sort of sculptured Egyptian cat or Peruvian mummy, moving nothing but his black eyes and looking absolutely non-human. This image and my fear entered into a species of combination with each other.

[98]

That shape am I, I felt, potentially. . . . There was such a horror of him, and such a perception of my own merely momentary discrepancy from him, that it was as if something hitherto solid within my breast gave way entirely, and I became a mass of quivering fear. After this the universe was changed for me altogether. I awoke morning after morning with a horrible dread at the pit of my stomach, and with a sense of the insecurity of life that I never knew before, and that I have never felt since. It was like a revelation. [1967:138]

Here certainly we see the forceful appropriation of an image by a state of feeling and thinking ("fear," "philosophic pessimism"). But to what agency should we bill the shattering effect of the image of the epileptic youth? Not to any cultural meaning attached to the image by an outside social or traditional authority, and certainly not to any hopeful or self-transcendant notion privately detected in this image, for the "revelation" that entirely transformed this subject's sense of self and world was anything but hopeful and self-transcendant. Existential satisfaction or socially shared doctrines pointing in the direction of such seem altogether remote from this experience. It would appear instead—as the author states—that an intense condition of mind sprang up of its own and then (simultaneously) memory supplied a suiting image for it. The "profundity" of the vision was already in the process of coming into being before the image crystallized it and gave it implications.

Even within experiences that satisfy all the points of the meaning-reorganization argument, one can detect more going on than the meaning-reorganization model—by itself—allows us to understand. Below is an example extracted from the contemporary literature on religious experience. Although it does not take place in the context of a ritual, it is the experience of a man who had had considerable religious training (he was a former divinity student), who was actively seeking a resolution to his ambivalent feelings about his religion, and who had in pursuit of this aim chosen to contemplate a religious symbol—the cross. Here is what happened.

I found myself observing its every facet with fascination and a kind of awe because every facet, every glinting particle became—when I focused my attention—some historical episode in the story of the cross.

I saw Jesus crucified and Peter martyred. I watched the early Christians die in the arena while others moved hurriedly through the Roman back streets, spreading Christ's doctrine. I stood by when Constantine gaped at the vision of the cross in the sky. I saw Rome fall and the Dark Ages begin. . . . I watched peasants trample [the cross] under their feet in some obscene forest rite, while, across the sea in Byzantium, they glorified it in jeweled mosaics. . . . My hand trembled, the cross glimmered, and history became confused. Martin Luther walked arm in arm with Billy Graham, followed by Thomas Aquinas and the armies of the Crusades. . . . Savonarola saluted a red-necked hell-fire and brimstone Texas preacher. Bombers flew in cross formation and St. Francis preached to the birds. A hundred thousand episodes erupted from the glinting facets of that cross and I knew that a hundred thousand more were waiting for their turn. But then, and I don't know when or how it happened, I was immersed *in* it; my substance—physical, mental, and spiritual—was totally absorbed in the substance of the cross. *My* life became the glinting, sparkling episodes of the history of the cross, and the hundred thousand remaining events were those of my own life's history. The shame and victory of the cross were endlessly repeated in the minutiae of my own life. *Mine* was the shame and *mine* was the victory. I had been inquisitor and saint, had falsely damned and sublimely reasoned. And, like the cross, I, too, had died, and lived, and died, and lived, and died to live again and again. And perhaps once more I would die. But now I knew (and now I know) that redemption is a constant thing and guilt is only transitory. [Cited in Masters and Houston 1966:222]

The experience was clearly an intense one. Both the display of the subject's affective dilemma and the mapping of self-pattern onto cosmic pattern seem to have been important factors in the sense of resolution that was achieved. Moreover, a religious symbol with its abundant culturally acquired meanings served to initiate and to a degree organize the psychological process that unfolded. Still, one must suspect that, given his religious training, this man had contemplated crosses on numerous occasions before—without result. What happened this time? And we note too that the inner experience was an incredibly "busy" one, as is the case with so many intense visionary experiences; that it encompassed a swarm of imagery and meaning, and that intriguing sudden shifts in perspective occurred, such as the leap into a total identification with the cross. Yet, except for the moment when the cross trembled and "history became confused," this wealth of inner activity is not matched by any corresponding activity (much less planned manipulation) in the external symbolic apparatus being employed. The impression is strengthened that there are qualities and movements within the visionary process that may be unrelated, or only loosely related, to external event—including the external presentation of symbolic paraphernalia. How to account for these qualities and movements?

We do not have any immediate explanation for the experience cited by James. In the second example, the subject was "tripping" on LSD. In fact, the example was selected from a collection of bizarre and visionary states reported by subjects experimenting with hallucinogenic substances. Any number of other examples could have been chosen from this collection that correspond in tone and general structure to the examples of religious experiences found in such classic studies as James's.

The reader probably does not have to be reminded that popular and scientific experimentation with hallucinogens during the 1960s provoked a new round of analysis of religious experience. In this new phase of the discussion, attention was turned away from the symbolic sources of vision and belief and directed toward the often neglected techniques of religious practice that, even divorced from their usual ritual/ceremonial settings, seem to produce states of mind in which the meaning of things is significantly enriched and transformed. The new line of inquiry has, to be sure, bred its new forms of vulgar materialism—the idea that all religions stem from mushroom-eating, for instance—but such oversimplifications need not distract us from the central point, which is that unusual states of mind of the sorts that figure importantly in religious (and often psychotherapeutic) revelation, may be generated by a-symbolic instrumentalities of which LSD is only one—though perhaps the most dramatic—example.

Surveying the field of religious and depth psychotherapeutic activity, we find that often, in fact usually, the central practice (or practices) of ritual, vision-questing, mysticism, or psychotherapy, boils down to a consciousness-altering technique of some sort: drug ingestion, rhythmic chanting or dancing, dreaming, sensory deprivation or bombardment, mind voiding, the enforced contemplation of a paradoxical object or concept such as the Zen koan, or the use of a rule of thinking that goes contrary to the ordinary thought process, such as the rule of "free association" in psychoanalysis, or the Scientology auditor's insistence upon spontaneous, nonlinear, thought and imagery. Not all these practices have the immediate and uncontrollable impact of chemical hallucinogens, and there are, as might be anticipated, differences in peripheral qualities between the states induced through different agents. The rather slow and calm pace of free association, auditing, or short bouts of meditation, seems to disrupt consciousness more slowly and, up to a point, more controllably than, say, marathon sessions of harassment or sensory bombardment. Nevertheless, close inspection of the mental results of sustained use of any of the afore-mentioned practices reveals a broad similarity in impact.

Before we get to what this impact is, it should be noted that cultural anthropologists have not been altogether blind to the presence or use of altered states of consciousness in ritual and religious visionary activity. Nancy Munn touches upon it frequently, without however, developing her observations. The full context of her statement quoted earlier is that in ritual "it is not merely a kind of object or meaning content which is being transmitted, but also a *particular form or mode of experiencing the world* in which symbols of collectivity are constantly recharged with intimations of self" (my emphasis).

The importance of special "modes of experiencing" in ritual is inescapable when hallucinogenic drugs are utilized, as they are in a surprisingly wide range of cultures (see Furst 1972). But there are numerous nonchemical means of gaining special access to the ritual message. Geertz, whose predominant focus is upon symbolic manipulation in ritual, nevertheless observes about the Balinese "Rangda" and "Barong" ceremony which he has studied:

> There is no aesthetic distance here separating actors from audience and placing the depicted events in an unenterable world of illusion, and by the time a fullscale Rangda-Barong encounter has been concluded a majority, often nearly all, of the members of the group sponsoring it will have become caught up in it not just imaginatively but bodily. . . . In part, this entry into the body of the ritual takes place through the agency of the various supporting roles contained in it. . . . But mostly it takes place through the agency of an extraordinarily developed capacity for psychological dissociation on the part of a very large segment of the population. . . . Mass trance, spreading like a panic, projects the individual Balinese out of the commonplace world in which he usually lives and into that most uncommonplace one in which Rangda and Barong live. To become entranced is, for the Balinese, to cross the threshold into another order of existence, . . . the realm in which those presences exist. [1972:116, 118]

Walbiri Iconography, Munn's fine study of the sources of Australian Aboriginal ritual symbolism, illustrates beyond any quibble that the sacred realm the Aborigines call the "Dreaming," or the "Dream-

[102]

Time," did not come by its name accidentally. Rather it is through the most readily available and widely used "altered state of consciousness"—the dream—that the Australian Dream-Time is entered and its imprint extracted for conveyance to the ritual artifacts (Munn 1973:117). In Freudian or Jungian psychoanalysis, by the same principle, the imprint of a deeper ("primal," "archetypal") reality is extracted from the dream material and fantasies of the patient.

Nonetheless, despite cultural anthropology's passing appreciation of the use of extraordinary states of consciousness in ritual and religious activity, no attempt has arisen from this quarter to integrate the psychological literature on consciousness alteration—a literature which now subsumes earlier psychological studies of religious experience such as that of James—with the symbolic manipulation (or "meaning-reorganization") theories so brilliantly developed in studies of the ritual process. At most anthropologists speak of techniques to "heighten suggestibility" without delving further into what this entails.

The failure to integrate the two viewpoints in part reflects a failure to perceive that there are two viewpoints to integrate. The tendency in cultural anthropology is to treat consciousness alteration and meaning reorganization as virtually the same thing, and to assume that, having worked out the whys and wherefores of the latter, one has automatically taken care of the former. The strong core of truth in this assumption—that whatever alters consciousness reorganizes meaning and vice-versa—is in many respects flattened and turned into mere cleverness if it is not appreciated, or if appreciated not shown, that some disparity must exist, some analytic gulf must be bridged, between the system we call "mind" and the one we call "culture." Processes that go on in the realm of shared and publicly accessible meanings—the manipulation of symbols in ritual, the exchange of interpretations between therapist and client—inevitably impinge upon the private symboling processes of those participating (otherwise the ritual therapeutic effort would not be made), but the two sets of processes are not therefore of the same order, nor do they operate in a point-for-point correspondence. This being so, we can hypothesize variation in the modes of impingement, depending upon what sorts of psychological processes are brought into conjunction with what sorts of cultural formats. It is this variation that demands to be explored.

A more important reason for anthropologists' neglect of psychological perspectives on religious experience resides in the deficiency of these perspectives. Psychology has provided us with a wealth of phenomenological accounts of unusual experiences, some of them, like James's study, so organized as to make quite clear how important special states of mind are to religious culture. But this wealth has not been undergirded by an equally rich psychodynamic account. If we look at the literature on visionary states and consciousness alteration, we find that the great mass of it leads us in one of two unsatisfactory directions. On the one hand there are the models that relate unusual states of mind to certain physical, neurophysiological, or stimulus-response correlates: "transmarginal inhibition" of the higher brain functions, "holographic crises" in the brain, and so on. Typically favored by theorists who see the cultural uses of altered states of consciousness as "brainwashing" (that is, as inevitably associated with forceful indoctrination), these explanations say little more than that certain techniques cause confusion, heighten suggestibility, and make people act in ways they normally wouldn't. We knew this already and it isn't the point. What the cultural anthropologist needs is an explanation that outlines the structural particulars of the presumed "confusion" (never mind the neurophysiological or chemical correlates of it) and does so in such a way as to make possible systematic theoretical connections between these mental particulars and the cultural particulars to which they are, in ritual or psychotherapy, related. Working at the level of meaning, the anthropologist asks the question: if "meaning" is being altered or reorganized within the mind through who cares what neurophysiological quirk, how does this alteration unfold and how may this private reorganization of meaning be related to one that is culturally planned? Brain chemistry and reflex models leave us flat here because they skip over the level of meaning and, in doing so, neglect much of the anatomy of the experiences they purport to explain.

The other direction in which psychological explanations of altered states proceeds is back to Freud or back to Jung, and of course back to the problems of depth psychology I have already discussed. There is in fact much that is useful here, but it must be disentangled from much that is misleading. If that is not done we wind up once again in occult dead ends with, for example, statements to the effect that consciousness-altering techniques activate the Unconscious (how? what is the Unconscious?) or cause regression to various presumed early experiences—life in the womb, birth trauma, nursing, and so on.

It is not really surprising that, faced with a choice between brain-wave patterns and archetypes, cultural anthropology has chosen the conservative route of merely noting that religious practices seem to have some intensifying or disordering effect upon experience, and retreating back into the realm of culturally organized meaning manipulation. This is after all, the anthropologist reasons, his or her proper domain.

Not all of the psychological theorizing about consciousness alteration is so discouraging, however. Some of it, having its roots in structuralist psychology, can be nicely fitted to the structuralist perspective that I began to set forth in the preceding chapter, and, once so fitted, used to rework and make better sense of the important insights that depth psychologists, in particular Freud, have given us. I turn now to this task. Although I will use rather broad strokes in painting it, I think the resulting portrait of altered states of consciousness will be sufficient to enable us to place in proper perspective the roles played by psychological process and cultural process in the special situations of ritual and psychotherapy we are considering, and finally, to round out our understanding of "revelation."

Altered States of Consciousness

In contemporary cognitive studies of altered states of consciousness, there is a certain amount of agreement that ordinary wakeful consciousness is a product of the proper operation of widely ramifying interpretative structures which, in a sense, "hold" the real world in place. Arthur Deikman (1969) speaks of these structures as arising out of automatized mental habits and likens their acquisition to the acquisition of motor skills such as walking and bike riding. Ronald Shor hypothesizes a "generalized reality orientation": "The usual state of consciousness is characterized by the mobilization of a structured frame of reference in the background of attention which supports, interprets, and gives meaning to all experiences" (Shor 1969:242). The constant feedback/correction process that goes on between these pattern-giving mental structures and that enduring source of regular stimuli called "the real world" informs the entire interpretative system with certain principles that could be spoken of as a "grammar" of reality.

In these hypothesized interpretative structures, or structured frames of reference, we find again Piaget's concept of acquired mental schemata. It is also not hard to see that the production of an "altered state of consciousness" is, as the cited authors maintain, in one way or another dependent upon an attack on these structures and on the structuring activities of the mind. There are a number of ways that this may be accomplished. It seems to be the case that the psychochemical supports of habitual mental activity are interfered with under conditions of fatigue, sleeplessness, malnutrition, or ingestion of hallucinogenic substances. Or the mind may be cut off from the regular and predictable feedback of the environment which keeps it in balance—both stimulus deprivation and stimulus bombardment act to this effect. Finally, deliberate mental countereffforts of one sort and another are remarkably effective in causing reality disruption. Benumbing repetitions, mind voiding, and concentration on a narrowly limited stimulus field are among the common practices of various mystic disciplines. The strategy pointed out by Deikman of "putting the mind in a bind" by turning attention back upon the attending process itself—thus "deautomatizing" it in much the same way as the renewal of attention disrupts ingrained motor skills—is raised to a fine art in the Zen koan task. Some meditative practices enjoin a free as opposed to a goal-directed mental flow, a practice that has a gently errosive effect.[2]

The sort of mentation that results from this frustration of structuring activity could be called, in Piagetian terms, a disequilibrated thought process. In ordinary thinking, a balance obtains—or more accurately, continuously reasserts itself—between the molding of mental schemata to the attributes of the world, the process Piaget calls "accommodation," and the mental remodeling of the world to fit already existent schemata, the process he calls "assimilation." The side of the pair that suffers in all of the practices listed above is "accommodation." Reflection, self-consciousness, consciousness of one's activity and its meaning are all acts of accommodation forced upon the subject by the resistance of realities indifferent to the will. With the waning of accommodation, the subject becomes progressively "unconscious" of self and of what self is experiencing, even though the experiencing of it may be very rich and full. The waning of accommodation also means, reciprocally, the predominance of assimilation in the thought process. Reality is uncritically shaped to the preexisting structures of

2. See Naranjo and Ornstein, 1973, for an exhaustive account of mystical practices and their effects.

the subject, producing distortions and "projections" that become more personal and at the same time more unwitting as accommodation recedes from mental activity. As Piaget points out, we see the diminishment of accommodation and the primacy of assimilation in the symbolic play of children, in adult reverie, and to a greater degree in dreaming. I would add that the primacy of assimilation is remarkably prominent in hallucinogenic drug trips and visionary states.[3]

It would stand to reason as well that the function of "organization"—the coordination of schemata and the precipitation from this process of the higher principles of operation that inform mature thinking—also comes under attack with the use of consciousness-altering techniques. The higher principles of mental operation most often cited by Piaget (he admitted the list is not fully worked out) are "reversibility," "reciprocity," "conservation," and "decentration." A mental operation is said to be reversible when its opposite exists within the mental system, when for instance, addition implies subtraction, when conclusion can be traced back to premises. "Reciprocity" refers to the appreciation of relative relationships, for example that if A is greater than B, B is lesser than A. "Conservation" refers to the ability to effect mental compensations so as to preserve a property invariant under transformation—as for instance when the weight of a lump of clay is perceived to remain the same despite changes in its shape. "Decentration" involves the ability to assume different viewpoints and perspectives and, implied in this, the ability to take into account various features of an object or concept. In the absence of these higher mental operations, conceptions of class, hierarchy, causality, and seriation would be impossible. As I shall point out in a moment, in altered states of consciousness these principles and these concepts do indeed degenerate.

A simpler way of stating what happens when basic functions of mental structuration are diminished is that mental activity becomes less structured! Arthur Deikman, in a study of meditation, points out what the Piagetian system largely implies, namely that the disruption of structured thinking is similar in consequence to its lack of development in the first place. Mental material undergoes simplification and dedifferentiation; the thinking of the disrupted mind behaves in a general way like the thinking of the child (Deikman 1969:32–34). The

3. The predominance of accommodation is to be seen in imitation, rote learning, and other forms of what we are inclined to call "mindless" conformity.

states of mind that win the label "altered states of consciousness" are merely those in which this weakening of structure has reached dramatic proportions.

It would be tedious to cite masses of specific experiences here, so in order to review more specifically the evidence of structural de-differentiation in fantasy, dreams, hypnogogic states, drug trips, and mystical experiences, I will summarize what others have repeatedly abstracted from these data.

First, even at shallow levels of destructuration—reverie, mild intoxication, presleep states—formerly distinct trains of thought begin to collapse into one another, giving rise to novel combinations, off-beat intuitions, puns, and rebuses. Piaget speaks of this as the free play and "mutual assimilation" of schemata—the clustering together of schemata along virtually any line of similarity or association. We are familiar with such phenomena in psychoanalytic theory under the rubric "condensation." In it we see a manifestation both of the primacy of assimilation and the diminishment of organization. The clustering of multiple schemata tends to give way, at deeper levels of destructuration, to the appearance of grand, general, and more amorphous schemata, as evidenced in the fact that the images appropriated by the mind become grander, more global, and more ambiguous. Another manifestation of the movement from "stronger" into "weaker" structure is simply the replacement of verbal with pictorial representation.

The deterioration of the higher principles of thinking is evinced in visionary (and "tripping") subjects' tendency to experience the collapse of hierarchical distinctions between persons, creatures, values, and so on, with the resulting sense of "universal brotherhood," or in Victor Turner's terms, "communitas" (see Turner 1969: chs. 3 & 4)— here the principle of reciprocity is diminished. They tend to see efficacy in terms of effort (usually their own, e.g. the room brightens when the subject moves to turn on the lights)—here the concept of causality is primitivized. They tend to become entranced with, or to mentally overemphasize, one feature of an object or concept, ignoring all the rest (people are seen as caricatures, textures and surfaces bedazzle, a single utterance colors the entire meaning of the conversation)—here the ability to decenter is not fully operating. They tend to lose trains of thought in conversation, lose track of persons or objects that have left the sensory field, lose their own way geographically, and so on—reversibility is becoming more difficult. They tend also to experience a change in a minor feature of some object or person as a total transformation of character—conservation is impaired. Disorders in the sense of time (typically the experience of existing in a timeless realm), the increased enjoyment of paradox (contradictory thoughts no longer repel each other), the sense of persons, objects, situations as "classical," "archetypal," or the manifestation of Platonic essences, and so on also can be traced to diminishment of the higher operations of thinking.

Finally, in dedifferentiated cognition, we find that the self/nonself (or self/other) distinction, a product of self-conscious accommodated thinking, suffers impairment and its diminishment brings into being a magical realm in which the environment is experienced as an emanation of the self or vice-versa. Ultimately world and self may be fused in a mystic egolessness. The pinnacle of mystical insight is reported to be "all is one." This, certainly, is as far as one can go in the direction of dedifferentiation.

I have already taken exception to the prevailing view that the imagery through which structural dedifferentiation manifests itself is necessarily preexistent in the mind, but "unconscious." Now it is necessary to take exception to the modified view of the Unconscious proposed by Lévi-Strauss and Lacan, who suggest that the Unconscious is a realm of special structuring activity, comparable in a way to a grammar. It should be apparent from the foregoing that what is seen in visionary outpourings is not a special structure, but a vicissitude of structure. It is structure falling apart. Furthermore, it is not "hidden" and coming to light; it is simply happening.

This so far largely cognitive portrait of altered states can be matched by one that puts the emphasis on affect and emotion. As a matter of fact, it must be so matched if we are to continue to follow a Piagetian perspective. Mental structures are simultaneously cognitve and affective, according to Piaget. There is no organization of affect that does not have its cognitive component and vice-versa. This is not to say that a certain broad division cannot be made: some areas of structuration develop largely in relation to the world of material objects and processes, others in relation to the world of persons and interpersonal relationships. Piaget's main interest was in the former. His only extensive excursion into the topic of interpersonal structuration is *The Moral Judgment of the Child.* In this work he traces the development of social rule-governed behavior, making clear that with the development of the mental apparatus, the individual comes to construct a relatively stable system of values and beliefs informed by certain high-er-order principles such as those of interpersonal reciprocity, obligation, justice, and the like.

Ignoring as it does the erotic dimension of the interpersonal, Piaget's work fails to intersect with Freud's in a way that would allow of any easy synthesis. One can note of course that Freud's hypothesized stages of psychosexual development might be cast into a structuralist-developmental framework; but the dominant tone of Freud's message, and one with which I am inclined to agree, is that there is a certain inveterate primitiveness to the erotic and aggressive organization, and this would defeat the sort of thoroughgoing theoretical systematizing that Piaget so successfully applied to the formations of the intellect—just as, in the life of individuals, these instinctual forces continuously rise up to threaten the reality adaptations of the ego. The expression "all's fair in love and war" is folk wisdom's acceptance of the fact that the higher principles of reciprocity, justice, and so on, usually fail to hold in these areas. Indeed, following Freud's reasoning in regard to the instinctual underpinnings of affect, we would be inclined to treat these as enemies of structure and perhaps put erotic and aggressive drives into the category of consciousness-altering mechanisms.

I prefer, for present purposes, to bracket this problem and continue to work out the model of altered states of consciousness along certain lines where one finds a Freudian and a Piagetian in rough agreement. Equilibrated thinking on the one hand, and, on the other, the dis-equilibrated, "wildly" assimilatory activity we have just discussed, parallel Freud's "secondary process"—the reality-adapted thought of the adult—and "primary process"—the magical wish-dominated thinking of the child, and of the Unconscious as the latter manifests itself in dreams, neuroses, psychoses, and other "regressive" states. The secondary process is governed by the "reality" principle and is a function of the ego; the primary process is governed by the "pleasure" principle and expresses the patterns acquired by the instincts. There are thus two origin points of "regressive" ideation in the Freudian system: (a) a too powerful thrusting forward of instinctual drives with their archaic, primary process, mode of expression, and (b) a diminishment of the ego functions and thus a lapse in reality-governed thinking.

I do not wish to draw into this analysis all the tangled threads of psychoanalytic reasoning that have entered into the concept of the "ego." Nevertheless, even noting the difficulties of this concept and limiting myself to speaking of structured (equilibrated) thinking as an "ego function" rather than the sum of the Freudian "ego," I think it essential to our understanding of the affective phenomena that appear in altered states of consciousness that we borrow from Freud certain themes developed in regard the concept of "ego." One theme is that ego functions require a certain quantity of psychic energy for their support. While a percentage of this energy may be conceived of as neutral and as "belonging" to the ego as its own, a more significant percentage is "borrowed" from the instincts. Those operations of the mind that relate the person to the world in a realistic way are of great relevance to the instincts since ultimately "reality" is the only route through which instincts may be satisfactorily discharged. Instinctual energy becomes invested in and supports the higher processes inasmuch as these provide pathways to gratification. But this investment may be withdrawn—to the detriment of the higher processes. When it is withdrawn, of course, "regressive" ideation replaces realistic ideation.

This way of looking at the source of primary process mentation appears at a number of important points in Freud's model. That most commonplace regressive process, dreaming, is made possible by sleep, Freud notes, and sleep can be characterized (psychologically, not biologically) as a "withdrawal of interest" from the outside world (1958:92). Similarly, the bizarre world of the psychotic is called into being by a radical withdrawal of emotional investment from the "object world" (real world) and the consequent turning inward of libidinal energy. The neurotic symptom, itself a regressive formation, arises not just from the fixation of libido in past childhood pleasures, but from the coincidence of such fixations with a contemporary frustration. It is the latter, an externally imposed shutoff of reality outlets, that sets in motion the inward (or, in temporal terms, backward) flow of emotional energy into symbolic representations of an earlier satisfaction (1958:355; 1963:108–9). Lastly, there is the daydream, a somewhat primitive thought form, and this Freud quite readily saw as a happy escape from the "reality" principle. In all these instances of "regressive" or "archaic" thinking, the affective correlate singled out for us by Freud is the migration of desire away from its points of (what I will call for the moment) "worldly" attachment and into fantasmic constructs.

The missing element in psychoanalytic reasoning that would allow us to link it up directly with the structuralist perspective is the idea

[111]

that while desire (that is, libidinal energy) *supports* cognitive structure, it is also *mediated by* cognitive structure. What Freud is calling a withdrawal of interest from "reality," or the "world," is better stated as a withdrawal of interest from those objects which structured thinking has brought into being for the subject, and what he would characterize as a vesting of interest in symbolic substitutes can be stated as a migration of desire into those objects which *less* structured thinking has brought into being for the subject.

The cognitive apparatus and the emotional apparatus are in a sense flip sides of a single structural coin. It makes sense therefore that an assault upon one dimension must have inevitable consequences for the other. Structured thinking ceases to sustain a "world" from which interest has been withdrawn because the very withdrawal of interest effects a diminishment of ego energy, of "structured thinking" energy. Conversely, the destructuring of "reality" that takes place when cognition is thrown into disequilibrium through a purely cognitive assault such as drug ingestion is inevitably accompanied by a migration of desire away from its usual loci of attachment and into the fantasy constructs that simplified mental activities have appropriated as their objects. If only temporarily, these constructs become the new loci of attachment, and the same feeling values previously associated with things in the ordinary world now become associated with things in the nonordinary world of the fantascist.

A version of this reasoning is used by Arthur Deikman as a means of explaining one of the phenomena I have been trying to explain here: the intensely "real," self-evident, quality of visionary experience. Deikman writes:

> It is assumed by those who have had a mystic experience, whether induced by years of meditation or by a single dose of LSD, that the truthfulness of the experience is attested to by its sense of realness. . . . "I know it was real because it was more real than my talking to you now." But "realness" is not evidence. Indeed, there are many clinical examples of variability in the intensity of the feeling of realness that is not correlated with corresponding variability in the reality. . . . Thus it appears that . . . the *feeling* of realness represents a function distinct from that of reality *judgment*, although they usually operate in synchrony. . . . When one considers that meditation combined with renunciation brings about a profound disruption of the subject's normal psychological relationship to the world, it becomes plausible that the practice of such mystic techniques would be associated with a significant

alteration of the feeling of reality. The quality of reality formerly attached to objects becomes attached to the particular sensations and ideas that enter awareness during periods of perceptual and cognitive deautomatization. [1969:37–38]

As William James suspected, there is a detachable "sense of realness" to which even quite unimaginable notions may under the proper circumstances lay claim. Somewhat ironically the significance of this sense, that it is the experiential manifestation of a generalized libidinal investment, derives from the thinking of Freud who, at least when arguing for the existence of primal scene experiences, took it for what it is not: evidence of "realness."

The investigation of the emotional correlates of altered states can be pushed further by taking into account observations others, notably the mystics, have made about the emotional dimension of unusual states. In altered states of consciousness, not only is emotional charge with its attendant sense of reality directed at new, structurally weaker, constructs, but accompanying this redirection is a commensurate amplification of the emotional charge. The new "reality" is experienced as *more* real, richer, more meaningful, than the old. One might say that *more* emotional energy is captured in it. Whence this more? The mystics are helpful here. They speak of withdrawing from the given world as a process of "re-collecting" the assorted strands of interest heretofore engaged by ordinary reality and the fusion of these strands into a unified spiritual center. The senses are gathered back into the self, in St. Teresa's imagery, like bees returning to the hive to begin the making of honey (Underhill 1967:316).

This amalgamation of affective forces leads to a loss of their specific identities, as separate strands of feeling are increasingly divorced from their old aims and consolidated into a rich, unified affect. In higher-level visionary ecstasies, this consolidation of desire is often experienced as an overwhelming influx into the self of light, warmth, wind, or some other analogue of pure energy (see Underhill 1967:249, 421). In these mystical metaphors we hear stated in the idiom of affect what we have already noted in regard to the cognitive dimension of mental destructuration. Multiple differentiated schemata collapse into one another and give rise to simpler, grander, and more global formations. On the level of concept, this process is manifested in the apperception of grand general insights and images. At the level of affect, the process is manifested as an intensification and enrichment of feeling. As mystical cognition moves toward a pinnacle of an imageless, "all is one," gnosis, mystical desire moves toward a pinnacle of ultimate satisfaction. This pinnacle, says Evelyn Underhill, "is to the intellect an emptiness, and to the heart a fulfillment of all desire" [1967:304].

Disequilibrium and "Regression"

The structuralist model of altered states of consciousness, considered from either the cognitive or the affective angle, has much in common with the psychoanalytic notion of "regression" (hence my occasional use of this term above), and before I turn to the implications of this model of altered states for the understanding of ritual and psychotherapeutic effectiveness, it is useful to inquire how the viewpoint stated here differs from the more familiar psychoanalytic viewpoint and whether or not the latter might have been a perfectly satisfactory stand-in for the idea of cognitive dedifferentiation and affective involution just outlined.

If by "regression" is merely meant a process that parallels cognitive-emotional development in reverse, then the term is suitable for what I have been describing. And, in a general sense, this is what is meant by the psychoanalytic usage. There is, however, more specific baggage attached to the idea, both in Freud's formulation of it and in subsequent elaborations, that dissuades me from adopting it wholesale.

In order to maintain his notion of the Unconscious as a special realm of the mind, Freud was driven to speak of cognitive regression as "topographical," that is, a shift from one "area" into another, while libidinal (emotional) regression was simply "temporal," that is, a return to an earlier state. The two dimensions of the regressive process tend in this usage to lose their comparability. Furthermore, in regard to either dimension, Freud's speculations arising from the Wolf Man case show that for him the notion of a developmental recapitulation was only imperfectly disentangled from the notion of a historical recapitulation. It is understandable that a confusion of history with development should arise, since cognitive-emotional regression does in fact stir up and revivify old memories; but it is mistaken concreteness to make a mode of experiencing characteristic of an early stage synonymous with an early experience.

The inclination to conflate a structural progression with a historical one is simply a subspecies of the confusion of structure with content

[114]

criticized earlier. Further manifestations of this confusion are apt to crop up when we are trying to identify what it is about an adult experience that may be correctly called "infantile." Deikman reminds us that the adult continues to differ from the child even when he may be experiencing the world from a comparable cognitive vantage point (1969:36). Again, it is in structure rather than in content that we find the equivalence. The dreams and symbolic play of children are heavily concerned with pets, parents, and going to the bathroom, while much more sophisticated cultural/symbolic materials are being broken down and rearranged in adult visionary states. The notions and metaphors seized upon in the mature visionary's experience derive from adult culture and the resulting brew is a good deal richer in messages of potential relevance to adult social and intellectual life than are the productions of actual children. Adults are, as it were, playing with bigger toys. There is also the factor that the adult can, by shifting modes of consciousness, reflect upon his or her destructured apprehensions from a more structured point of view, thereby bringing to articulate focus the potential social and cultural relevance of visionary insights. The consciousness of the child is also subject to fluctuations, but these are of much narrower scope.

Another difficulty with "regression" in the Freudian system is its overwhelming connotation of pathology. Either such apparently harmless (and certainly common) regressive phenomena as dreaming and mourning must be, in Freud's words, "normal prototypes" of pathological states, an unilluminating distinction, or else all regressions are at bottom symptomatic of neurotic weakness. About dreams, Freud found himself in the position of saying: "It would be illogical to account for the dreams of neurotics in a way that would not also hold good for the dreams of normal people. . . . The healthy man too is . . . virtually a neurotic, but the only symptom he *seems* capable of developing is a dream" (1958:464–65; his emphasis).

In the view I have taken here, this assumption of pathology cannot be made. It is true of course, even within a Piagetian framework, that the failure or lapse of accommodative and organizing mental activity and the predominance of sheer assimilation betokens a mind that is "out of balance." And it is true too that this may occur, just as Freud argues, because of developmental deficiencies that have left the subject's acquired psychic organization ill equipped to deal realistically with a given situation. Indeed, even in the case of the adequately developed individual, when accommodation is nullified through sleep or a cultural manipulation such as religious practice, his or her assimilations will tend to gravitate to emotional involvements that are currently problematic. In dreams, unresolved concerns of the day make their appearance; in induced religious visions, the visionary's life troubles are often writ large. In a word, the *un*assimilated areas of a person's life experience will occupy the foreground of any increased assimilatory activity.

But the range of those matters that require further psychological digestion is, for any individual at any given time, so broad as to render nonsensical the attempt to make "normality" coincident with the absence of this sort of psychological work. The commonness and easy occurrence of heightened assimilatory states and their obvious linkage to certain routinely encountered impairments to accommodation, such as sleep, fatigue, and frustration, should overrule our impulse to automatically attribute an ominous significance to them.

It may be more promising to argue that there are regressions and regressions; some are pathological, others are not. This is the drift that more recent psychiatric writings on the subject have taken. Some speak of "regression in the service of the ego," of which artistic inspiration and religious experience are the most frequently cited examples, and this type is opposed to the pathological regressions of neurosis and psychosis (see Kris 1964; Prince and Savage 1966). Two often poorly differentiated axes of distinction seem to be operating here.

The first is the distinguishing of regressions in terms of their outcome. The regression that resolves positively (or at least neutrally) for the individual or has cultural value is put into a different category from that which produces the psychiatric patient. The principal objection that can be raised to this typology is that it opens the door to letting cultural values rather than psychodynamic principles dictate the diagnosis. The religious conversion experience is seen variously as "regression in the service of the ego," or as the rise of a neurotic symptom, depending upon the classifier's attitude toward religion in general or the particular religion in question. Comparably, deep and extensive mourning phenomena are judged as healthy "working through" of loss if the loss involved a family member, but as something else again if the loss involved only a pet or possession. Disequilibrated states will reflect the pattern of a person's emotional attachments and the direction of his or her wishes. These are expected to concur with prevailing cultural values. When they do not, it will be for this reason that harsh judgments descend upon the regressive condition.

While cultural values do not provide an adequate psychodynamic basis for distinguishing regressive states, still it cannot be ignored that such values, by influencing the interpretive and social response to regressive behavior, may in concrete cases alter for good or ill the further progress of the regression itself. This means of diagnosis, biased from the start, also has a self-fulfilling tendency in it.

The other axis of distinction has to do with the degree to which regression pervades the personality organization as a whole. Regressions may be likened to tumors in this regard: some are "encapsulated," others "invasive." In the first instance we think of a relatively compartmentalized phenomenon which, while certainly affecting thought and feeling for the duration of its occurrence, does not impair bodily functions or cause an infantilization of overt behavior. Most people dream and daydream without peculiar behavioral carry-over, for instance, and even superior mystical experiences have been achieved with no particular disruption of the subject's day-to-day activities. In the second instance, we are apt to encounter the psychiatric patient, neurotic or psychotic, whose physical functioning and social behavior show obvious peculiarity, who may have to be cared for to the point of feeding, or whose activities must be monitored to forestall violence. In the first instance, regression appears to be subject to the individual's control; in the second, he or she is no longer in full control, and the need for intervention is assumed. There is some correlation, though far from a perfect one, between the degree of pervasiveness in a regression and the depth of cognitive-affective destructuration discussed above.

The business of keeping the "good" regressions analytically separate from the "bad" ones raises important questions about the qualities and outcomes of regressive states, but it may do so at the cost of fragmenting the identity of the phenomena under scrutiny. It helps to remember that these distinctions are the particular obsession of modern secular psychotherapy and that there are good social and cultural reasons why the issue of distinguishing should be raised to the status of a dilemma in this tradition. Secular psychotherapy has traditionally had as its clientele persons whose regressions have, for the moment, slipped their control or offended family, friends, and community. At the same time, there has been little or no acknowlegment of the possibility that the psychotherapeutic treatment for this condition might itself be regression-inducing; if anything, the therapeutic effort is presumed to work in the opposite direction. Consequently, patients who continue to manifest regression will tend to be written off as "inaccessible" to treatment, while those who regain control of the regression or bring it to a positive resolution are interpreted as having responded to the *counter*regressive effects of the treatment. All that remain to be explained are the apparently benign lunacies of the nonpatient population, a disturbing puzzle indeed. What is obscured by this combination of client condition and assumptions about treatment is the possibility that pervasive, unpleasant, or culturally undesirable "regressions" might constitute simply a moment in a larger process that has its benevolent transformations as well, a process that may be, in many cases, largely self-correcting.

In the mystical traditions, by contrast, there is usually acknowledgment of the fact that the spiritual journey has its downs as well as its ups, and the lives of religiously trained "regressors" testify to this. Accounts of those undergoing the "dark night of the soul" in medieval Christian mystical practice, for instance, leave no doubt in my mind that these saintly souls would be immediately institutionalized were they, in their condition, to appear among us today; and not just because our faith in their goals is nowadays diminished. They needed tending, and in fact they received it—in religious institutions (see Underhill 1967: ch. 9).

In the 1960s and early 1970s some schools of psychiatry embraced a similar sanguine view of regressive states and attempted to treat schizophrenia as an essentially fruitful, if extreme, personality reorganization process (Barnes and Berke 1971; also cf. Foster 1975). In this respect they share the buoyant attitude of the Christian mystics. I should add here, however, that mysticism's "dark night of the soul," which has strong similarities to psychosis, lasted in some cases ten or fifteen years; it is questionable whether modern psychiatric optimism can endure so long.

The larger point remains. If regressions cannot be automatically adjudged pathological, they cannot be automatically adjudged harmless either. Rather there seem to be both benign and malevolent transformations on the same underlying process, and these shift about over the course of a regressive episode. All the variables of the condition so far mentioned—depth, pervasiveness, pleasantness or unpleasantness of feeling tones, even cultural implications—may vary widely, and not necessarily in synchrony, within the compass of a single experience. Over the course of a career of fairly intense experiences, and we encounter such careers when turning to the religious life, it is not surprising to see all shades of spiritual light and dark, psychiatric health and disease. What should determine the moment at which we freeze the frame and declare that this person is undergoing a normal or an abnormal experience?

In order to avoid the unwanted connotations of the term "regression" and to bring to the foreground the element in disequilibrated mental behavior that I feel is most relevant to the reequilibrations that religions and psychotherapies strive to effect, I will adopt the Western mystic's term "renunciation" for the joint cognitive-affective process outlined above and speak of it hereafter as "the process of renunciation." Schematically, what we see in the process of renunciation is an (affective) movement out of and (cognitive) dissolution of one set of desire-mediating structures and, resulting from this—operating out of the same materials, as it were—a (cognitive) construction of and (affective) movement into a new, and hierarchically simpler, set of structures. For the renouncer, the "world" as previously constituted or, more usually, some aspect or element of this world is abandoned, while by the same process a new and richer reality or, more usually, a new and richer dimension of the old reality is envisioned and embraced. "Renunciation," as the mystics do not tire of telling us, is the path to fulfillment. It remains to be shown quite how this is so.

To square away this last formulation of the argument, let me return to the questions with which the chapter began, the questions of how revelation is produced within the ritual or psychotherapeutic setting, why it is profound, and what relationship obtains between spontaneous visionary states and those that are culturally induced. As these questions are reviewed in light of the structuralist explanation of altered states of consciousness, we will be able to see how the psychological process stimulated by religious and psychotherapeutic activity fits together with the sorts of cultural apparatus that typically accompany this activity.

Renunciation and Cultural Form

In ritual and psychotherapeutic situations, the consciousness of participants is being altered (gradually or abruptly) through the use of techniques that set in motion the process of renunciation: a joint dedifferentiation of thinking and the involution and intensification of desire. Cast into this mental mode, participants become not simply passive appreciators of the messages encoded in the symbolic dramas or discourses of the session, but hyperactive generators of emotionally charged autistic constructions. These constructions are invariably personally relevant, for inasmuch as accommodation to external reality has been lessened, the activity of the mind turns increasingly to the display and spinning out of its existent patterns. Qualities of "realness," "meaningfulness," and fascination attach to these autistic constructions both by dint of their subjective origin and by dint of the pooling of affective energy that renunciatory practice engenders. At the same time, the forms appropriated by mental activity become, as cognitive destructuration occurs, nonordinary, bizarre, archetypal, and ultimately "beyond thought." The reality with which ritual or psychotherapeutic participants find themselves in touch is an unaccustomed one, yet it speaks directly to their hearts—after all, it is for the moment the bearer of their desires.

This portrait of religious and psychotherapeutic revelation by no means contradicts or undermines the "meaning-reorganization" view of ritual/therapeutic activity discussed earlier, but rather broadens our angle on it. The symbolic tradition brought to bear upon participants in these special activities, in addition to furnishing a way of looking at the world or providing resolutions to social and cultural contradictions, serves most immediately as a set of glosses upon participants' supercharged perceptions. Carved as they usually are from the productions of earlier visionaries, both religious idiom and the deeper imagery of the depth psychotherapies have about them the same rich, elemental, paradoxical, and circular qualities as destructured mentality itself. They are structurally appropriate to the special states of mind engendered by ritual and psychotherapeutic practice. Thus participants are more readily able to discover within themselves, experience with their own (altered) senses, those elements of reality that the tradition assures them will be there, and these dramatically experienced elements then act as a powerful leverage point for the belief system as a whole.

A more detailed examination of this fitting together of autistic construction and cultural form will unfold as I turn to illustrations of it in subsequent chapters. For the moment I have merely attempted to summarize in broad outline what it is that religious and psychotherapeutic practice and its psychological effects do for the doctrine or belief system under the auspices of which the practice proceeds.

This summary having been made, it is possible to see that a belief system or doctrine is also doing something for the special states of mind that support it. Primarily, cultural glosses act to focus, stabilize, and lend reinforcing collective agreement to special perceptions that might otherwise, like dream images, slither away with the dawning of ordinary consciousness. Carlos Castaneda, the now famed apprentice to Yaqui sorcerer don Juan, makes this point especially clearly when summing up the effects of don Juan's teachings. He writes: "By directing the extrinsic and intrinsic levels of nonordinary reality, don Juan exploited the different hallucinogenic properties [of the drugs used] until they created in me, as the apprentice, the perception that nonordinary reality was a perfectly defined area, a realm separate from [the] ordinary . . . whose inherent properties were revealed as I went along" (1968:249). Out of the often chaotic melange of visionary constructions, a cultural tradition selects some materials and neglects others. It thus acts to interpret and *direct* the renunciatory process, leading it to certain outcomes and away from others. The favored outcomes will be, on the one hand, ones that validate the belief system, as I have just stated. On the other hand, we may, I think, safely speculate that the favored outcomes are ones that are experienced on the individual level as a return of emotional and cognitive equilibrium.

With these points in mind, let us inquire finally about the relationship between culturally controlled and spontaneous visionary experiences. By implication, the latter are simply renunciatory episodes taking place without benefit of any systematic intervention on the part of mediators of a doctrine designed for this sort of intervention.

It should be made clearer at this point how it is that visionary and special states arise spontaneously. With drug experimentation or the deliberate mental manipulations undertaken in ritual and therapeutic situations, one can point to relatively discrete instigators of mental disequilibrium, but in "ordinary" unsupervised living, what mechanisms are at work? To be sure, there are the routine disequilibrations that occur as a normal part of everyday experience—relaxations into reverie, fatigue-induced mental lapses, the dreaming occasioned by sleep. But if one wishes to find uninstigated forces that operate more continuously and dramatically upon mental organization, then surely the most prominent candidates for this role are those singled out by Freud—frustration, loss, trauma. In these situations, "reality," having inflicted an injury, loses for a time its emotional appeal, and the stage is set for the withdrawal of desire from the reality-constituting

[121]

operations of the ego—the accommodative operations. The subsequent predominance of free assimilatory activity is both the willy-nilly consequence of this lapse in accommodation and, simultaneously, a type of search for a more satisfying reality or for a compensatory illusion about the given reality that will render bearable an actual or impending privation. It is no coincidence that the cultural traditions in which are to be found the institutionalization and control of the process of renunciation are those traditions that have as a principal mandate the resolution of loss, frustration, and emotional shock.

Earlier the possibility was raised that the process of renunciation might be, in the long run, inherently self-correcting. It is necessary to look more closely at what this might mean. Can we speculate, for instance, that—apart perhaps from certain types of psychosis where stubborn biochemical imbalances may be involved—most people would recover their psychological equilibrium simply by waiting it out? One can certainly point to numberless cases where this seems to have happened. No priest, therapist, or magician was called upon to intervene; the person in question simply suffered through a regressive episode and eventually recovered. But the question is, was this recuperation effected simply by letting the time pass? Close scrutiny will generally reveal that it was not.

While it is true that in the face of suitable life vicissitudes, the process of renunciation seems to get the steam up on its own, even so, the spontaneity of its beginnings gives way in countless concrete instances to deliberate manipulation. Those trying to overcome a trauma or privation can often be detected speeding the process along, as it were. They interrupt their normal schedule to make way for periods of inner absorption; they drink, they try drugs, they render themselves sleepless, they undertake mental exercises aimed at driving the offending reality from their minds, which efforts, in effect, go contrary to normal thinking; and so on. In a word, they unwittingly innovate religious and therapeutic practices. It must be remembered that the psyche, in a renunciatory mode, is indisposed to "wait." Those in the grips of this process not only turn to instrumental aids of one sort and another, they also seek out and batten onto symbolic materials with a peculiarly obsessive force. We cannot say that they are bereft of cultural guidelines even when ostensibly left to their own devices, for, unlike people in ordinary states of mind, spontaneous renouncers have a talent for finding guidelines everywhere.

Some years ago, in a newspaper article the reference to which I have forgotten, a journalist described his descent into a profound personal depression. The episode began to occur, coincidentally, at the time of the second major gasoline shortage in the United States, and as the lines at the pumps grew longer and the orange "No Gas" signs proliferated along the highways, this man experienced himself as—like his country—rapidly running out of "energy." Having hitched his mental wagon to this publicly shared succession of events, he found himself emotionally lifted once again when the orange flags disappeared from the service stations and green ones emerged, signaling the return of an adequate fuel supply. By the time the energy crisis ended, so too had his depression. The mind was not at a loss.

More often than such quaintly secular props as the energy crisis, we find the distressed gravitating to ideas and images that do not merely resemble but are actually purloined from established traditions of renunciatory control. Even having eschewed official religious and psychotherapeutic intervention, they may nevertheless be found casting the *I Ching* and brooding over its messages, reinventing "automatic writing" so as to contact a deceased loved one, devising private rituals, and so on. By imperceptible degrees these maneuvers grade into an open acceptance of established religious and psychotherapeutic traditions. Finding a "pure" case of renunciation uninfluenced by the prevailing traditions of control is no easier than finding a genuine "idiolect" unrelated to the surrounding languages.

Switching from the viewpoint of the individual to that of established traditions, we see the affinity between the spontaneous and the ordained operating from this direction as well. As is well known, new religious traditions spring up from the acceptance of initially "wild" visions, and established traditions continuously reach out to enrich themselves with visionary insights erupting from situations they may not have authored. This reaching out and absorption of novel and idiosyncratic materials may take either a positive form—the legitimation of new ideas—or a negative one—the labeling of heresies; indeed, both aspects of encompassment are important if a doctrine is to be comprehensive without being utterly amorphous. (Some would argue that secular psychiatry has overspecialized in negative encompassment, leaving its positive vision relatively implicit and unformed.)

In overview, it can be posited that the same relationship that obtains between psyche and cultural form *within* the ritual or psychotherapeutic context obtains as well, but in a more haphazard and unpredictable fashion, between spontaneous renunciatory states and

[123]

the prevailing "cultures of renunciation" articulated in religion, or, in modern society, psychotherapy. In either situation, there is a constant movement toward the dialectical engagement of private meaning systems with shared ones, a groping for alignment between autistic construction and collectively authorized form. In even broader overview, this dialogue between private and public "symboling" is not different in its mechanism from that which takes place between mind and culture generally. What one sees in situations of renunciation, whether spontaneously erupting or artifically induced, is simply a more urgent, ambitious, and superheated version of it.

In the chapters to follow, I will illustrate the way the process of renunciation is put to work in Scientology, concentrating in turn on auditing, which is the system of techniques used to initiate the process; the Scientology world-view that furnishes the projective format and system of glosses to which participants' special perceptions are fitted; and the various ways in which this fitting together take place—how, in other words, participants come to experience directly the truths that Scientology asserts. Finally, I will turn to certain broader issues in the careers of religious and therapeutic renouncers, in particular the appearance of negative transformations of renunciation and the expanded practices and beliefs that typically rise up within a tradition to encompass these transformations. Throughout I will have recourse to the comparisons, already initiated here, between Scientology, mysticism, and psychoanalysis.

It is important to point out before beginning, that Scientologists do not see their practice as "renunciatory," for it is typically experienced as gratifying and relieving. Nor do they see the orientation of their religion as "world-rejecting," as I implicitly do. On the contrary, Scientology's promise is to enhance the individual's worldly success and enjoyment. Just so. The sign of a renunciation successfully conducted is precisely a sense of gratification and relief, and worldly success is often linked to the acquisition of a certain healthy disdain for the immediate and apparent world. This is the magic that a renunciatory discipline can work.

[5]

Scientology Auditing Techniques

For several reasons it is necessary to treat Scientology auditing and training methods at some length. The chief reason is the extent to which Scientology techniques are embedded in the Scientology belief system. In the preceding chapters, I distinguished religious and therapeutic practices from the symbolic systems to which these practices are adjunct, the better to bring out theoretically the ways in which each dimension operates upon the mind and interacts with the other; the distinction is one to which I will return. In ethnographic reality, of course, we do not find this sort of distinction being made. Rather, to proponents of a belief system, the practices of that system are seen—like everything else in the world—as manifestations of the principles set forth in the beliefs, and practice is justified in these terms. Mesoamerican mushroom-eating cults, for instance, consciously enjoin mushroom eating not in order to obtain an intoxicating effect that then can be put to use, but instead because mushrooms are thought to contain a divine principle—as witnessed by the intoxication they induce. Similarly, mystics withdraw from the concerns and pleasures of the world not in order to obliterate the regular feedback of reality upon mental structure, but because, in their belief, the world is a distraction and a barrier between soul and divinity.

This encompassment of technique by belief system is developed to a high degree in Scientology, paradoxically *because of* rather than despite Scientology's emphasis upon the virtues of a (supposedly) demystified technological approach. While Scientology does recognize that a great range of techniques, including drug ingestion and the practices of other religions and therapies, all produce states of mind similar to some of those encountered in Scientology practice, it argues that only the Scientology methods operate upon the mind in a precise and useful manner because only Scientology theory accurately understands the human spirit. Other practices are simply groping in the dark, hitting and missing unpredictably. By contrast, Scientology methods, guided as they are by correct theory, offer pinpoint control. Each auditing procedure is understood to be aimed at the uncovering and elimination of some specific type of mental content, preconception, or reflex, as set forth in Hubbard's theory of the mind, and the procedure is guided with this specific goal in view. The nuances of auditing style and the behavior of the skin-galvanometer, which is used as a sort of bio-feedback device in much of auditing, are similarly understood and monitored in terms of a detailed theory. Therefore, the description of Scientology practices is, in a sense, the first chapter in the description of the Scientology world-view, and much of the detail given here will help to situate items of belief that are discussed in subsequent chapters.

At the same time, I am trying to show that Scientology auditing and training are the means whereby the process of renunciation is triggered and its psychological effects controlled. To some extent, I am forced simply to assert this, since, for readers personally unfamiliar with religious or therapeutic practices, it may remain forever unclear how giving answers to the same two questions over and over again, or staring for hours into someone's face, or imagining one's mind attached to the four corners of the room—to mention only a few Scientology methods—could have any mental effect other than boredom. But this problem arises in the analysis of any religious or psychotherapeutic methodology. The details about auditing given here will be more useful to those who, having some acquaintance with other methodologies, wish to make comparisons between methods and thereby inform their judgment of my conclusions or arrive at conclusions of their own. In this respect I think it important to show that Scientology techniques are systematic and sensible in terms of the effects sought. Too often we think of the "conversion" methods of marginal sects as either sheer hocus-pocus, that is, having no real effect other than what the gullible wish to imagine, or conversely, as "brainwashing," that is, automatically effective even against the resistant. The techniques of mainstream religions and psychotherapies are not subjected to either of these distorting interpretations, and what I wish to make clear is that Scientology methods do not differ in

[126]

general character and effect from the practices of other systems, including the most respected. I must, therefore, establish that what goes on in the auditing session and in auditor-training is neither *ad hoc* propagandizing on the one hand, nor will-destroying coercion on the other; but rather a monitored induction into states of nonordinary experience and insight.

A final reason for lengthiness here is that there are numerous facts about auditing which I have simply not gone into up to this point but which must enter the picture if we are to avoid confusion later. The most important of these from the viewpoint of future clarity is that parts of auditor-*training*, and not simply auditing proper, must be classed as types of consciousness-altering techniques. I refer in particular to the "training routines," or "TRs" that a Scientologist must repeatedly practice if he or she is to become an effective auditor. In fact all Scientologists practice, and are urged to practice, the TRs, whether training to be auditors or not, and these are the first exercises taught to newcomers in order to give them some understanding of Scientology "reality." Thus the collection of consciousness-affecting practices I have hitherto loosely called "auditing" should be understood as including these key elements of training as well.

The reader must also be updated on the main developments that auditing and training underwent after the Dianetics days. I will begin the discussion with this updating and move from there to the salient components of early 1970s auditing and training. It should be noted that while the general principles of Scientology practice (and belief) have remained relatively stable over the past decade or so, minor changes in procedure go on continuously and undoubtedly many have occurred since I ended my research in 1971. The following account purports to be accurate in detail only to that year.

Scientology Auditing

Certain features of auditing remain unchanged from the Dianetics period. All auditing takes the form of command and response, or, more usually, question and answer. The role of the auditor is to issue a command or ask a question, and to attend to and acknowledge the response. The role of the pre-clear is to respond. Auditors do not interpret responses but rather use various indicators in the pre-clear's behavior and mode of responding and, in some cases, indicators with-

in the response itself, as signals determining which of various standardized steps is to be followed next. The session is brought to a close
upon the appearance of certain changes in the pre-clear's attitude and
answers, changes which are taken to indicate "release."

Within this general framework there has been a tremendous expansion over time of both the lines of questioning and the strategies used
for eliciting pre-clear cooperation and for guiding the session. The
search for locks, secondaries, and engrams of the Dianetics years is
now only a subfield of a much larger field of introspective searches,
and the techniques utilized in Dianetics are but a small sample of the
auditing procedures now available. Furthermore, auditor-training no
longer consists of merely reading a book or two and attempting to
follow their instructions, attending an occasional demonstration and
practice session for supplement. There are now a series of courses to
cover the history and practice of each major area of auditing inquiry,
and the training routines and other exercises have been developed in
which auditors must repeatedly drill in order to keep their skills in
session-control at an adequate level. The use of a small portable skin
galvanometer, called the "E-Meter," is now a routine part of most
auditing actions, and the auditor must master this instrument.

Another innovation is the introduction, at the more advanced levels
of auditing, of what is called "solo auditing," a solitary method in
which the practitioner assumes alternately the role of the auditor and
the role of the pre-clear. He or she must learn to compartmentalize
his or her behavior and mental operations so that the two roles do not
interfere with, or blur into, each other. It goes without saying that in
order to progress to these more advanced levels of auditing, which
include the milestone of going "Clear," a Scientologist must acquire
auditing skills—if only to be able to "solo" properly. Typically, those
wishing to progress to the solo-audited levels take one lower-level
training course that involves practicing auditing skills on others. After
this, they learn the theory and practice of solo auditing as part of the
program, or "course," that reveals to them the special processes (commands and questions) they will be using in their solo audit. The first
course of this sort is called, appropriately, the "Solo Course"; but
"Clear" and the levels of auditing beyond Clear are solo-audited (for
the most part) and thus also include a training component.

A last development to be mentioned is the tenfold burgeoning of
Scientology jargon. Though many of the concepts glossed by this
terminology are similar to those found in the mainstream culture or in

other therapeutic or religious disciplines, Hubbard took pains to ensure that Scientology not be confused with other practices and therefore, whenever possible, he devised unique terms. Many of these are acronyms of English phrases, some are neologisms, but the majority are common English words coopted to a specialized meaning. There are several Scientology glossaries available to the practitioner and careful attention is paid, in both auditing and training, to the correct understanding of the glossed concepts.[1]

In all these developments, there has been a marked trend toward what Hubbard aptly called "standardization." His goal was to make auditing a precise standardized technique, uniformly administered and producing uniform results which unfold in a predictable sequence.

In regard to the training of auditors, this movement toward standardization was implicit even in the early days. Special training in auditing technique began as soon as the first Dianetics foundation was established, and developed in complexity with the evolution of the belief system. In 1959, when Hubbard moved to England and set himself up in Saint Hill Manor, an estate in East Grinstead, Sussex, auditing and training were increasingly brought under bureaucratic control. Hubbard began to communicate the latest word via mimeo bulletins and to package Scientology materials into courses that could be taught at any authorized Scientology establishment; the network of authorized training establishments developed accordingly. It became possible for Scientologists to receive a good many stages of training and auditing without having to go to wherever Hubbard was located. The requirements for any particular course always involve reading one or more of Hubbard's books, although the books have come to take second place to bulletins and taped lectures, in which the bulk of the important information is conveyed. Many of the instruction bulletins and tapes are available only to students registered on a training course; only a select few can be purchased independently. The trend has long been to bring auditing and training more and more under the personal supervision of the duly qualified—and thus more and more under the control of Hubbard—and to make the Scientology world more private. Indeed, the advanced levels of Scientology auditing and training are secret, as we shall see.

1. Throughout the text I will have occasion to refer to official definitions of Scientology terms. These definitions, however, do not always correspond to actual usage among Scientologists and when there is a discrepancy, I have based my own analysis and interpretations upon actual usage.

As an important part of the expansion, routinization, and control of Scientology knowledge, auditing and training are now set out in a series of "levels" through which practitioners must graduate in sequence. These levels are outlined in the "Classification, Gradation and Awareness Chart" first put out in 1965. As regards auditing, each level encompasses a series of auditing actions that deal with a particular area of the pre-clear's life and awareness. Each level is aimed at bringing about, on the one hand a "release" from certain problems, and, on the other, a "recovery" of certain abilities. For instance on "Grade 0," one is released from any difficulties regarding communication and thus recovers the ability to "communicate freely with anyone on any subject." On "Clear," one is "released" from the Reactive Mind (the "Bank") altogether and recovers the ability to "be at cause over mental matter, energy, space and time on the first Dynamic," which means, in translation, that one is in control of one's own mind.

The stages of auditing fall into three rough groupings. At the bottom rungs of the hierarchy one finds an assortment of levels designed to acquaint the newcomer lightly with Scientology, patch up certain common problem areas such as poor recall, mental interferences stemming from prior drug use, and so on. Capping these levels is the "Dianetic Case Completion," which amounts to the new pre-clear's first experience recalling old locks, secondaries, and engrams, as described in Chapter 2. Upon finishing the Dianetic Case Completion level, the pre-clear typically purchases in one large package Grades 0–IV, called informally "the Grades" (more recently called "Expanded Grades" since Hubbard added new dimensions to all of them). "The Grades" are the principal exoteric levels of Scientology auditing. Like the levels below them, they are available at all Scientology establishments and they are administered to the pre-clear by a trained auditor. At the completion of Grade IV, the pre-clear undergoes another and deeper bout of Dianetic auditing.

After the Grades and the second round of Dianetics, matters become more complicated because the pre-clear then proceeds to the "Confidential Levels" of auditing and, eventually, to solo auditing. Around 1965, Hubbard decided to cordon off all processes and techniques beyond Grade IV, so that the uninitiated would have no prior knowledge (other than that gleaned from cryptic statements) of the sorts of questions and commands to be encountered on these levels, the special nuances of technique used to audit them, or the special theories explaining the significance of each level. Furthermore, the pre-clear must go to an Advanced Organization in order to receive these Confidential Levels for it is only at these highly regulated establishments that adequate control over secret materials can be maintained.[2] The effect of these arrangements obviously is to make the Confidential Levels tremendously tantalizing, a focus of any number of private hopes and fears.

The lowest two Confidential Levels, Grades V and Va, are the last levels to be administered entirely by another auditor. After Va, one must acquire auditing experience oneself and learn solo auditing. Training in the latter begins on the "Solo Course" and is repeated with additional refinements on the succeeding levels. In terms of its confidentiality, what is perhaps of greater significance than either the auditing processes or the solo technique is the mass of esoteric theoretical material to which pre-clears entering the solo-audited levels are exposed. Beginning with the Solo Course, the practitioner is taught the deepest and most fearful secrets of the Bank, its precise structure, its history, and the alarming pitfalls that must be avoided if one is properly to eradicate it. On later levels, further portentous secrets are revealed and new spiritual powers (and dangers) sketched in. On several of the Confidential Levels, then, but particularly on "Solo," a good deal of new knowledge must be mastered before the practitioner is allowed to begin auditing.

Having mastered the requisite materials and learned to solo audit, the practitioner proceeds in two stages—"Solo" and "Clear"—to audit away, that is eliminate, the Bank. He or she is then "clear" of any irrationality and in conscious control of his or her mental processes. This is a significant watershed in the career of a Scientologist, but in fact auditing does not cease with the disappearance of its principal target, the Bank. Confidential Levels beyond Clear, called the "OT Sections," consist of auditing exercises designed to teach Scientologists how to "operate as thetans" ("OT" means "operating the-

2. I was, of course, never made privy to the materials on the Confidential Levels. Some knowledge of them circulates in Scientology "scuttlebutt," and advanced Scientologists are not averse to giving loaded hints. The most revealing hint, which I heard repeatedly, was that many of the secrets actually appear in Hubbard's earlier, and still available books—the point is that the uninitiated don't know which ones, nor do they know what new significances have become attached to these old ideas. A more useful source on the Confidential Levels is the publications of defecting Scientologists, who have had no qualms in exposing some of the secrets. Taking all these sources into consideration, I feel I have a generic knowledge of the Confidential materials sufficient to support the generalizations that will appear here and in later chapters.

tan"), that is, to emancipate their consciousness from the laws of the material universe. According to informants' accounts and the many testimonials appearing in the periodical published by the Advanced Organization, an important aspect of learning how to operate as a thetan is the cultivation of special "OT" powers such as telepathy, telekinesis, out-of-body travel, and subtle influence over the minds of others (see *Advance* 1972–75). Most of the OT Sections are solo-audited, although there are components of some that must be other-audited. These sections are available only at Advanced Orgs.

Even with this rough breakdown of the Gradation and Awareness Chart, one has not encompassed all the auditing done in Scientology establishments. As it turns out, there are many things that can go wrong in a pre-clear's progress up the levels, and many of these require additional steps and remedies that also take the form of auditing actions. It used to be the case that the necessary repairs were determined and then administered by a "review" auditor, who took the problem pre-clear into a session and ran through with him or her a comprehensive list of things that might be wrong, patching up each problem as it was located. "Review" was sold by the hour and bought as needed. In the early 1970s, many of the old review procedures were consolidated into special "intensives," not unlike levels, which must be purchased as a complete package. An intensive differs from a level solely in that it is not routinely required but undertaken only if it is established that a pre-clear is having some special difficulty in proceeding through the normal stages. There is a tendency, however, for intensives to find their way onto the chart as routinely required levels. The Drug Rundown, for instance, originated as a special intensive (during the late 1960s a lot of drug-saturated members of the counter-culture found their way into Scientology and Hubbard discovered, or decided, that they presented special problems); it subsequently became a necessary level for everyone.

The movement of special remedies into a normative status is only one aspect of a larger tendency: the ongoing expansion of the Gradation and Awareness Chart through the insertion of new steps. When Scientology was in its youth, in the early to middle 1950s, Hubbard's continual invention of new "processes" was typically presented as the discovery of faster and more effective routes to "Clear." As new discoveries made their appearance older methods were often derogated, at least partially. While not declared wrong, they were considered slow or limited. As a result, some techniques fell into disuse, others were demoted to an introductory or beginner's level. The old form of Dianetic auditing, for example, the procedure of locating and abreacting engrams, was relegated to a minor introductory status until the late 1960s. The articulation of a hierarchy of "levels," however, provided a logical solution to the problem of what to do with the accumulation of old methods as new ones were developed. By various lines of reasoning, it was possible to argue that certain things must precede (or follow) certain others. For instance, the pre-clear must be able to recall things in general before he or she can be asked to recall engrams; therefore, the Recall Release process (which cultivates recall ability) was put before Dianetic auditing. Similarly, one cannot hope to attain rarefied levels of awareness if one's attention is distracted by physical suffering; therefore, Dianetic auditing, which deals with physical and psychosomatic ailments, must precede Scientology auditing, which deals primarily with rarefied awarenesses. Old Dianetic auditing thus has been refurbished and inserted at two levels of the auditing hierarchy. It could also be reasoned that some of the older methods had only apparently been inefficient because they were thrust upon pre-clears not yet ready for them. Inserted at a higher level of auditing experience, these older methods took on a new life. Some of the derogated older processes now appear, according to advanced Scientologists, on the OT Sections. And so on. This sort of logic governed the crystallization of the Gradation and Awareness Chart, and still operates, justifying both the insertion of new auditing actions into the sequence and the refurbishment of neglected procedures from past years. The clearer the significance of the different levels became (in Scientology theory), the easier it was for Hubbard to find a slot for data that previously didn't seem to fit anywhere, or posit gaps in the existing data which he could than proceed to fill with a new level or special intensive. The additions have always had the effect of appearing eminently sensible. Over the years, this mechanism has allowed for a continuous expansion of Scientology "reality," a continuous need for those already audited as far as they can go to come back and get some level "put in," and a continuous source of profit for the Church of Scientology.

Corresponding to the levels of auditing are levels of auditor-training, called "classes," which qualify Scientologists to audit others. To qualify to audit someone else on a particular level, one must have graduated from the class corresponding to that level and all classes preceding it on the training ladder. So too, one may not supervise someone else's auditing of another, or of self in solo auditing without the corresponding training and certification. It is also the case that one may not audit another on an area or level one has not oneself received auditing on. This last restriction is routinely overcome by the policy of having students on training courses audit each other and lower-level students as part of their training.

Since the training course requirements involve practicing one's skills on fellow students, one incentive for going "on course" is that one will receive auditing from student trainees at no additional expense. For Scientologists who are willing to have their "cases" handled by relatively inexperienced student auditors, it is a cheap way to attain desired levels. But auditor-training is popular with Scientologists for other reasons as well. The drilling, the study of tapes and bulletins, the long hours spent surrounded by fellow Scientologists, allow students to immerse themselves deeply in the subject that fascinates them; the situation provides opportunities to put the "technology" to work on a daily basis and is a constant source of new insights and personal "highs." If enthusiasm for Scientology and a desire to put it to work on a daily basis are sufficiently great, an individual will often consider "going the professional route"—that is, contracting as a staff auditor at a Scientology establishment, or setting up a Scientology Mission of his or her own. Launched along this path, the person has every incentive to advance up the training ladder. The higher the level of training, the greater the range and diversity of auditing situations one is qualified to deal with, both as auditor and as supervisor of lower-level auditors, and the more in demand one's services. A common Scientology dream is to make a living this way.

Just about every aspect of auditing and training is strictly controlled by the Church of Scientology. There are certain minor Scientology procedures, called "assists," that may be employed at one's own discretion to alleviate small ailments or tune up the senses. Scientologists may practice the training routines among themselves without formal supervision, and of course much of Scientology lore has its applications to the understanding and manipulation of ordinary life situations. But it is firm Church policy that one does not audit oneself or anyone else without supervision by a certified other and that one cannot acquire any officially recognized training outside of a supervised training course. Course supervisors, who run the training classes, and case supervisors, who oversee the work of auditors, themselves follow strict rules and policies laid down in their own training.

They are not licensed to innovate or in any way alter Hubbard's word. To do so is to be guilty of "squirreling," the distortion or alteration of Scientology data. Misuses of Scientology are grounds for disciplinary action within the group, or ultimately for the removal of certifications and disbarment from further participation.

Let us move now from this larger context to the specifics of contemporary auditing. In what follows I will always treat auditing as a two-person interaction, for even in solo auditing two roles are involved, that of auditor and that of pre-clear. (I will also use the term "pre-clear" in the generic sense it has acquired in Scientology: the person receiving auditing. Technically one should say "pre-OT" when referring to someone beyond Clear.) In broad terms, the Scientology auditor, closeted with the pre-clear in a private room or space, engages the pre-clear in the distinctive style of interaction fostered by the training routines, uses a skin galvanometer to help guide the session, and asks standardized sequences of questions (or issues standardized commands), acknowledging the pre-clear's response.

I will deal with each of these features in turn.

The Training Routines

The most essential feature of auditing resides in the auditor's ability to engage the pre-clear in a highly focused form of communication wherein, within the limits set by the auditor, maximum space is given to the display of the pre-clear's innermost thoughts and feelings. The auditor acquires the skill for doing this through repeated practice of what Scientologists call the "TRs."

The term TRs (usually said in the plural since there are several training routines) has a double use. Technically, it means "training routines"—drills one goes through to develop one's auditing skills. But this meaning is overshadowed by its use in signifying the skills themselves, or more subtly, the subjective state that these skills bespeak. A Scientologist will say, "Her TRs are magnificent," or "Your TR-1 [to cite a specific one] is feeble," much as one says, "Your timing is excellent," or "His driving is appalling." It is perfectly correct, then, to say that the drill TR-1, for instance, is the exercise done to develop one's "TR-1."

The TRs are distillations of Hubbard's own auditing style. They are principles designed to generate a certain mode of interaction and they can be used—and are used—not only in the auditing session but also, as Scientologists put it, in one's "life and livingness." In fact, the introductory course in Scientology, the Communications Course, teaches the first five TRs, which are the most important ones, purely as self-improvement/life-improvement techniques, with little stress on their use in auditing. These same five TRs are repeated again on every subsequent training course and to the highly trained Scientologist the skills become almost as natural as breathing.

In the first and most fundamental training routine, TR-0 (said "TR-Zero"), the student sits facing another person (usually another student) just as the auditor will sit facing the pre-clear, and devotes all attention simply to "being there" (Hubbard 1975b:151–53). He or she must hold this position and this attention for two hours, no easy feat. Another word for TR-0 is "confronting," and the two-hour confront is another name for this sitting exercise. The emphasis is upon a totally calm but unswerving attention, a simple manifestation of presence devoid of motivated interest. Any flinching or evasion of the other person's face, doping off, yawning, or fidgeting is grounds for a "flunk" on the drill, as is "breaking the confront" by responding—even by a flickering side glance—to some stimulus outside the dyadic setting. In theory, one must not retreat into a fantasy or other inner self-amusements, although a certain amount of this may, in practice, pass undetected. Usually two students will practice their TR-0 simultaneously, being checked at regular intervals by a supervisor. If either is flunked, the clock is reset and the two hours start over again.

Once the simultaneous "confront" is ended, the drill called "bull-baiting" begins. In this drill one student assumes the role of attentive auditor, while the other begins to act like an imaginary pre-clear, spouting unsettling remarks and stories. The imaginary pre-clear also serves as the coach, and supervises the other's handling of the drill. In order to test the student's TR-0, the coach "bull-baits" him or her with words or behavior designed to provoke laughter, anger, or other sorts of "nonconfront." Bull-bait gambits are entirely up to the coach, and everything that human wit can devise has by now undoubtedly appeared in Scientology bull-baits. Scientologists revel in repeating those that really cracked them up or that they used to demolish another's "confront." If a student's TR-0 appears especially uncrackable, another student or the course supervisor may join the bull-baiter in the effort, setting up a riff between them about all the amusing, remarkable, and scandalous things they can think to attribute to the student; and the joint effort of two against one will usually weaken the sturdiest sangfroid. An auditor, Scientologists explain, must be ready for anything that a pre-clear might hurl out in a session: "he may tell you he fucks chickens or murdered his grandmother, you never know." Hence the provocative tenor of the "bull-bait."

Breaking the student's "confront" is spoken of as "finding a button"—a thing that one can press to provoke a reaction. Having found a button, the coach says "Flunk," followed by "Start"—meaning resume your confront; he/she then proceeds to press the same button, by repeating the gambit, over and over until it is "flat," that is, until there is no more reaction. The coach then looks for another button and so on, the exercise continuing until the student can, to the coach's satisfaction, maintain a long period of imperviousness. Icy rigidity or a distracted look of having mentally left the scene is not acceptable. The student must "be there" with all faculties engaged and put out a feeling of generally positive regard for the bull-baiter.

The key to good bull-baiting is to make it personal. Among the most effective gambits are those that draw the student into imaginary scenes and stories that expose his or her latent interests and identities as vain, silly, or craven. In many ways bull-baiting is a test of the coach as well, for it demands a considerable presence and sensitivity as well as a willingness to be, in Scientology terms, "causative"—or in common parlance, dominant. Not surprisingly, the key to a good "confront" is much the same thing. In either case, a detachment from one's own egoistic subjectivity is crucial.

The remaining training routines require the same seating arrangement and the same student-coach relation as that of bull-baiting. Also, each succeeding TR presumes a mastery of the previous one, so that if one's TR-1 is poor, one's TRs 2, 3, and 4 will suffer, and so on, TR-0 being the foundation of them all.

TR-1 rehearses the student in communicating intention (Hubbard 1975b:153–58). He or she must, as a good auditor, be able to ask questions or deliver commands in a way that completely captures the other's attention but is at the same time motivationally neutral, benignly impersonal. Students practice "intention" by reading aloud phrases taken from *Alice in Wonderland*—phrases chosen, in other words, for contextual meaninglessness. If real auditing phrases were used, it is thought, students might become jaded through constant exposure to them, or worse, provoked into thinking about their own inner lives when they should be merely practicing the drill. In uttering each phrase, the student is instructed to find where the coach "is" and send the utterance direct to that spot. He or she must neither overdo it ("take the coach's head off") nor let the phrase fall lamely short of its target. It is important too that the student speak the phrase each time with absolute freshness, or, as the instructions say, "newly and in a new unit of time." Through a series of trials, the student gradually learns to adjust voice projection and expressiveness in perfect concordance with the partner's level of attentiveness and receptivity.

TR-2 is a practice in "acknowledgment." The acknowledgment of another's communication is very important in auditing. It completes the "communication cycle," lets the other person know that his or her communication ("comm") was received with full attention and understanding (Hubbard 1975b:158–163). Standard acknowledgments are preferred: "Good," "Fine," "All right," "OK," "Thank you," sometimes for emphasis, "Thank you, I got that," and, in Los Angeles at least, an occasional "Cool." Acknowledgments must be delivered not only with due regard to TR-0 and TR-1, but with accurate timing. Coaches may test for timing by lagging their utterances, putting "uh" at the end of the sentence as if not quite through, staring off into space as though racking their brains for a further word, and so on. Acknowledgment should come only when an expectant look or a subtle relinquishment of effort indicates that the speaker is ready for it. Late acknowledgments mean that the student is not really listening; premature ones that he or she is not really interested. The coach is instructed to ask the student from time to time what really *was* said.

In TR-3, the student must ask a question, get an answer, and acknowledge the answer, keeping the preceding TRs intact (Hubbard 1975b:163–69). The question is a mock auditing question, not a real one, and the standard ones used in practice are "Do birds fly?" and "Do fish swim?" The coach watches for and flunks "automaticity," that is, becoming mechanical in the routine or blurring questions together, and tries at the same time to throw the student off by saying something that is not an answer to the question ("Do birds fly?" "Cottage cheese."), by prefacing the answer with long monologues ("Cottage cheese, apple pie, eggplants, yes.") or by engaging the student in a stalling line of counterquestions ("Do birds fly?" "Aren't you hungry?" "Yes." "Flunk."). When the coach does not answer the question, the student must say "I'll repeat the auditing question," then repeat it. This is called "returning the pre-clear to session."

TR-4 teaches the student to distinguish between pre-clear "originations" and mere stalls and distractions (Hubbard 1975b:169–176). An "origination" is not an answer to the question but it is a statement that genuinely refers to the pre-clear's own condition or state of mind, such as "I'm beginning to feel dizzy," or "I just thought of something." It is self-referential. Thus, even though it may not be an answer to the question asked, it must be acknowledged: it must be given its moment of understanding, however brief. The point is that in a real auditing session, the pre-clear is there to deliver up his subjective self, and the squashing of some small spontaneous interjection may destroy rapport. So the student auditor acknowledges originations before announcing, "I'll repeat the auditing question." Anything that is not an origination is classified as a "comment." The indicator here is that it is not self-referential: "You look funny," "It's time for lunch." Comments are not to be acknowledged; instead, the student persists with "I'll repeat the auditing question." As far as the drill goes, ambiguous utterances—"You're beginning to look funny to me"—are not dwelt upon, nor is the coach encouraged to make remarks that are syntactically "comments" but voice-cued to sound like "originations," or vice-versa. For simplicity's sake, the coach reads from a list of preselected "comments" and "originations." The coach furthermore continues to bull-bait and attempts to throw the student off, as in the previous drills.

To an outsider, an evening spent practicing the training routines may sound like a prescription for boredom. But students find that they must be alert as Zen swordsmen to get through the exercises without repeated "flunks." Experienced Scientologists will often go through the drills on their own initiative, to pep themselves up and tune their faculties.

In the course of any extensive involvement with Scientology, the individual will have occasion to practice the TRs repeatedly. In addition, one is encouraged to use the skills so acquired in one's daily interactions both inside and outside Scientology circles. Obviously, phrases such as "I'll repeat the auditing command" are dropped from ordinary interactions, but the principles of "being there," communicating with intention, acknowledging, and, when the occasion demands it, getting one's question answered, are retained.

Beginning Scientologists are prone to apply the TRs mechanistically and self-consciously—engaging their fellows in uncompromising eye-locks, compulsively interjecting "OK" and "Fine" at every available

[139]

opportunity. But these manifestations, the more sophisticated will point out, are not really the TRs. "Being there" (TR-0), for instance, does not involve doing any one concrete thing such as staring into a person's eyes; it simply involves "being there." If one's TR-0 is "in," one's entire demeanor indicates this; if not, there is no way to fake it. Similarly, an acknowledgment can be given without saying a word. Any indication of recognition and understanding that is genuine constitutes an acknowledgment. Essentially, what is meant by "good TRs" is a sensitivity to interpersonal situations so developed that one can know or feel exactly what is happening with the other person and respond to it in a manner that calls no particular attention to oneself. This is a *real* TR-0. The remarks of one Scientologist expand upon these points:

> A very interesting thing about when you're auditing and when you're not. Uh, does one apply [auditing principles] in life and all that? And, uh, I tend to say sometimes yes sometimes no, and I like it and I don't like it, and it comes and goes. And no matter how strange you think [a person's] ideas are they're probably the best they've got, and so you just kind of listen . . . and you don't go in for heavy "Good!"'s and things like that. That's quite brutal and I do not do that. You know the volume you need . . . the sound volume that you need in your TR-1 is inversely related to how good your TR-0 is. And if you have a good TR-0 and you go around saying "Good!" (slightly forced) to people, you unmock [negate] your own TR-0. And it makes it unreal for them because they know that they're being understood if you're understanding them! Y'know, they can see it in your eyes. And if you say, "Ooh, I *got* that!" they think you're crazy. And you are! [Taped interview]

In their ultimate extension into the abstract, good TRs may very well be manifested by refraining from the more concrete auditor-like applications of the training routines. The more concrete applications inevitably carry with them the connotations of that situation out of which the TRs were developed in the first place: the control or "handling" of an immanently irrational other, a pre-clear, a person who is—as they say—"being a case." In some situations, then, an obvious "TR" can be an insult, and advanced Scientologists will react to it as such:

> When I told her about the mistake she didn't believe me. Then I started to [get upset]. Then she began to "act like the auditor"—y'know, "OK. . . . Fine . . ."—that made me even madder.

[140]

This does not mean, however, that auditors actually engaged in auditing can simply skip all the formalities in the pursuit of interactional purity. To be sure, a purity of understanding that transcends mere form is the mark of a good auditor. At the same time, the concrete actions rehearsed in the drills—verbal acknowledgments, eye contact, and the rest—serve in a real auditing session as reassurances to the pre-clear who has come to expect them that the auditor is properly assuming the auditor's role.

The effect of good TRs in auditing is both to give the auditor unflappable control of the session and also to make him or her a safe person to whom the pre-clear can relinquish control. Nothing that a pre-clear can do should throw the auditor off course. Meanwhile, the auditor should be "doing nothing" to the pre-clear except benevolently auditing. The stated purpose of TR-0 is to train the student "to confront the pre-clear with auditing or with nothing" (Hubbard 1975b:152).

Scientologists speak of good auditing—thus good TRs—as engendering a distinctive atmosphere. Its general push is for both auditor and pre-clear in the direction of the sort of "deautomatized awareness" that Deikman (1969) speaks of in regard to meditative states. The clatter and frenzy of outside stimuli are hushed, interpersonal maneuvering is rendered pointless, attention is focused, and the thought process subsides to a quiet guided flow. If done right, each auditing move—the question, the expectant wait, the answer, the look of understanding, the acknowledgment—is, as one put it, "clearly etched and separated from everything around it" (Kaufman 1972:125). Another Scientologist wrote of the auditing encounter: "The space was so clean, it was as if time didn't exist" [Flyer of testimonials from AOLA]. From the perspective of a pre-clear, with the major noises of living stilled and the subjectivity of one's interlocutor no longer a matter requiring attention (or counteraction), little thoughts previously crowded out of awareness, or seemingly so trivial that one never saw fit to give them much consideration, suddenly make their tiny voices heard and begin to take their place in an unsuspected pattern of meaning. In due course it will seem that some of these thoughts have been niggling for eons, festering thorns in what one thought was a reasonably sound and impervious self-concept. The inner self revealed in auditing, when all the little whispers are heard, turns out to be a creature of great fragility and surprising cunning. The pre-clear may have never acknowledged this delicate inner self before; the auditor does.

During the sessions, the auditor too experiences a slowing of time and a heightened distinctiveness of every detail; however, it is the other's condition that is the object of attention. Every change in the pre-clear's face, eyes, voice, body, telegraph their meanings to the auditor undistorted by the static of the auditor's own impulses and calculations. With mastery of the TRs, the auditor gains an assurance that what he or she sees going on in the pre-clear (or the other person) really is going on. It is not something stirred up by the auditor's own self-serving ploys or personal projections. A high-level Scientologist whose job in the outside world involved conducting interviews and administering tests explained:

> I found more and more, as my TRs got good, I can depend on these. . . .
> Now in psychological jargon, in psychological mystique, you have your "instruments," y'know. They're always talking about instruments and calibrating your instruments. . . . well, I can depend on my TRs, I can depend on my confront. It's standardized. Now—any feedback I get I know is not caused by me directly; it's a resultant, in me, of the person interacting with me. And it's pretty pure. I sit down with [someone] and give him the test, and after I'm through I notice how he made me feel. If he made *me* feel that way, I'm not the only one. It's a standard bit he's doing. So . . . that's the internal view. I'm using myself as the "instrument." [Taped interview]

The E-Meter

Advanced Scientologists sometimes will assert that the TRs are really the only "instruments" necessary to auditing; but there is another, quite material instrument involved: the E-Meter, a skin galvanometer the electrodes of which the pre-clear clutches during the auditing session. Auditors must learn to read the needle and dials of this mechanism with the same lightning comprehension they apply to the pre-clear's behavior.

Before launching into meter use in auditing, I had best acquaint the reader briefly with what a skin galvanometer is and what sort of galvanometer the E-Meter is. Skin galvanometers, such as may be found in many psychology labs, measure the electrical resistance (or conductivity) of the skin by passing a current along it between two sites where electrodes have been attached. Technically, there are two ways to measure: by keeping current constant and letting voltage vary, one gets a measure of resistance. By keeping voltage constant and letting current vary, one gets a measure of conductance—the reciprocal of resistance. The E-Meter in use at the time of my research was a conductance meter. In this discussion, I will continue to speak in "resistance" terms, however, since Scientology meter terminology uses "rise," as indicated on the meter dials, to mean what is in fact a rise in resistance, and "fall" to mean a fall in resistance.

Skin galvanometer experiments have shown that resistance fluctuates in certain ways, depending upon where the electrodes are placed. In particular, on the so-called active sites, chiefly the palms of the hands or the soles of the feet, the rise and fall of skin resistance seems to follow—instantaneously—changes in alertness, or, more generally, changes in central nervous system arousal (Burch and Griener 1960; Hebb 1955). Measured from an active site, this "galvanic skin response" (GSR) will have a discernible but nonspecific correlation with one's subjective state. That is, stimuli or thoughts that excite, startle, or arouse tension—even minutely—will cause a drop in resistance. Conversely, boredom or drowsiness is accompanied by rising skin resistance. The proximate cause is said to be ion shifts in the cutaneous chemistry (Forbes 1964:27). The GSR appears even when there is no measurable change in skin moisture, although an increase in skin moisture (sweating) which often accompanies increased tension or arousal will contribute to the drop in resistance (Darrow 1964: 24).

Because of the correlation with subjective excitement, galvanometer readings have been incorporated as one of the graphs in the contemporary lie-detector, or polygraph. Alone, however, the galvanic skin response is not a reliable indicator of lies since, on the one hand, any matter exciting to the subject will provoke drops in resistance and, on the other, some liars, it is said, are blithe. In Scientology, the meter is used to find "charged" areas—subjects that produce excitement or tension in the pre-clear—and to keep track of how much "action," in terms of rises and falls, is being produced by an auditing procedure.

A skin galvanometer first appeared in auditing use in 1951, when Hubbard experimented with a primitive version designed by an inventor acquaintance. (He also tried out oscilloscopes and and other equipment that might be employed to register inner states.) Several models of the E-Meter were put out during the 1950s, but Hubbard's enthusiasm for it seems to have waxed and waned until 1957, when a transistorized model became available for general use. Around 1961

[143]

he formalized instructions for use of the meter; the basic principles articulated then were still in effect in 1971.

The E-Meter with which I am acquainted, like earlier ones, was designed especially for Hubbard and according to his requirements. It is not, as often reported, a "crude" device; nor was the 1971 price (135 dollars) unreasonable given that it was being manufactured for a small market. The meter's inner workings include a rather expensive needle-action, and two amplifiers that increase needle deflection and make it possible to pick up very minute resistance changes. Because the amount of current required for getting "reads" does not exceed 100 microamps and may be as little as a fraction of a microamp, and because the electrode surface is unusually large, the chances of electrode polarization are virtually eliminated.

The electrodes are, in fact, two tin cans. Ordinary soup cans or juice cans are preferred. The pre-clear clasps one in each hand if he is being audited by another (see Figure 1). In solo auditing, the cans are pushed over the ends of a plastic or wooden post that keeps them separated from each other yet close enough together that they can be

Figure 1

Figure 2

grasped in one hand, leaving the other hand free to write and to regulate the dials (Figure 2).

Unlike many laboratory galvanometers that involve a stylus flickering against a moving band of graph paper, the E-Meter produces no printout. Instead, the auditor watches the movements of a needle set on a dial face (Figure 3). Movement to the right indicates falling resistance; movement to the left rising resistance. In effect, watching the needle is like watching the stylus instead of the printout, but with the significant difference that the interpretation of certain types of "reads" depends less upon the actual distance the needle moves than on the quality of the movement. Does it dart, jerk, drift, or loll? Various needle-movement "gestalts" are more salient to someone watching the needle than they would be to someone watching a printout.

The other meter indicator that the auditor watches, and also adjusts, is the tone arm, usually called the "TA." The TA is a potentiometer that is used to recenter the needle as resistance rises and falls. The TA dial is marked off into six divisions, with the number 0

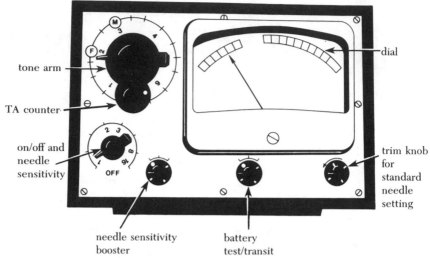

tone arm

TA counter

on/off and
needle
sensitivity

OFF

dial

trim knob
for
standard
needle
setting

needle sensitivity
booster

battery
test/transit

Figure 3

representing the bottom of the meter's measuring range (zero ohms), and 6 the top (about 1,500,000 ohms). Any full sweep of the needle, at its lowest deflection level, across the dial in either direction necessitates resetting the TA up or down one full division.[3] The tone arm gives the auditor a sense of the relative level of resistance of the preclear at any given point during the session, and this figures into interpretation of what is happening in the session. Another function of the TA is to give the auditor an idea of whether the session actions are tending to increase resistance ("drive the TA up") or decrease it. The auditor makes jottings of the different TA settings as the session proceeds, and may check back to see what the drift has been. Useful in this regard is the TA "counter," a device usually affixed to the tone arm knob when any lengthy period of auditing is contemplated. Since downward movement (indicating falling skin resistance) is the salient movement in auditing theory, the counter is constructed to register a number for every division of downward movement and to ratchet on the upward movement, thus leaving a record of downward movement only. At points during the session, or at the end of it, the auditor is able to note at a glance how many divisions of TA have been pro-

3. While the numbers of the TA dial go up arithmetically, the number of ohms resistance registered increases geometrically; thus 1 to 2 on the TA dial covers a 4700-ohm range; 2 to 3, a 7500-ohm range; 3 to 4, a 16,500-ohm range, and so on.

duced, and thus to judge how much "action," psychologically speaking, has occurred.

Because of the function of the tone arm, the term "TA" has acquired several senses in Scientology. Sometimes it denotes the tone arm knob itself. It is also used as the equivalent of "resistance"; one will say, "My TA was high," for instance. In certain contexts, it means, more specifically, gross amount of fluctuation over a period of time, as in the statement, "This auditing produced tons of TA."

In auditing, the meter is propped on its lid, facing the auditor, the face of it shielded from the pre-clear's view. Before the session begins, the auditor must briefly check the potency of the meter's battery and set the instrument to a standard starting point; he or she then connects the electrodes and asks the pre-clear to squeeze them lightly in order to determine an adequate sensitivity (needle-deflection) setting for that pre-clear. At the start of any auditing session, the auditor makes a note of the beginning TA and sensitivity levels. Then auditing may begin.

Ordinarily, if a person is told to pick up the cans and then just left alone, the meter behavior will be quite uninteresting. Resistance falls for a while, the needle moving sometimes in a sharp driven fashion, sometimes in a monotonous drift with little halts and rises. Eventually it reverses itself, begins to rise again, and usually will continue to rise, haltingly, until—if nothing is done to distract the subject—resistance may wind up even higher than at the start. Heavy breathing, talking, coughing, laughing, or sneezing will bring the TA down sharply and cause it to stay down for a while. Little hand and body movements—from which the pre-clear is begged to abstain as far as possible during session—will cause needle fluctuations but usually not enduring "drops." (Body-movement reads come to be easily recognizable and can be read out of the record as far as auditing goes.)

Once the person holding the cans is engaged in an interaction with someone else, as opposed to being left unattended, the skin response begins to "follow" the interaction to a certain extent; and the more focused the interaction, the more regularly does the "following" occur.[4] It is out of this relationship that the auditing use of the meter arises. It is also in this regard that the auditor's TRs become extremely important. Given that the pre-clear is interested in being audited in

4. The concept of a "focused" interaction or encounter is borrowed from Goffman (1961).

the first place, good TRs serve to focus the encounter so that the pre-clear becomes increasingly responsive to the auditor and decreasingly responsive to outside distractions or to private musings unrelated to the auditor's questions. This responsiveness is spoken of as being "in session," and it is accompanied by a pattern of galvanic skin responses that can be meaningfully connected to the things going on in session. If the meter reads begin to lose their nonrandom attachment to the events of the session, or, as not infrequently happens, the needle becomes tight and sticky and the TA begins to rise into the upper ranges, the auditor is alerted that the pre-clear's attention is no longer on the session.

During a session, the auditor will wrap a hand lightly around the left side of the meter, so as to be able to adjust the TA with the left thumb. (There are reversed meters for left-handed people.) The pre-clear should not be allowed to see and thus be distracted by the meter dials, and most auditors prop a book or folder behind the meter to screen from sight their own minor hand movements. With his or her free hand, the auditor makes notes on the progress of the session, jotting in abbreviated form the questions asked, the answers given, and, as specified for the particular auditing procedure being used, the accompanying meter changes. All auditing procedures are, in essence, flow-charted to cover any eventuality that may arise in the course of the session, including its running aground entirely. Besides the verbal and gestural responses of the pre-clear, the behavior of the meter guides the auditor in determining which of several possible steps to take next. Since each step places a particular demand upon the pre-clear, the meter comes to serve as a "bio-feedback" device that can route the pre-clear's responses and thus his or her subjective state in definite directions. If this turns out to have been the wrong direction (in Scientology theory), the auditor and the case supervisor should be able to spot from the record of the session where things went astray.

There are some twenty-seven E-Meter drills of varying complexity which students master as they advance through the training hierarchy. Some auditing actions do not require extensive use of the meter; others depend upon it heavily and require lightning interpretive reactions on the part of the auditor. The interpretive system used to distinguish and explain different meter reads cannot be described in depth without getting into the heart of the belief system itself, but I will try to outline some of the basic principles and deal with those meter phenomena that are of the most general relevance.[5]

Scientologists recognize the concept of electrical resistance; in fact, it is cleverly woven into their otherwise quite nonmaterial view of human behavior. They attribute this resistance to the mind, or, more specifically, the Bank, as explained in the description of Dianetics. The Bank contains "mental image pictures" and sensory impressions which are "charged" because of their painful content, and which in their passive repressed state constitute mental "mass." This mass, though mental, is held to be materially real. However infinitesimal its weight and volume, it is essentially a form of matter. Mental mass registers on the E-Meter in the form of an electrical resistance *higher* than that which the body alone presents. The normal level of body-resistance, according to Hubbard, falls between 2 and 3 on the tone arm dial. Anything more is coming from the mind. According to one account:

Phil was explaining mental mass to Harvey after the second Comm Course class. He said that it is an actual solidity in the mind. It consists of mental images that are not confronted. They are stored but never inspected, or never inspected closely. The more closely one inspects them and confronts them, the more they lose their mass. The existence of mass registers on the E-Meter as a "rising needle." This is because the body forms a circuit with the meter and the more resistance there is in

5. I have not been able to find anything in the existing literature on skin galvanometry that would enable me to give an explanation in orthodox scientific terms of some of the reads Scientologists see and interpret during an auditing session. Obviously, no conventional research situations using the skin galvanometer were ever designed to duplicate the conditions found in auditing, so comparison is restricted. The nearest approximation to auditing is the situation of an interrogator using a polygraph on a subject. The findings from these situations concerning the GSR are in line with the findings of Scientology: some topics and questions trigger greater alertness in the subject than others, depending upon context and subjective factors. The standardization of polygraph interrogators' behavior, however, is less refined than is the standardization of auditing skills, polygraph readings are usually not used to guide the interrogation, and the states of mind sought in Scientology and thought to be correlated with certain sorts of meter reads are not only probably entirely unheard of by the average polygraph expert but also unlikely to occur in the implicitly antagonistic exchange between polygraph examiner and subject. I can only testify that all of the reads to be discussed here (with the exception of "Stage Four," see footnote, p. 153), are ones that I have myself observed in practice auditing. The reads named by Scientologists do occur, in other words; the question is what do they mean?

[149]

the body the less free flow in the circuit. "Think of two electrical terminals with a wire connecting them. The material of the wire causes some
resistance to the free flow of electricity. But think if you went and
chopped the wire at intervals between the two terminals, so that instead
of passing straight through the wire, the charge has to arc to bridge the
gaps; well, that's the effect that stored images have on the passage of
charge through your body. They are blanks that have to be bypassed."
Harvey still wasn't sure how to view it, so Phil told him to mock-up
[imagine] an image of an elephant. Harvey said, "All right." Phil said,
"Now you've just brought a mass into your mind. It may weigh as little
as .000000001 of an ounce, but it does have solidity." Later Harvey said
that he'd heard that well-trained mystics can stand on a scale and make
themselves as much as 35 pounds heavier, by thinking. Phil agreed
instantly. "Or," he added, "35 pounds lighter."

Subjectively, "mass" is associated with dullness, woolly-headedness,
a clogged, dense, unresponsive feeling (or manner, if referring to
another). I have heard Scientologists say: "I know when it's there, I
can feel it. It comes and settles around the back of my head like a
weight." (Headaches are attributed to excessive mass.) Or: "The people around here are higher-toned than in the east: their faces are
lighter, not as massy." One way of viewing auditing is that it "blows off
the mass"—makes it vanish. This is demonstrated by a drop in resistance on the meter.

The other image used—"charge"—is experienced differently but
treated similarly in regard to meter interpretation. The Scientology
Dictionary defines "charge" as "harmful energy or force accumulated
and stored within the Reactive Mind, resulting from the conflicts and
unpleasant experiences that a person has had. (Auditing discharges
this charge so that it is no longer there to affect the individual.)"
(Hubbard 1964). In this sense, a drop of the meter needle or a
lowering of the TA indicates that a charged area has been hit and the
charge is discharging.

"Charge" is subjectively experienced, at its simplest level, as a
reaction, an impulse, an urge or tension pushing one into action or
making one cast about for a resolution. In its more extreme forms it is
felt as irritability, anxiety, or a flood of uncontrollable emotion. Impulses that are stirred but not successfully resolved become, in Scientology terms, "bypassed charge." Scientologists point out a number of
behavioral manifestations of "charge" and "bypassed charge." When
someone has "charge" on a subject, he or she may frigidly avoid

[150]

discussing it or else talk about it rather too obsessively. Heightened tension, jumpiness, and pupil dilation are indicative of "charge." "Bypassed charge" is sometimes more obvious because it can usually be seen connected to some blockage of impulse: the antagonistic remark that follows having one's conversation interrupted by another, for instance. One Scientologist found an apt illustration. He had just issued a sharp "No!" to his cat who was poised to jump onto the kitchen table. She paused but her tail began lashing violently. "Bypassed charge," he commented. The expression "bypassed charge" derives from auditing where it applies to situations in which the auditor misses a meter read and thus does not probe for the thought behind it, or cuts the pre-clear off before the pre-clear is quite through expressing something. Bypassed charge registers on the meter as a "dirty needle"—a needle that, rather like the cat's tail, "ticks" or gets tight and jerky, then begins to rise. If not caught in time, bypassed charge will send the TA up and lead to a failed session.

There is an implicit conversion theory behind the use of the two images, "mass" and "charge," although I cannot find where, if anywhere, Hubbard fully articulated it. One Scientology student worked it out very simply:

John pointed out the interconvertibility of Mass and Energy in Einstein's law, and suggested that mental mass be considered Mass in the form of matter, while charge is the same thing in the form of Energy. "In other words, mass can be converted into something that can move and flow, and flow away—charge. And that's what happens. If all mental image pictures are mass, then what you're doing when you look at them is you're starting to convert them into charge which you can discharge and it will go away and the picture "erases"; there's no more mass there. And vice-versa, energy or charge can turn into mass.

In many contexts the terms "mass" and "charge" are used interchangeably. Some Scientologists also speak of "mass" as "encysted charge."

The overall purpose of auditing is to "take charge off the case," and "erase masses." The meter acts as a means of locating charge and of guiding the pre-clear in the direction of discharge. This does not mean that resistance is relentlessly driven downward. On the contrary, it is recognized that that which comes down must first have gone up, and there are some intervals in the auditing session when the meter is

temporarily ignored and nothing is done to intervene in a rising TA—
if it happens to be rising. But the pre-clear is allowed to drift off into
his or her "mental masses" only in a limited way. Auditing is conceived of as "selective restimulation." A little bit of the Bank is contacted and "blown," then another little bit, and so forth. Nor should
the auditor allow the TA to drop way down. The bottom-most limit
acceptable in auditing is 2. If the TA goes below 2, the pre-clear is
considered to be "overwhelmed" (indeed, panic states will register as
very low TA), and if the TA does not rise again, the session must be
ended.

Besides the general theory of mass and charge, there are more
specific interpretations of a number of needle movements. We will
not concern ourselves with all of them—several are quite arcane—but
only with those that are pertinent to most metered auditing actions.

In a great many auditing actions, the auditor is called upon to search
out charged areas in the pre-clear, using meter reads as a guide. The
more charge on a subject, generally speaking, the greater its current
significance to the pre-clear's "case." The student auditor is taught to
classify and recognize needle reads as "nul" (no reaction), "change of
characteristic" (the needle does not fall, but it stops what it is doing
and starts doing something else), "tick," "short fall," "fall," "long fall,"
and "long fall/blowdown" (a fall that necessitates resetting the tone
arm downward). These are listed in order of increasing amount of
charge indicated.

In doing what is called an "assessment" in auditing, the auditor will
call items from a prepared list, noting after each call how much charge
(if any) was indicated by the needle. These readings then determine
further auditing action. It may be that all "reading" items must be
followed up with further questions, or, in some plans, only the most
charged item is singled out for further auditing, after which the list is
reassessed. In any of these assessment procedures, the auditor-trainee
must learn to distinguish between a read that comes in response to a
question or the calling of an item, and one that comes from elsewhere,
for instance, an outside stimulus or an unrelated private rumination
going on in the pre-clear. In general, he or she looks for the read that
occurs right as the question or the called item "hits home," which,
given a good TR-1 on the part of the auditor and an interested pre-
clear, is right at the end of the last uttered word. (In practice, the pre-
clear may have to be coached not to try and anticipate the auditor's
meaning.) A read that begins before the last word is called a "prior
read"; it is discarded, and the auditor repeats the item or question.

Reads that occur a split second or two after the item are called "latent reads." These may or may not be relevant to the question asked; in some sorts of assessment they are taken into account, in others, ignored. Making the distinctions between real, prior, and latent reads is not in fact possible in the absence of adequate TRs, and many a trainee is sent back to the TRs when his or her meter drills collapse into random guessing.

The student must also learn to recognize and ignore body-movement reads, and to repeat an item or question if body movement interferes with the assessment. In addition, he or she must be able to recognize the signs of a failing session mentioned above: "dirty needle," relentlessly rising TA, too low TA, and "out of session" randomness.[6]

A last needle phenomenon that is of crucial importance in auditing is the "floating needle," also called "free needle" or "F/N." A floating needle is one of the indicators that alerts the auditor to the fact that the auditing has reached a successful conclusion: a "release" in the pre-clear. It is one of the end phenomena (E/P) of an auditing session, the others being a "cognition" (an insight), and "good indicators" in the pre-clear's manner: a happy or relieved look, brightness, and extroversion. An end phenomena free needle must occur when the TA is in the 2–3 range, or so Hubbard decided, in accord with a belief he held about the normal level of body resistance. If the TA is higher, there is still mass around; if lower, "overwhelm." It is a rule in auditing that whenever a "release" F/N appears, the auditor must inform the pre-clear, "Your needle is floating" or "You have a floating needle." In this way, pre-clears come to recognize the subjective state(s) associated with the F/N. Like a good "acknowledgment," the auditor's indication of the floating needle should be properly timed so as not to interrupt the pre-clear in the midst of a "cognition," as this may squelch the cognition. The auditor is instructed to wait until the pre-clear turns attention back to the auditor before indicating the "float."

One trouble with F/Ns is that they are notoriously hard to demon-

6. Another, fairly uncommon, needle phenomenon which is counterindicative to auditing is one called a "stage four." Here the needle rises, sticks, falls; rises, sticks, falls—in the same pattern over and over and nothing the auditor can do will change it (although pre-clear body movement will interrupt it). No one is quite sure what this means except "no auditing." Hubbard remarks in an early publication on the E-Meter that it means "the preclear is from Noplace as a case" (Hubbard 1967c:19). One auditor told me that it should be interpreted as a form of "overwhelm" and that she had seen it once in a fairly high-level Scientologist—"he was fine after he got over the thing that was overwhelming him."

strate to the student. They are defined entirely by the quality of movement, rather than by size, range, or repetitiveness of pattern— although any given F/N may adopt a range and a pattern within which it repetitively moves. Hubbard tried to capture the quality of the F/N in words:

> *Free needle.* This is probably the least understood term and needle action in all of E-Metering.
>
> It means an idle, uninfluenced motion, no matter what you say about [the subject] being audited. It isn't just nul, it's uninfluenced by anything (except body reactions).
>
> Man, it's really free.
>
> You'll know one when you see one. They're really pretty startling. The needle just idles around and yawns at your questions on the subject.[7] [Hubbard 1967c:18]

In *The Book Introducing the E-Meter*, Hubbard explains, "The needle just floats over a wide area and anything the p-c says or thinks has no influence on the very smooth movement. Further, you will have difficulty in controlling the needle with the Tone Arm just as you would have difficulty balancing a long stick on your fingertip" (1967b:46).

In spite of Hubbard's assurances that "you'll know it when you see it," in the days before auditors had been instructed to look for the other end phenomena that should accompany the "float," many claimed to have missed it as often as they saw it. Even today, inexperienced auditors live in trepidation that they will squash a blossoming "cognition" by blundering ahead with another question after the needle has begun to float. Part of the reason, as I have said, is that the read is defined solely by the quality of movement. It neither drags nor is it driven. It "floats." The range it covers may be very small (one-half inch), or it may be dial-wide: it may flit by in a second or it may last for several minutes. Short ones may do only a single downsweep or a single upsweep. The F/N is impossible to demonstrate mechanically, by twisting the trim knob or the TA knob by hand, the way many other reads are demonstrated, or by moving one's fingers about on the cans. (Hand movement causes too much jerk in the needle.) Coaches may attempt to demonstrate it by taking the cans and recalling a

---

7. Nowadays auditors are supposed to recognize it without testing the pre-clear with further questions.

moment of "release" in their own past auditing, but sometimes they are not able to do so, or the float may be so brief that by the time they say to the student "There it went," it has gone. Of late, videotape demonstrations have been devised that are rather more successful. To help things out, since few auditors seem to have trouble spotting the "big ones," all auditors are now instructed to nurse anything they suspect of being a tiny "float" by waiting calmly to see if it develops into something bigger and more definite. Since F/Ns are expected to occur shortly after the pre-clear has unburdened himself of a heavy incident or confession, bringing down the TA, the auditor may begin to nurse possible F/Ns at this point. In practice, this often takes the form of glancing expectantly at the pre-clear who, if he or she is anticipating a "float" at about that point also, may oblige the auditor by getting on with it. Experienced auditors tell me that different pre-clears will have characteristic pre-float needle patterns that the auditor who works with a pre-clear for any length of time comes to recognize. Hubbard commented too that an F/N is often preceded by the needle "popping" to the left as if coming unstuck from something.

Because the floating needle is supposed to mark a release in the pre-clear, it becomes in itself a means of validating that such a thing as release occurs, or, given that releases occur, that one *is* occurring at this or that particular point. (In a similar way, the rising and falling of the needle and TA are a validation of the concepts of mass and charge and their elimination.) Yet given the nonspecificity of the emotional/cognitive states that are detectable on a neurophysiological measuring device, it would be surprising to find an instrument reading that appeared only under the precise conditions of an uplifting insight and none other. As it happens, an F/N may appear for reasons other than a release. In Scientology the most generally recognized additional cause of an F/N in session is paradoxically, a sudden drop in rapport between auditor and pre-clear. These sudden drops (whether between auditor and pre-clear or between any two parties) are called, in Scientology, "ARC breaks." Subjectively, an ARC break is experienced as an upset. (The anatomy of ARC will be explained in greater detail in Chapter 6.) As to how one distinguishes a release F/N from an ARC break F/N some auditors have assured me that a release F/N will occur when the TA is between 2 and 3, leaving me to suppose that ARC break F/Ns occur only at other TA settings. But there is evidence to the effect that either type can occur at practically any setting. Even advanced Scientologists have remarked that they have occasionally experienced releases accompanied by F/Ns when the TA was higher than 3, but because Hubbard defined an *acceptable* F/N as occurring between 2 and 3, these releases could not be validated. By corollary, ARC break F/Ns occur in the 2–3 range; and indeed there are cases reported of auditors validating as release F/Ns that were in fact expressions of pre-clear disenchantment (Kaufman 1972:250). Sophisticated auditors resolve the problem of differentiating F/Ns by the simple formula: look at the pre-clear—do you see upset or happiness? Nevertheless, following Hubbard's directives, they will not validate a release unless the TA is between 2 and 3.

Inasmuch as one can speculate about the mental correlate of a floating needle, it would seem that the element which all F/Ns— happy or angry—have in common is that slight sense of mental mastery, the arrest of the thought process which occurs when some comprehensible pattern suddenly clicks into place. Along this line, one Scientologist told me that a person given a list of words to memorize will "F/N" at the point of having mastered the list. In the release phenomenon, the F/N is correlated with a "cognition"; in ARC breaks, there is a sudden shift from one perspective to another, more baleful one, as the pre-clear realizes, say, that his auditor is a nincompoop.

A final point about the Scientological understanding of the E-Meter is that the meter reads just below the level of conscious awareness. The auditor will see a read slightly before the pre-clear begins to articulate a thought; indeed, in many auditing actions, the auditor is instructed to wait, or probe gently ("Is there something else?" "I have a read here; what do you consider that could be?") in order to bring the preconscious thought to the surface. In certain other actions, the auditor steers the pre-clear toward a reading item by saying "That" each time the particular read occurs. Sooner or later a response blossoms in the pre-clear's mind.

In a very real sense, the meter can be used just like the "flash answer" technique of Dianetics or Freud's head-press to mark the next formulated idea as significant, or, in the Scientology case, "charged." One may well ask whether any given galvanic skin response is, in fact, correlated with preconscious ideas. Couldn't "steering" with the use of the E-Meter simply cause the pre-clear to rationalize or fabricate? But this question assumes that the line along which fabrication takes place is psychodynamically distinct from that along which preconscious ideation takes place, and there is no ground for making this assumption. It is best to say that what "reads" on the meter is an impulse pure and simple. Its appearance may be a sign that a recollection is struggling to the surface or that a total fabrication is being summoned into articulable form; whatever articulation surfaces, its epistemological status must be determined by its content. The meter alone will not distinguish lying from thinking, nor confabulating from remembering.

In fact, in Scientology there are two ways to greet the news that the auditor has just observed a read on the meter. The most usual way is to search one's mind for what it might be or deliver up what one already suspects it is. If, after this is done, the "item" (marked topic) no longer reads, one accepts that the thing delivered was "it." If there is still a read, one searches again. Whichever, the subjective experience of "finding" something with the use of the meter is often as not that it was "there" all along in some sense—one "recognizes" it as it reaches the level of articulation. One feels that the only reason one did not say it sooner, or think of it sooner, is that it seemed too insignificant or inappropriate to the context. Usually, however, *some* answer can be found if searched for. But not everyone searches. Sometimes higher-level Scientologists who are well acquainted with auditing, when told there is a read on an item, may interpret it to mean "protest" or "disagreement." They will say so to the auditor, for instance, "I know I'm clean on that item so the meter is registering my protest at being asked that question." This response is valid in Scientology theory. Protest generates charge, and Hubbard said bluntly that the meter "reacts on thought *and* disagreement" (Hubbard and Hubbard 1968:35). It is usually only high-level Scientologists who take this tack or from whom it is accepted. After you have been in Scientology for a while, they explain, "you begin to get your own certainty." You also begin to get your *bona fides* as a person of high-level awareness. Far be it from an auditor to question the "certainty" of an OT VI.

Because, according to Scientology theory, the meter reads on matters just below the surface of consciousness, there is a ready explanation for the surprising fact that some matters one would expect to carry charge may, for some people, not register on the meter at all. The nonread may mean, of course, that the pre-clear genuinely has no charge on the item. On the other hand, it may mean that charge is there but so deeply buried that it does not show up on the meter. The pre-clear is "not yet ready to confront it." He or she may be ready in the future, in which case the item will begin to read. Subtle plays of

[157]

interpretation can be brought to bear upon this business of what does and does not read. If a Scientologist enters a session with a bothersome thing in mind, yet finds that this produces little or no reaction on the meter, he or she may be reassured that all that thinking about it before the session has taken off a good deal of the charge already; in thinking about it before the session, one has already partially "confronted" it. It may happen, too, that an item or subject on which a person has already been audited to a release will heat up again in the future and start causing reads. This means that the previous auditing got only part of the charge off—enough to "key-out" that piece of the Bank, but not to totally erase it. Some deeper level of charge may still lurk.

The Processes

The final constituent of the auditing session is, of course, the lines of questioning addressed to the pre-clear. These are usually spoken of as "processes," and auditing is frequently called "processing." There are literally hundreds of processes in Scientology. Most of them are organized into packages of one or more which make up a level (as described in the treatment of the hierarchy of auditing) or an intensive.

A "process" is a set of questions or a set of commands aimed at bringing about a certain result in the pre-clear and accompanied by instructions as to how the "process" is to be run. These instructions amount to a flow-chart designating what step to take first, what to do with the reaction produced by this step, when and whether to go on to the next step, and so on. Often "assessments"—the calling of items from a prepared list—are used as forerunners to other processes. Having found what to audit from an assessment, the auditor then audits it via a separate set of questions or commands. Similarly, there are other common auditing actions which amount to full-scale processes in their own right, but which may be inserted into a session dealing with other things if certain eventualities arise. The processes usually undertaken to correct auditing mistakes may be so inserted, if the auditor discovers that he or she has "goofed." For example, there is an ARC break assessment that can be used to locate the reason for a session ARC break; this is followed by another process to deal with the ARC break. If the auditor is not trained to do ARC break assessments and processes, and the pre-clear does ARC break in session, the auditor must end the session and route the pre-clear to an auditor who can handle the matter. Generally speaking, any process is run until it produces the end phenomena described above: a floating needle, a "cognition," and "good indicators."

Most of Hubbard's processes fall into four basic types: listing actions, incident running, paired question processes, and imaginative exercises. (These categories are mine; they overlap with Scientology ones to a great extent but not entirely. I have coined the term "paired question processes" to cover a type for which there seems to be no current term in Scientology, and "imaginative exercises" to cover a lot of what Hubbard called Creative Processes, but other things as well. "Incident running" is a Scientology concept, but this type of auditing is usually either called by a term referring to the specific subject area, for example, Dianetic auditing, or loosely labeled "Earlier Similar." Most of the processes that I call "listing actions" are so referred to by Scientologists unless a more specific name is given according to subject or purpose.)

Listing Actions: Here the auditor is auditing from a prepared list of items, either to find an item to "run" via another process, or because the listing is a process in itself that is a way of "taking charge off the case." Often an element of both is involved. Lists typically comprise categories of behavior, categories of mental or physical phenomena, and types of situations that Scientology theory considers likely to carry charge for most pre-clears, or for pre-clears in certain situations or conditions. Typical disappointments and upsets in life, psychosomatic and neurotic complaints, old guilts, new guilts, characteristic misunderstandings about Scientology, characteristic foul-ups in auditing, commonly found preconceptions about existence, spirituality, and higher levels of awareness—these sorts of things are strung out in the form of lists which the pre-clear is asked to react to, item by item, as the auditing session unfolds. It may be that the pre-clear in a previous session has itemized his or her personal problems and then with the guidance of the auditor broken these problems down along Scientology lines to yield a list of subcategories or of angles from which to consider the troubling topics; the "listing action" is then used to find which particular aspect of the troubling topic is *most* troubling. More often, the list is simply a standardized one, composed of items held to be relevant to any pre-clear under the appropriate conditions—any pre-clear having difficulty auditing, any pre-clear with a drug history, any pre-clear just beginning the X or Y level of auditing, and so on.

A list may be run in several ways. It may be simply conducted as a "metered" interview, as in the "p-c assessment" form, which asks for general background information on the pre-clear's life; but this is hardly considered a process. The major ways of auditing from a list are:

(1) Assessment: here the auditor reads off the list to the pre-clear, checking the meter at each item, in search of an item with a certain type or size of read. The chosen item will then be "run," using a different process, to end phenomena. The same list may be assessed over and over again, with new items added as the pre-clear thinks of them. Or it may be used only once for a very specific purpose.

(2) General cleaning of a list: the auditor reads from a list—usually in this case a list of questions covering a number of experiential phenomena—and for each item that reads asks for the pre-clear's thoughts on the subject. As long as the item reads each time it is called, the auditor continues to "pull" thoughts from the pre-clear. When it no longer reads, the auditor goes on to the next item. The list is run until (the discussion of) an item produces the end phenomena.

(3) Listing and nulling: here a list is devised from the pre-clear's contributions and called straight through with all reading items marked and all nonreading items scratched off. The process is repeated over and over, eliminating nonreading items, until only one item is left that continues to produce reads, or in some cases, a particular type of read. This item may then be run using a different process.

(4) "Platen" lists: this is an unusual type of listing action that takes place, according to ex-Scientologist Robert Kaufman, on the Clearing Course. As far as I know, it is not used at lower levels of auditing. Here the solo auditor/pre-clear is given a list of Scientology concepts all of which are assumed, a priori, to be highly charged—that is, they should all produce reads. He or she begins by calling the first item, recording the read, calling it again and recording, until the item no longer produces reads. He or she then goes on to the next. (The thought—if any—associated with a read, apparently need not be expressed.) If, at any point, the next item does *not* read, this is taken to mean that there is still charge left on an earlier item or items. The auditor must thus backtrack until finding an earlier item that has begun to read again, "flatten" it again, then return to the point where he or she broke off and continue down the list. The list is presumably run to end phenomena (Kaufman 1972:141–42, 144).

There may be other listing actions with which I am unacquainted,

[160]

but the general idea is conveyed. (Bits of lists and references to lists will appear in subsequent parts of this book where the terms have a bearing upon the subject under discussion.)

Incident Running: An "incident" is defined in the Scientology Dictionary as "an experience, simple or complex, related by the same subject, location, perception or people that takes place in a short and finite time period such as minutes, hours or days; also, mental image pictures of such experiences" (Hubbard 1964). No "incident" is run, however, just for the sake of its being an incident. It must be—in theory at least—an incident of a certain type. On the broadest level, any incident can be classified—as we saw in the second chapter—as either an engram, a secondary, or a lock. Usually, however, incident-running processes will be searching for something more specific, for instance, engrams, secondaries, and locks containing an ARC break, or ones containing a particular body sensation. In these situations, the auditor will use the general term "incident" to cover all three types. The sort of incident looked for is determined by the sort of problem the auditing is meant to eliminate: if pain or body ailments, then one tries to find incidents containing pains and other sensations; if a tendency to become easily upset, then one looks for incidents containing ARC breaks. In incident-running processes, the auditor first asks the pre-clear to "locate" an incident of the type specified. Technically, it does not matter what method of location the pre-clear uses as long as he or she comes up with something, although certain ways of finding it—to be described later—are hinted at and preferred. If, in practice, the pre-clear comes up with an incident that is not of the type specified, the auditor must accept it as well intentioned, whatever it is—interrupting with dictionary clarifications only if the session seems to be bogging or if a gross misconstrual is apparent. The auditor has the pre-clear run the incident by simply going over it ("scanning" or "moving through" it) in his or her mind, letting whatever charge is connected to it come off in the course of this running.

With a few exceptions, to be described below, incidents are expected to occur in "chains." Any particular incident will have others associated with it through some similarity of content. If the running of the first-located incident does not produce the end phenomena, the pre-clear is asked to locate an earlier incident of the same type, or an earlier incident in which a particular item appears. (Thus, incident running is sometimes designated "Earlier Similar," since the auditing

[161]

question will usually be either "Is there an earlier similar incident?" or "Is there an earlier incident containing ——?") An incident may be run through more than once if it is "producing TA"; if not, the pre-clear is sent earlier. This continues until the running of some incident results in the end phenomena. The end phenomena are taken to indicate either that the chain has temporarily "keyed-out," or that it has erased entirely. In theory, all chains have a "basic," "basic" being the chronologically first incident on the chain. If the basic is erased, then the entire subsequent chain erases with it—if not, the entire chain may "key-in" again later. There is, in fact, no way to tell either from the meter or from the pre-clear's behavior whether the end phenomena mean erasure or merely "key-out." Some Scientologists as pre-clears report a difference in subjective experience, but not all are able to do so. Generally, the proof of the pudding is in the eating—if one hits the same incident, or chain of incidents again in later auditing, or if one continues to have problems related to this chain, well, it must not have erased the first time.

Dianetic auditing of old was essentially incident running. Contemporary Dianetic auditing, now called Standard Dianetics, is still incident running, but with a specificity that was lacking before. Now, instead of looking for any old engram, secondary, or lock, running that, then looking for an earlier one, and so on, auditor and pre-clear first make a list of the pre-clear's complaints. Each complaint is broken down into a capsule description of the sorts of sensations, emotions, pains, and discomforts found in the major complaint. A "sore throat" may be broken down into "tightness in the throat," "rawness in throat," "burning sensation in back of nose," and so forth. If, in the course of breaking down the symptom, any such capsule description produces a "blowdown" of the TA, the auditor stops the list construction and asks the pre-clear if he or she wishes to run that item. If so, the pre-clear is asked to locate an incident containing the (capsule description) item. A chain is run to E/P; then the auditor returns to the listing procedure for a new item.

Whatever the type of incident or the principle along which chains are formed, in the majority of incident running it is the pre-clear who furnishes the actual incident. But there are important exceptions. On some of the Confidential Levels, the incident or incidents the pre-clear is meant to run have been furnished by Hubbard (see Kaufman 1972:160–63). It appears that in such cases the incident is presented in a very schematic fashion; the pre-clear is not told quite how to position himself within it, so a great range of subjective reactions is possible. To facilitate the running of such furnished incidents, Hubbard sometimes presented them in pairs, the solo auditor/pre-clear being instructed to alternate back and forth between the two; or additional processes may be given to employ if running of the incident bogs down.

Paired Question Processes: The most common auditing action on the Scientology Grades consists of addressing a subject through a pair of questions (or commands), asking first the one, then the other, then the first again; back and forth, in effect sandpapering off layer after layer of thought until the bare grain of the matter lies exposed to the pre-clear's view. A very simple version of this type is simply shifting perspective back and forth from negative to positive: "Tell me something you wouldn't mind remembering," followed by "Tell me something you wouldn't mind forgetting," for example. Or, for a deeper and more focused sequence, the answer to the first question may be the departure point for the second question: "What are you willing to talk to me about?" Pre-clear says "X." "Good. If you were talking to me about 'X,' what exactly would you say?" And so on. The effect of this sort of process is similar to that of running incidents by chain, except that the pre-clear's answers need not be formulated by incident or fitted to a temporal sequence.

Imaginative Exercises: While I will use the term here in a more specialized sense, in actuality just about any "process" can be viewed as an "imaginative exercise." All processes present the pre-clear with a particular mental task. If he or she is not able to perform the task, or if the performance of it produces no upsurge of feeling, idea, or insight, a second task is presented. If, in turn, this fails to bite, either a third task is presented or the pre-clear is returned to the first task. The auditing will continue along this course until something takes and E/P are achieved.

In most of the auditing just described, the tasks presented all have some obvious bearing upon the pre-clear's life and past thoughts and experiences. Some tasks, however, are concerned purely with the pre-clear's mental/perceptual apparatus *per se*, the not unreasonable premise being that it is through this apparatus that life experience in general is organized, and thus the auditing of mentation in and of itself will provide the pre-clear with hierarchically higher insights into the way in which he or she approaches and experiences the world. This is the sort of auditing I am here designating "imaginative exercises." Many of Hubbard's early Scientology books outline numerous processes of this type. They are conceived of as ways of determining, for instance, how the pre-clear "handles energy," whether he is able to create and destroy illusions, how he is located in space and time, and so on. Examples:

> This is a list of the things a preclear must be able to do with an illusion [a mental construct]:
>> Create the condition, energy or object [in his/her mind];
>> Conserve it;
>> Protect it;
>> Control it;
>> Hide it;
>> Change it;
>> Age it;
>> Make it go backwards on a cycle of action;
>> Perceive it with all perceptions;
>> Shift it at will in time;
>> Rearrange it;
>> Duplicate it;
>> Turn it upside down or on the side at will;
>> Make it disobey MEST [material universe] laws;
>> Be it;
>> Not be it;
>> Destroy it. [Hubbard 1965:116–17]

> . . . [have] the preclear close his eyes and move actual places on Earth under him, preferably places he has not been. Have him bring these up to him, find two similar things in the scene and observe the difference between them. Move him over oceans and cities. . . . [Hubbard 1965:125–26]

Many of these exercises Hubbard termed Creative Processing, and the stated purpose behind them was precisely (though in Hubbard phraseology) the destructuring of the pre-clear's "ordinary reality" apparatus.

This, then, is Scientology practice. In combination with the unusual state of introspective lucidity engendered by the training routines, the presentation by the auditor of a preordained and inexorable sequence of questions and the auditor's use of the E-Meter as a means of directing the pre-clear into personally relevant areas of response have the effect of bringing to the foreground and, if all goes well, defeating the pre-clear's customary defenses and self-image concerns. Pre-clear attempts at hedging are circumvented by the auditor's undistracted return to the question at hand ("I'll repeat the auditing question") and by the auditor's ability to communicate through correct auditing style that this is not a contest between two personalities but simply the working through of a prescribed mental task.

The pre-clear's customary defenses and self-image concerns are all of a piece with his ordinary modes of thought and, at bottom, ordinary thinking in all its manifestations is the activity that Scientology "processes" are geared to undermine gently. Like meditative exercises and the numerous modern psychotherapeutic techniques that it resembles, auditing has the capacity to bring about a disruption of the practitioner's reality schemas and a heightening of assimilatory activity. Deep reverie states occur in some pre-clears, who report losing consciousness of all their surroundings save for the auditor's voice. On the higher, solo-audited levels, mystical states are reported: the sense of self suffusing the universe, the experience of reaching a point of blissful utter stillness, the sense of possessing vast ineffable knowledge. One nonordinary experience frequently reported, because commonly looked for, is the sensation of being out of one's body—the condition of "exteriorization," in Scientology terminology.

Spectacular sensations need not invariably arise in auditing, however, and an auditing session is not discredited if they fail to appear. Any auditing is considered successful as long as it produces the characteristic end phenomena; the floating needle, the "cognition," and an influx of positive feeling. A correct ending such as this, and especially a series of such endings experienced over the course of an extensive bout of auditing, will, according to Scientologists, leave a person in a subjective condition of "lightness," "freedom," "clarity." This is not to say that auditing invariably produces the desired effects. For reasons that will be the concern of a later chapter, auditing's disruptions may be experienced negatively or the whole effort resisted. But these reaons being absent, the general upshot of an auditing procedure is to launch the pre-clear upon a little journey along the unexpected avenues of his thought process. Encouraged by the safety of the auditing situation and at the same time stripped of defenses, the pre-clear finds the movement into spontaneous associations and imagery to a great degree unavoidable and, in many respects, appealing. Plunging in, the pre-clear takes it on faith that his outpourings contain within them some meaningful pattern and that at some critical juncture in this exercise the meaning will be revealed.

When the pre-clear's moment of insight arrives, it will almost invariably appear as a validation of Scientology theory. This brings us to a final, and crucial, point concerning the auditing procedures. Though enormously varied in content, all Scientology processes have in common the fact that they are phrased in Scientology terminology and employ Scientology concepts about the mind, life, and behavior. Further, there is little in the mind, life, or behavior for which Scientology lacks a concept. When being "run" on a process then, the pre-clear is essentially enlisted in the task of fitting his or her thoughts and experiences to the principles of Scientology. This operation goes on out of session as well. Indeed, the pre-clear must have received a certain amount of instruction in Scientology before he or she will be able to understand and respond to the auditor's questions and commands. Before the pre-clear is allowed to begin any auditing sequence, he or she will be given books and bulletins to read that explain some of the principles involved in that particular auditing action; he/she will be checked for comprehension. In addition, the auditor must, before beginning the process, "clear the commands" with the pre-clear by making sure that the latter understands the Scientology definition of every Scientology term that appears in the auditing questions, and the standard dictionary definition of every non-Scientology term that so appears. If, during the session itself, conceptual confusion becomes evident, the auditor may temporarily interrupt the session, probe for the "misunderstood," and refer the pre-clear to the appropriate dictionary. It is a violation of the rules of auditing, embodied in the Auditor's Code, for the auditor actually to interpret *for* the pre-clear; that is, take the pre-clear's productions and "fit" them to Scientology concepts—or any other concepts (Hubbard 1956:100). But in a real sense such interpretation is unnecessary anyway. All the principles of the Scientology world-view relevant to the session should be familiar to the pre-clear already (or, be lying close to hand in a dictionary). There is no need for the connection to be made by the auditor. The pre-clear has a life and a set of ideas and experiences that he or she wishes to talk about; he or she also has a set of Scientology notions and terms and an understanding of their ostensible meaning. Auditing is designed to steer each in the direction of the other until the pre-clear

[166]

"discovers" the connections between them in an intimate way. In Chapters 7 and 8, we will see examples of how such connections are discovered. First, however, we must get some handle on the welter of concept and belief that constitutes Scientology "theory," and to which the terms used in auditing procedures refer.

[6]

Scientology Beliefs

The Scientology belief system, called by Scientologists, "Scientology data," is encyclopedic and labyrinthine. The fact of its sheer complexity can be understood in part as the result of a continuous attempt by Hubbard to abstract, from the behavior of the mind in the auditing situation and the behavior of Scientologists in relation to their practice, principles applicable to human behavior in general and to the cosmos at large. Projected onto larger social and cosmic maps, these abstracted principles assume additional, larger meanings that then feed back upon the situations from which they initially derive: the auditing situation and the relationship of Scientologists to Scientology. Hubbard executed this abstraction 'loop' repeatedly.

In his books, bulletins, and taped lectures, which Scientologists are constantly engaged in digesting, Hubbard preferred to start out at the abstract level and work down to particulars, letting the latter appear almost as incidentals to his main point. Let us say he had in mind the behavior that people not infrequently display in the auditing situation—and in life—of unconsciously mimicking the style, gestures, and attitudes of someone else. This is called, in Scientology, "going into the valence" of another, meaning assuming the other's identity, in whole or in part. Hubbard was wont to begin the discussion so loftily that one had no idea where he was heading. For instance: "There are three conditions (circumstances, qualities) of existence (apparency, reality, livingness). These three conditions comprise (make up, constitute) life. They are BE, DO, and HAVE" (Hubbard 1956:26). One then learns the Scientology concepts of BEINGNESS, DOINGNESS, and HAVINGNESS. There will be a formal definition for each. BEINGNESS, it turns out, is "the assumption of a category of identity." There is a relationship between the three conditions we are told, to wit, BEINGNESS is the most fundamental of the three; one must first BE before one can DO, and DO before one can HAVE. Finally, the auditors, whom Hubbard was always implictly addressing, find something they can sink their teeth into: it may be that the pre-clear who has gone into another's "valence" is suffering from a *scarcity of identity* (BEINGNESS).

> The preclear is often found in valences (other identities): his father's or mother's or marital partner's or any or all of thousands of possible people. He is unable to achieve or obtain (he thinks) enough identity or an identity of his own. He decries or criticizes the identities of others (fails to grant beingness to them). . . . To be with such a person is therefore an uncomfortable experience. . . . The "cure" for this is elementary. [Hubbard 1956:28]

There follows a series of suggested auditing procedures for remedying a pre-clear's scarcity of identity.

> A clever Auditor . . . would see that while he [the pre-clear] was in father's valence, it was really mother's attention that was sought. . . . He [the auditor] asks the preclear to lie about . . . identities that would attract mother's attention. Then, when the preclear can do this, the Auditor would have him invent identities that would attract mother's attention. [Hubbard 1956:29]

These observations nestle into other sets of observations. *Lying about* and *inventing*, for instance, appear in other lectures on the nature of CREATIVITY; and those who have read Hubbard's Dianetics works will recognize that "going into valences" was used to explain why so many people, remembering past lives, turn out to have "been" the same famous historical personage—Julius Caesar, or Jesus Christ, for instance; they were actually remembering an old "valence."

The same behaviors and mental phenomena may, in other Hubbard lectures, be approached from some rather different theoretical angle, used as illustration of some further principle. Fortunately, an exhaustive account of the Scientology system is not needed for present purposes, since such an account would be virtually impossible. The complexity and redundancy of Scientology "data" must be noted, however, because it is an important source of what one might call

[169]

"noetic satisfaction" for Scientologists. The multiple, overlapping and intertwined lines of reasoning are productive of multiple interconnected insights and a sense of ever-expanding comprehension.

Further, all the experiential phenomena noted by Scientology and all the varied lines of explanation for these phenomena feed into and support certain core tenets. To a great extent, these core tenets have been abstracted for us by Hubbard and coordinated into a set of axioms, "The Axioms of Scientology." I will have recourse to these axioms in presenting the overview of Scientology beliefs that begins below.

In addition to the voluminous abstract and technical principles that compose Scientology "data," there is a stratum of more concrete, so-to-speak mythological material having to do with what Hubbard called the "history of Man." Scientologists believe in the immortality of the self and thus in prior existences. What their special history consists of then is speculations about life in other (earlier) times, in other galaxies, even in alien "universes," and more particularly about crucial episodes of this bygone time through which *all* people, considered as immortal beings, may have passed. Like the individual engram, to which some present-day aberration in the individual is attributed, collectively experienced traumas are used to account for problems we all have in common. At the heart of these common problems is the existence of the Bank itself, and Scientology mythology suggests that the "core" of the Bank, its central cluster of components, is the result of certain past horrors to which all Beings were subjected—universal incidents.

It is perhaps slightly misleading to speak of Scientology's speculative history as mythology, for to some scholars this term suggests sacred narratives that have acquired the status of dogma. This is not quite the situation in Scientology. Hubbard was careful to emphasize that these accounts of the past are speculation, not established fact. The theory of immortality predicates that such a past is discoverable and every individual, through recollection, comes into contact with bits of it, but its exact outlines may never be completely established; what we know about it is impressionistic and subject to revision. Hubbard's tapes and writings toss off what can best be described as a "collage," rather than an ironclad sequence, of past incidents, managing in this fashion to give the idea of the sorts of things that happened back then without committing him to a definitive version. (His sense of humor often surfaces in these tales and some Scientologists find the tongue-in-cheek tone disquieting.) In many ways, Hubbard's interest in the universal incidents was less in their character of unalterable revelation than in their usefulness as a springboard for his technical abstractions. He related them to specific structures in the Bank, set forth rules for how to audit these, and so on.

Nevertheless, Scientology's "history of Man" even though not grasped in a fundamentalist manner, cannot be said to be devoid of an aura of sacredness, especially if we consider sacredness to be a quality that implies danger as well as holiness. The most important events on the collective "Time Track" (or "back on the Track," as Scientologists informally put it) are held to be so highly charged that they cannot be remembered or properly "confronted" without Scientology guidance. Any contact with these incidents outside a controlled auditing and training situation could cause profound psychological disturbance. Therefore, their nature is not revealed to the practitioner till he or she has reached the Confidential Levels of auditing.

The Scientology "Track" is analogous in many ways to the Australian Aboriginal "Dream-Time." In either case, anyone may enter this realm through the appropriate mental mechanism (dreaming for Aborigines, recollecting for Scientologists), but only the specifically privileged are initiated into its more portentous secrets. And in both cases, circumstances of the present are accounted for in terms of events in a magical past.

In a rough sense, the mythologic stratum of Scientology belief and the more abstract stratum of axioms and principles correspond to two different emphases in auditing. In Dianetic auditing—in its present form as in the past—the pre-clear is directed to the uncovering of "incidents," that is, narrative episodes from his or her past, and this sort of auditing emphasis is generative of reconstructed histories and narrative modes of explaining current situations. The emphasis on repressed incidents reinforces the traumatic conditioning theory of neurosis so salient in the early period of Dianetics. In most of the auditing procedures developed after Dianetics and broadly called "Scientology auditing," the emphasis is shifted from the uncovering of incidents to the uncovering of previously unarticulated thoughts, decisions, viewpoints, and impulses first adopted or experienced in the past but still operative in the present. Scientology has several general terms for these ideational components of personality: "postulates," "considerations," and "computations" are the most commonly used. More specific types of motivational vectors may be sought in auditing such as (hidden) "purposes" and "goals" or "Stable Data" (fundamental assumptions). But these are deemed forms of "postulate" or "consideration." When auditing emphasis is upon finding these sorts of behavior components, then explanations of the pre-clear's personal problems will highlight the implicit "ideology" (my term) that the pre-clear uses to organize his or her experience. The traumatic conditioning theory of neurosis recedes in favor of something resembling an "existentialist" or "game theory" model of behavior, wherein the individual is seen as an active agent in his/her own history and personality development. It is the latter emphasis that prevails in Scientology as a philosophical system, and indeed Scientology auditing with its emphasis upon hidden, self-constructed ideologies is seen as superordinate to Dianetic auditing with its emphasis upon traumatic experiences. The two theoretical emphases do not stand in contradiction to one another. Rather they are coordinated by the general theme that people ("Beings" in Scientology terminology) unwittingly but actively create the conditions of their own traumatization, trauma then gives rise to "aberrated" ideas and postulates which help in turn to create further potential for traumatization, and so on. In this way, the two auditing emphases are quite complementary. Of course, in any particular auditing session, the pre-clear will wind up both articulating previously implicit thoughts and orientations and recalling/fantasizing past happenings. In the auditing of one type of phenomenon the other is always to some degree also evoked.

The rough division between "ideology" and "event" in the auditing search can serve to organize the presentation of Scientology beliefs. I will (like Hubbard) work from the abstract to the concrete, dealing first with the basic tenets of Scientology, excerpted from the "Axioms," then illustrating in turn (*a*) selected mental/behavioral principles, the belief in which is elicited and reinforced by the Scientology auditing search for hidden "postulates," and so on, and (*b*) the events of the collective "Track," the belief in which is reinforced by the Dianetics-style emphasis upon recovering past incidents.

Basic Tenets: Thetans and the MEST Universe

In Chapter 2, I indicated that with the articulation of the doctrine of Scientology, Hubbard divided the cosmos into the material universe called, in his usage, the MEST universe (from Matter, Energy, Space, and Time) and the "theta" universe, the realm of spirit. More specifically, all sentient creatures are conceived to be spiritual beings: "thetans." Thetans, also called "Beings," the usage I will usually follow here, are nonmaterial in every sense of the word. Axiom 1 of the Scientology Axioms states: "LIFE IS BASICALLY A STATIC. Definition: A Life Static has no mass, no motion, no wave-length, no location in space or in time. It has the ability to postulate and to perceive" (Hubbard 1958). Hubbard was quick to correct any misimpression that he was talking about an "infinite mind" of which we are but manifestations. Every thetan is individual and each individual is "infinite mind" in itself. Since thetans exist prior to the MEST universe, one can conceive of a time when the distinctions between them were "immaterial," so to speak, but the individuality was nevertheless there.

Because thetans can "postulate and perceive" they are capable of making things and perceiving what they have made. There is a trick to this. Ordinarily, a thetan-created thing vanishes at the moment of its creation; it has no persistence.

> Axiom 11. . . . AS-IS-NESS is the condition of immediate creation without persistence, and is the condition of existence which exists at the moment of creation and the moment of destruction, and is different from other considerations in that it does not contain survival. [Hubbard 1958]

In order to bring about a persistence in a thetan-created thing (an AS-IS-NESS), the thing must be altered (ALTER-ISED) and the alteration denied or unrecognized. Thus all persisting things (outside of thetans, that is) contain a "lie." The best way of lying—or ALTER-ISING—something is to create it and then "assign other authorship" to it than one's own. Thus the basic lie is that one is not responsible for what is.

Persisting things are IS-NESSES—"apparencies." The way to undo them, cause them to vanish again, is to recreate the thing exactly "as-is" minus the alteration. Since, according to Axiom 12, "THE PRIMARY CONDITION OF ANY UNIVERSE IS THAT TWO SPACES, ENERGIES, OR OBJECTS MUST NOT OCCUPY THE SAME SPACE [then] WHEN THIS CONDITION IS VIOLATED (PERFECT DUPLICATE) THE APPARENCY OF ANY UNIVERSE OR ANY PART THEREOF IS NULLED" (Hubbard 1958). Another way to put this is that in the creation of a perfect duplicate, one must "spot the lie." Both the creation of a perfect duplicate and "spotting the lie" are spoken of as AS-IS-ING, just as is the creation of a

[173]

thing in the first place. The act of creation and the act of destruction are the same. The attempt to deny something or annihilate it by force is spoken of as NOT-IS-ING. NOT-IS-ING, however, never really vanquishes a created thing.

But we still have not yet quite accounted for the presence of the given MEST universe. For the formula of persistence just described does not distinguish purely mental constructs (which can persist) from materially real ones. The key to the latter is that thetans must jointly agree upon a persistency in order for it to become a solid reality. "Reality is agreement."

Axiom 26: REALITY IS THE AGREED-UPON APPARENCY OF EXISTENCE.
Axiom 27: AN ACTUALITY CAN EXIST FOR ONE INDIVIDUALLY; BUT WHEN IT IS AGREED WITH BY OTHERS IT CAN THEN BE SAID TO BE A REALITY. [Hubbard 1958]

In sum, the material universe is simply a big "solid" agreement by thetans busily denying that they are responsible for it in the first place. But why?

Axiom 39: LIFE POSES PROBLEMS FOR ITS OWN SOLUTION. . . .
Axiom 42: MEST (MATTER, ENERGY, SPACE, TIME) PERSISTS BECAUSE IT IS A PROBLEM. [Hubbard 1958]

We begin to get an inkling here of what thetans are like: they are curious, creative, challenge-seeking gamesmen. They like to cause effects. "Axiom 10. THE HIGHEST PURPOSE IN THIS UNIVERSE IS THE CREATION OF AN EFFECT" (Hubbard 1958).

Thetans are basically good, according to Hubbard; it's just that even with the finest of intentions, things can get out of hand. In his chattier lecture style, Hubbard explains:

It's the long spiral down. It goes like this: A thetan mocks things up according to certain vibrations and it gets to be an automatic intention. Then he doesn't know what this automatic intention is [i.e. forgets its origins]. And then somebody comes along and gives him things for the automatic intention to mock up which are things that would be bad for him. Or they jam the machinery of his automatic intention and make him fight his own automatic intention. The next thing you know he's got a messed up time track. And the next thing you know he's solid. And the next thing you know he picks up a meat body. See how it goes? [From taped lecture 23 May 1963, reprinted in *Advance* (1972) 15:17]

As the person himself makes his own time track, even if under compulsion, and commits his own overts, even if on provocation, it can be said, then, that the being aberrates himself. But he is assisted by mammoth betrayals and his necessity to combat them. And he is guilty of aberrating his fellows. [1975b:82]

Three major themes stand out in the axioms cited and Hubbard's foregoing statements. One is the explicit assimilation of material reality to mental phenomena. This assimilation actually begins in the auditing context, with an observation that any auditor and any preclear can make. That is that mental constructions—ideas, fantasies, or whatever—are not all freely constructed and freely dismissable. The obsessive cannot get rid of his obsessive idea. The phobic cannot prevent the phobia from arising in its typical context. The individual bent on denying an impulse experiences the impulse nevertheless. And so on. Mental phenomena, at least some mental phenomena, may exhibit the same imperviousness to the individual will as material "reality." It is but a small step to conclude that mental constructions are a form of materiality. The reader will recall from the discussion of the E-Meter that Scientologists view mental phenomena as having a certain solidity and weight—"mass." That is the reason proposed for the appearance of resistance to the free passage of the E-Meter's electrical current.

However, electrical resistance and imperviousness to the will do not characterize all mental materials. There is at any time a great deal that is subject to the thinker's control, that seems to come into being as he or she wishes and to vanish again as attention moves on to other things. The experiencer does not become "hung up" in it. It is easy to see that the first type of mental phenomena, the uncontrollable, corresponds to the Scientology notion of "Bank," while the second kind, the controllable, represents mental activity in its Bank-free, "keyed-out" state.

The axioms are an attempt to account for the difference between "Banky" and Bank-free mentation, while at the same time projecting the explanation of these differences onto the cosmos in general. Like the Bank, the material world has an externality and imperviousness to the will; and it is held to be similar in its origin. At bottom, both Bank and world are the result of authorship denied, alteration of truth, "occlusion of origins." The principal difference is the element of mutual agreement between Beings that enters into the constitution of the material universe. While the Bank of an individual contains much that is "solid" and "real" for him or her but relatively unreal for others, the MEST universe presents much the same picture to everyone. Even this distinction becomes blurred at the higher levels of Scientology awareness, where it begins to become obvious that "Bank" and "world" are so mutually implicative that freedom from one is freedom from the other.

And the secret of this freedom? Auditing is the process used to break up and dispell uncontrollable mental phenomena. Auditing locates mental masses, converts these into charge—energy—which may become unbound and discharge. After that, no more mass. The paradigmatic situation here is that of the dispelling of affect and tension surrounding disturbing images, memories, ideas. Again any auditor or pre-clear can observe that after running a succession of emotionally disturbing (or compelling) ideas or images to the point of release, the pre-clear will find nothing left in these ideas or images to hold his/her attention. They lose their charge and with it their specific attraction or repulsion; they no longer haunt the mind. In fact some report themselves unable to conjure up the successfully audited ideas and images at all; it is as if these had simply erased. In terms of the axioms, the constructs in question have been "AS-ISED." All denials and distortions have been removed and the truth about the constructs, including their authorship, confronted; at this point, they cease to persist.

By extension, these same things can happen to the material world, at least from the viewpoint of any individual experiencer. This is part of the promise held forth by Scientology. One starts out by auditing "away" ostensibly "mental matter," by freeing Beings from their Banks. But the envisioned end-point is the freeing of Beings from the laws of Matter, Energy, Space and Time. The idea that this can happen and will begin to happen as a Scientologist progresses up the levels of auditing is significantly reinforced by experiences of destructured perception encountered in the auditing or training situation. For Scientologists, uncanny experiences that seem to defy empirical science paradigms are proof of Scientology's claim that Beings are not inherently constrained by the laws of the material universe.

A second major theme implied in the foregoing is the inferiority of

MEST to "theta." To the extent that a construct has materiality, it is to be viewed as coarse and imperfect, potentially harmful. The "massiness" of mental phenomena is an index of "aberration," and the existence of the Bank and the present-day material world are seen as representing the end-point of a dwindling spiral down which thetans have descended over the eons as they became progressively trapped in their own lies. The purpose of Scientology is to reverse this dwindling spiral.

The final principle which Hubbard's formulations underscore, and which is endlessly elaborated upon in the Scientology cosmos, is the value opposition between self-determinism and other-determinism, between being "at cause" and being "in effect." An undeteriorated thetan, Hubbard asserted, is the Cause of things; a deteriorated thetan is the Effect of them. This is true whether one is speaking of one's own mental phenomena or of that more solid mind-stuff called the MEST universe. Scientology posits that the majority of people are currently in a deteriorated state. As Beings, they find themseves surrounded by a physical universe that is harsh and unsympathetic to their desires; they occupy MEST bodies the afflictions and cravings of which they are little able to control; and they are possessed of "minds" which at their Analytic best are no better than "servo-mechanisms" like the body, and at their Reactive worst are the source of nightmarish suffering. The last is the crowning insult. Already hopelessly "in effect" of the material universe, an average present-day thetan can't even control his own mind. The prevailing state of other-determinism is equated with MEST, solidity, and low levels of awareness— including the inability to perceive Scientology truths. It is a devalued state. Self-determinism is equated with full theta powers, freedom from MEST laws, and high levels of awareness, including appreciation of Scientology truths. The thing that stands between the one condition and the other is the Bank, and the purpose of auditing is to eliminate the Bank and thus translate the Being from the devalued other-determined state to the valued self-determined state.

I have just described the Scientology belief system in quite schematic form. Now it requires fleshing out.

Thetans were born free, but everywhere we find them in chains. Implicit in the axioms are two ways of conceiving how this may have come about. One is through the application of a temporal metaphor: things came to be the way they are through a progression of events. The other way of conceiving the situation is to speak—as the axioms for the most part do—of certain principles of Beingness itself, or laws of thetan behavior: things come to be the way they are because Beings operate in certain ways. In line with the two major emphases in auditing described above, Scientology theory develops both approaches.

Let us look at some of the more specific principles of behavior that govern thetans and that thus account for the way things are, by examining highlights from the material learned on the different auditing levels.

Certain Principles of Thetan Behavior

Beginning with the Scientology Grades, the pre-clear launches into principles with increasing depth. Each level treats of some specific concept or cluster of concepts. Auditors training to audit these levels must have command of the entire body of lore surrounding each, and their pre-clears must be given some elementary instruction as well.

Grade 0—Communication—is a vast arena of information concerning the precise anatomy of communication, all the ways in which persons become aberrated in regard to it, and all the ways in which they may become less aberrated through the application of Scientology insights about it. One recalls Axiom 10: "THE HIGHEST PURPOSE IN THIS UNIVERSE IS THE CREATION OF AN EFFECT." In studying communication, one learns that the formula of communication is CAUSE, DISTANCE, EFFECT—"cause" being the source of the communication, "effect" its receipt-point. Thus communication is a manifestation of the highest purpose in this universe. Furthermore, good communication is seen as the thing that ultimately dissolves the Bank, and its theoretical importance is noted in the axioms. "Axiom 51. POSTULATES AND LIVE COMMUNICATION NOT BEING MEST AND BEING SENIOR TO MEST CAN ACCOMPLISH CHANGE IN MEST WITHOUT BRINGING ABOUT A PERSISTENCE OF MEST. THUS AUDITING CAN OCCUR" (Hubbard 1958).

As far as good communication goes, the ideal would be telepathic harmony between two Beings. Approaching this ideal is the lucid sensitivity of interchange cultivated by the training routines and put to use in auditing for the purpose of dissolving the pre-clear's Bank. There are coarser and more "massy" forms of communication, such as those employed by ordinary people, where Bank manipulativeness enters in, where there is resort to body language, shouting, and dramatization, and where, not surprisingly (to Scientologists), people manage regularly to misunderstand one another. At the grossest levels of communication, *things* are exchanged rather than ideas: bullets and bombs, for instance.

On Grade I, one learns that "problems" have an exact anatomy, again alluded to in the axioms. Problems are conceived to arise out of "equal but opposing forces," one of which contains a "lie." Such conflicts generate "chains" inasmuch as the solution to a problem tends to become itself a problem calling for a yet further solution. "The solution to the problem is the problem," to cite a Hubbard aphorism. Part of problems auditing (Grade I) consists of following such chains back down to the original conflict, finding the two opposing forces in it and "spotting the lie."

On Grade II, one deals with "overts" and "withholds." An overt is a wrongdoing. A withhold is a concealment, often, though not invariably, the concealment of an overt. Both should ideally be understood in terms of the Scientology moral system, which posits survival as the driving force of existence, moral good as the promotion of survival, and moral evil as that which goes against survival. "Survival" is not a simple thing, as it occurs across several dimensions, or, in Scientology terms, "dynamics." Beings strive to survive as individuals (FIRST DYNAMIC), as procreative or sexual units (SECOND DYNAMIC), as groups (THIRD DYNAMIC), as humankind (FOURTH DYNAMIC), as the animal kingdom (FIFTH DYNAMIC), as the physical universe (SIXTH DYNAMIC), as spirit (SEVENTH DYNAMIC), and finally as "the infinite," sometimes identified as the Supreme Being (EIGHTH DYNAMIC). The moral value of an act must be judged according to how many survival dynamics are affected by it for better or worse. Within this framework, an overt is a contravention of one or more of the dynamics.

In auditing practice, and in practical day-to-day affairs, Scientologists regard as an overt anything felt to be a wrongdoing by the party or parties involved, and as a withhold, any item a person is concealing from the auditor or others with whom he or she deals for whatever reason. Ratiocination may succeed in connecting felt wrongs with the survival dynamics, and concealments with felt wrongs, but in fact auditing interest in overts and withholds is less a function of ethical system-spinning than of the consequences of these matters for the pre-clear's case and thus for auditing action. Let us take withholds to start with. When a pre-clear is attempting to conceal something (consciously or unconsciously), this sooner or later affects the auditing of everything else, even subjects apparently unrelated to the with-hold. Withholds in general block the free flow of information from pre-clear to auditor that is essential to successful auditing. More particularly, there are certain behaviors into which the pre-clear will lapse if she or he feels that something concealed is in danger of being exposed. He or she will go out of rapport with the auditor quite readily and become critical—of the auditor, of the process, of Scientology in general. Typically the target of criticism is the party against whom an overt, now "withheld," has been committed. This sort of defensive criticism is called "nattering," and the appearance of nattering on the part of a pre-clear is a signal to the auditor that some withhold has been threatened, or, in Scientology jargon, "missed"— that is, the auditor has come close to it without uncovering it. Besides natter, the missing of a withhold stirs up "bypassed charge" in the pre-clear and this will often manifest itself on the E-Meter as a stubbornly rising or "tight" needle, making further progress through the session difficult. Finally, having withholds missed will often provoke a person to fall ill. In falling ill, the guilt-burdened individual simultaneously executes a punishment upon himself and elicits sympathy, and leniency, from the environment. (Illness will also preclude any further auditing for the time being.)

Of course all these repercussions of withholds appear in life as well as in auditing, but the auditing situation is tailor-made to bring them to a head. For some individuals, simply to sit down with an auditor, someone who operates that "mind-reading" device, the E-Meter, is to have all sorts of nameless guilts evoked. It follows that the best way to guarantee progress in auditing is to have the pre-clear lay all these hidden cards on the table. The auditing processes of Grade II are designed to bring about this result.

The deeper issue involved in the business of overts and withholds is why Beings commit wrongful acts in the first place. Thetans are basically good, said Hubbard; they do not willfully cause harm. As evidence of this he cited the tendency of wrongdoers to "avoid the injured area," that is, to try to put out of their minds and out of their lives persons or things they have harmed or imagine they have harmed. The presence of the injured makes the injurer feel bad, and a bad conscience is proof of an ethically good Being. Hubbard further argued that the reasons people typically give for their wrongdoings— retaliation, self-defense—are no more than justifications ("motivators") resorted to after the fact. Of course these "motivators," once latched on to, are then employed to inspire further misdeeds, so they are not to be ignored. In one of these sequences of cumulative deterioration to which Hubbard was apparently so addicted, motivator is seen to follow overt, inspiring more overts, which then require in their turn more motivators, and so on. This is called the overt-motivator cycle. And yet the original overts in these overt-motivator chains occur not because of thetan perverseness or even vindictiveness. They are to be traced instead to a "misunderstood" or an ARC break. The latter concepts are explored in depth on Grade III.

On Grade III, one learns that understanding has three components — "affinity," "reality," and "communication," for which reason understanding is spoken of in Scientology as "ARC." Affinity is liking or a feeling of closeness to someone or thing; reality is agreement (see Axiom 26 above) with someone or thing; and communication, as learned earlier, is the exchange of ideas or things. These three factors are observed to be interdependent and covariable. An increase in one will cause an increase in the other two. For instance, if one has occasion to communicate more frequently with another person whom one previously thought little of one way or the other, one's affinity for that person will rise, according to this theory, and one will discover more things to agree upon. Hence, understanding, as a whole, improves. Conversely, a decrease in any one of the variables will bring about a decrease in the other two. A sudden or sharp decrease in ARC (or one of its components) is spoken of as an ARC "break." An ARC break is manifested in an upset on the part of the ARC-broken party. It does not matter whether the upset takes the form of anger and disillusionment, or grief and self-flagellation—either is an ARC break.

ARC thus occurs along a high-to-low continuum and may, under appropriate circumstances, reach very exalted heights of intuitive sensitivity to another person, creature, or thing. In keeping with the idea that all positive conditions are those transcendant of material laws, Axiom 23 states: "TOTAL ARC WOULD BRING ABOUT THE VANISHMENT OF ALL MECHANICAL CONDITIONS OF EXISTENCE" (Hubbard 1958). On the other hand, low ARC, ARC breaks, and failures of understanding are to be blamed for the appearance of hostilities between Beings and the commission of overts, and these in turn are bound up with the rise of material barriers, "mechanical conditions of existence," and the Bank.

On Grade IV, one studies one of the more intriguing, not to mention entertaining, Scientology concepts, that of the "service facsimile." A service facsimile is a hidden computation (a piece of conceptual Bank) that a person uses to "make self right and others wrong, dominate others and escape domination, aid own survival and hinder the survival of others" (Hubbard 1964). Everyone has a service facsimile. In fact, everyone, theoretically, has many; but usually only the one acquired in the current lifetime is heavily in operation. The "serv fac" computation always resolves into a simple generalization about the way things are, such as "People will let you down," "Money is power," "Everybody likes a nice guy." The service fac is said to be formed during a moment or period in a person's life when he or she was extremely confused and needed some guideline for behavior. The generalization that most aptly summarized the confusing circumstances then became the means of orienting oneself in the original situation and in all subsequent moments of threat or confusion. All of a person's "make-guilty" mechanisms and dominance ploys can be shown to be covert ways of proving this false truism to himself and the world.

Without further explication, it is possible to perceive that each level picks up and brings a broader or slightly different perspective to bear upon previous levels, and all principles ultimately resolve into the axioms. Scientologists will remark that the data on any given level are "harmonics" of data found at other levels. One can see, for instance, that the dynamics of communication interlock with the dynamics of ARC and also with the dynamics of overts and withholds. Overts in turn manifest themselves in engrams; service facsimiles can be viewed as a way of solving a problem, and so on. I cannot bring out all the interwoven threads here, but conversations such as the following are typical among experienced Scientologists:

> Bart launched into the subject of Service Facsimiles and said that they're usually a computation that's made "before the basic [this lifetime] personality is formed," and that an Overt is always present at the time the computation is made. After the Service Fac is postulated (he also described it as a "postulate"), usually really early in childhood, like age 2, then the entire personality will tend to be formed around it. "You look at people, you look at a person and you can see that his whole personality, all his eccentricities and everything he does, is saying the same thing, you can't actually put your finger on the exact phrase, but you can tell by looking at him that it's all coming from his Service Fac." I asked, "Even when he's not in the process of making someone wrong?" "That's right, he doesn't have to be making you wrong, it's still there in his life and

livingness. Most people have the idea of the Service Fac as being one thing—the thing you use to make self right and others wrong. That's a Misunderstood. Like it says in the bulletin, it's what he's using to *dominate* others and prevent them dominating him. It's what he uses to aid own survival and *hinder* the survival of others. That's the Service Fac."

He went on to explain that auditing on the Service Fac has to be very precisely done and very cleanly done, otherwise, it never really "keys-out." He said, "You've got to get that Overt, the Overt that was committed at the time he made the postulate."

Louise entered in by saying that it was very important to "duplicate the exact moment in time" when the postulate was made and be able to AS-IS the circumstances surrounding it. She said that at that exact time, "you'll find a Misunderstood, an ARC break, and a Problem. And you have to audit out the Problem."

Bart came back in on having to get the Overt. . . .

This complex interlocking and redundancy of principles continues into the Confidential Levels, where every heretofore mentioned principle and then some puts in an appearance.

Robert Kaufman's description of the Confidential materials is my main source of information on these levels. The description is far from complete, but certain themes stand out. Grades V and Va (called "Power" and "Power Plus") apparently deal with the pre-clear's conception of how to handle "existing conditions" and with his/her conceptions of "source" (Kaufman 1972:88). The first theme is opaque to me, the second less so. "Source" is defined as "cause" or "point of origin," for instance the point of origin of a communication (as learned on Grade 0). This seems innocuous enough, but it is to be noted that in Scientology Ron Hubbard is often termed "Source"—with a capital S. We may surmise from this that on Grades V and Va, the pre-clear's feelings about Hubbard and Hubbard's authority within the movement would often become the object of introspection.

Solo and Clear, Grades VI and VII, are concerned with the core of the Reactive Mind, the deepest level of psychic organization. This deep level has certain resemblances to the "problems" treated on Grade I. The core of the Bank consists of a series of structures called goals-problem-masses, or GPMs. Goals are "prime intentions" of the thetan; GPMs result from the fact that these intentions have experienced opposition.

. . . the *goal* has been balked for eons by opposing forces. The *goal* pointed one way, the opposing forces point exactly opposite and against it. If you took two fire hoses and pointed them at each other, their streams would not reach each other's nozzles, but would splatter against one another in midair. If this splatter were to hang there, it would be a ball of messed up water. Call hose A the force the pc has used to execute his *goal*. Call hose B the force other dynamics have used to oppose that *goal*. Where these two forces have perpetually met, a mental mass is created. . . . This is the *goal problem mass*. [Hubbard 1975a:179]

The lore surrounding these levels is apparently dazzlingly complex. To be dealt with, GPMs have to be broken down into phrases—the Reliable Items. The conditions mentioned in these phrases are in turn linked to conditions that the pre-clear is continuously "dramatizing" (acting out) in his/her current life, and so on. Here and there in these complicated descriptions and instructions, the essence of Clearing emerges in plainer language: ". . . getting out of the road all these unrealized goals each one of which has been a defeat for [the pre-clear] at some time or another" (Hubbard 1975a:361). The ultimate reasons for the presence of GPMs is perhaps most succinctly if enigmatically stated in Axiom 39: LIFE POSES PROBLEMS FOR ITS OWN SOLUTION.

All the Confidential Levels past Clear are spoken of as "OT Sections," OT meaning, it will be recalled, "operating thetan." These levels are aimed at stabilizing the condition of Clear and making it possible for thetans to recover their innate abilities. The few sketchy fragments of information available about these levels make it apparent that Scientologists continue, on the OT Sections, to audit away at their Bank, even though one is given to believe that the entire Bank has been destroyed on the Clearing Course. This basic contradiction in Scientology theory is subject to a number of rationalizations. Some Scientologists argue that while the core of the Bank is "blown" at Clear, there are still disconnected "bits" of it lying around which interfere with the full potentialities of the thetan; therefore more auditing is necessary to put everything straight. Others advance a rather more impressive rationale to the effect that "cleared" thetans become, by virtue of clearing, so powerful that they are capable of re-creating, postulating, or "mocking-up" the Bank all over again, and furthermore will do so, since the "no-games" condition of Bank-lessness grows tedious after a while. The thetan is an inveterate gamesman; having no Bank to bother him, he reinvents one! A rather more ingenious, if slightly sinister, reason for continued auditing is suggested by reports concerning the materials of the OT III Section, one of the most important of the OT levels. Here, according to ex-Scientologist Robert Kaufman, the solo auditor is put to work auditing away the Banks of other (disembodied) thetans who have attached themselves to his or her body as the result of traumatic incidents in their (the disembodied thetans') pasts (1972:160–64). Advanced Scientologists, speaking to me elliptically about the OT III materials, were of the opinion that the main theme for this level derived from earlier days when Hubbard, less committed at that point to the notion of thetanhood as a unique spiritual identity, had toyed with the idea of racial memory and instructed pre-clears to audit out bits of genetic Track embedded in various parts of their bodies. These alien memory-lines were referred to as "genetic entities" (Hubbard 1961:13). If we combine these informants' speculations with Kaufman's account, it would appear that the old familiar "genetic entities" reemerge on the OT III Section as the attached "body thetans," little traumatized Beings who have battened onto the bodies of their healthier fellows and who must be audited by the latter to the point where they can disengage. While it poses the problem of having to audit a mind that is somehow available to one's consciousness without, however, being one's own mind, the concept of "body thetans" is not actually inconsistent with the Scientology construction of reality. Nevertheless, the idea comes as something of a shock even to sophisticated Scientologists, because they have become accustomed to the dominant flavor of the belief system which emphasizes the isolated autonomy of the free thetan.

Advanced Scientologists indicate broadly that much of the auditing on the OT Sections is derived from, or similar to, the imaginative exercises devised by Hubbard in the beginning days of Scientology; but I have no information on the specific principles addressed. Some of the OT auditing, however, especially that on the OT III Section, consists of running incidents, Dianetics-fashion. This brings us to the other branch of Scientology reality—the Time Track.

The Time Track

The Time Track, usually called in Scientology simply "the Track," is defined as follows in the Scientology Dictionary: "The consecutive mental image pictures or facsimiles recording the consecutive moments of 'now' through which the individual has lived" (Hubbard 1964). Theoretically, every person has in his or her mind a complete record of his or her past experience extending beyond the current lifetime into an infinity of previous existences. One can, of course, "remember" more or less what happened to one during the current lifetime except for those events that one has repressed because of their unpleasantness. Similarly, after overcoming the relatively slight barrier preventing one's recollection of past lives, one can remember what happened in them—except for those portions of the Track that have been, like this lifetime's repressions, "occluded" by pain and heavy "charge." Once one begins to uncover the latter, the whole history of the dwindling spiral unravels, one understands how thetans deteriorated through time down to their present lowly condition, and one can remember, increasingly, those early days of the Track when it wasn't all so bad.

Let us examine "early Track" for a moment. The fundamentals of how it all started are contained in the axioms, and here too is everything one needs to know—abstractly at least—about how it all got out of hand.

> Harry, a former Comm Course student, engaged Louise, a high-level Scientologist, in an ontological discussion. He wanted to know when it all started and where it all came from. She said, "Do you mean the MEST universe and the whole game we're in?" "Well, yes." She said look at Axiom 3. ("Space, Energy, Objects, Form and Time are the result of considerations made and/or agreed upon or not by the static, and are perceived solely because the static considers that it can perceive them.") "Thetans wanted a game so they began to mock the whole thing up, and began to agree upon their 'mock-ups.' Or at least some of them agreed, some didn't." She cocked an eye-brow. "Well, no," said Harry, that wasn't what he meant. "Like where did *thetans* come from?"
> Louise: "The origins of the static are in infinity. Think about that."
> Harry: "That's not conceivable to me. I mean, before they began mocking things up, how long had they—I mean, *we*—been around?"
> Louise: "How can you time it? Time is a consideration of statics; you can't have time before you have the consideration."
> Harry: "Oh well, but if all of these beings were there, see, and they were not aberrated because they hadn't done anything to cause aberrations, then why did they start mocking things up that could cause aberrations?"
> Louise: "How would they know it would cause aberrations?"
> Harry: "Well, if they had such a high level of awareness . . ."

[186]

Louise: "What have they got to be aware of? What would they have to
be knowledgeable about? If you have nothing to perceive you can't
perceive anything. Once you've made the consideration that there are
things to perceive and begun to perceive things, then you have something to be knowledgeable about. Not before."
Harry: "You mean they didn't know what they were getting into?"
Louise: (laughing) "How could they?"

The idea of innocence and ignorance is reiterated in the most prevalent line of speculation about how things went astray. Curious about
why thetans commit overts if thetans are basically good, I asked one
advanced Scientologist. He answered:

Beings are basically good, but they're really kinda stupid! They're given
to error. Y'know it starts with a misunderstood word. You know the cycle
of the Overt—. They misunderstand something and then they say, "I
unh, dunno, unnnh—that's the best I can do," and then they go off half-
cocked and make a mess and that's the Overt. And then after they've
done the Overt, they go "Well, mmm, something crazy here, I couldn't
have been all that wrong," and then they get a Motivator. Uh . . . now
why they get confronted with misunderstandable things I don't have
much of an answer. Except that you take your ordinary game. Do you
play bridge? [Yes.] Well, the fact is that you don't know what the other
person has in his hand. You're not able, within the rules of the game, to
understand fully what he has, so you misunderstand it, you make errors.
If you're gonna play a game, you make errors, and if you go into action,
"aberration" follows and there's no way out. Uh, a maxim from Hubbard:
"All games are aberrative. Some are fun." [Taped interview]

As to why Beings start playing games in the first place, most will
simply say that a "no-games" condition is too boring to be tolerated for
long.

Another line of speculation as to how innocent sport degenerated
into serious derangement, dragging the players along with it, has to do
with the fact that a pure theta universe would be totally anarchistic.
Without agreed-upon rules, no game—not even a fun one—could
endure for long without someone coming along and smashing it up.
Therefore, the agreements about Matter, Energy, Space and Time
arose as an original social contract, transforming anarchy into social
organization. "We made these agreements," said the Scientologist
just quoted, "to keep from being vastly destructive." But doing so had

its cost, for with enduring MEST came enduring wounds and enduring wounds are essentially what forms the basis of the Reactive Mind. What in neutral terms would be called a "social organization," in Scientology terms is transmuted into "an aberrated game of enslavement and control"—not a bad way of describing most contemporary social organizations, Scientologists are quick to point out.

The early portion of the Track, when things were only just beginning to congeal into potentially dangerous forms, is important in auditing, as we shall see later; but it is not filled with specific historical events as are the later portions of the Track. Early Track is, within the limits of the axioms, left to individual imagination. One leaps into concrete theta history somewhere further down the line when the aberrated game of enslavement and control is well under way. Broadly speaking, any "time" in between the ethereal beginnings and recorded (or archaeologically surmised) human history is a suitable stage for Hubbard's postulated universal incidents. Most of these are conceived as taking place in science-fictionesque settings millions, billions, and trillions of years ago.

Some idea of what this "solider" portion of the Track is like can be gleaned by seeing how Hubbard (re)constructed it. Once past-life incidents became permissible in auditing, pre-clears could "run" anything conceivable, and did. For a while Hubbard had everyone keep a "Track map" and send in their recorded recollections to him. He was the one with authority to generalize from all this material, and he proceeded to do so; but a kind of mutual feedback process was under way from the start. Hubbard could deduce what was of interest to the group from the sorts of incidents that people were running; at the same time, he needed only hint at what he thought was "back there" to cause a fresh crop of discoveries to take shape in his followers' memories. (A Scientologist who had been in the movement from the early days remarked to me blandly, "People will run what they think is there.") Thus a vogue for certain incidents or a certain genre of incident would sweep through the group like a prairie fire producing astonishing results, then subside to be followed by another vogue, and so on. These vogues were the original "universal" incidents.

In putting all the ideas about Track into some workable format, Hubbard's first problems were those of verisimilitude. Anachronism presented one such difficulty. Pre-clears were not averse to interjecting tidbits from seventeenth-century Spain into the last days of Pompeii or automobile accidents into the Stone Age. "Space opera" and other science fiction materials showed up in prehuman (or pre-Earth) times, but then so did the seventeenth century again. Rather too obvious borrowing constituted another problem: books, movies, verbatim incidents from another pre-clear's Track. And lastly, there was a redundancy of famous figures from the past. Too many pre-clears wound up having been Julius Caesar and sometimes Brutus at the same time. It didn't wash. Several devices served to sort all these difficulties out. For one, it was posited that history proceeds in cycles or spirals, and that periods closely resembling periods of Earth history have occurred in earlier cycles. Thus one need not worry about running into a Roman centurion or a Chevy four-door thirty-four billion years ago. It is perfectly conceivable that a civilization existed thirty-four billion years ago (or whenever) that possessed such features.

Similarly, the space age, which contemporary humanity is just entering, has been entered and gone through many times before—science fiction writers are only "running Track" when they write their stories. The prevalence of famous past identities is explained, as I mentioned above, by the theory of valence (identity) shifting. A person will assume the identity of another, act with the other's mannerisms, spout the other's opinions, and so on, if he or she perceives this other as the "winner" in a situation where the self is a "loser." (This mechanism can be seen readily enough even in present-day life.) It follows that most of the pre-clears who discovered themselves to have been Julius Caesar or Genghis Khan were probably no more than soldiers in the great man's army, or more likely his victims. As to borrowing: thetans are fond of collecting pictures or "facsimiles" from all sources and are apt to borrow whole memory-banks from other Beings, just as they may "dub in" to their own real record extraneous bits that strike their fancy. The test of whether it's real or not is whether it "runs out"—brings a release. If it does, then some of it must be more or less accurate. With all these details taken care of, it was possible for pre-clears to run just about anything to a "release" without tripping over considerations of plausibility.

It bears emphasizing that a good deal of one's Time Track is one's own; it is left up to one's imagination, preconceptions, or what-have-you. Most Scientologists will get into Track in their first bout of Dianetic auditing. Here they discover that over the eons they have been many places—other planets, galaxies, universes—in many different bodies: female bodies, male bodies, plant or animal bodies, robot bodies, doll bodies, even stellar bodies. They have been shot, strangled, electrocuted, crushed, blown up, drowned, stabbed, and dismembered in any number of wars, earthquakes, lynchings, executions, murders, and accidents, and for any number of reasons. They may discover that some of the people they know today are Beings they have known in other lifetimes, usually lifetimes in which love, hate, envy, greed were more openly acknowledged and played out to more dramatic denouements. Any or all of such discoveries may be "charged" and emotionally fraught and, naturally, running them out is beneficial. It "chips away" at the Bank. However, the charge contained in this idiosyncratic material is held to be secondary to and derivative from the overwhelming charge contained in the "basic" universal incidents that Hubbard has discovered.

The universal incidents that are still considered important in contemporary Scientology are all revealed on the Confidential Levels; they are often spoken of as the core incidents of the Reactive Mind, the "glue" that holds the Bank together. But contrary to the expectation of many a Scientologist just entering the Confidential Levels, these incidents, with the exception of a scattering on the OT Sections, are not directly audited as incidents in the Dianetic style. They are simply described or alluded to in the bulletins and tapes. The effect is to convey a general sense of theta history and an appreciation of how it is that the central irrationalities of the human mind (the "aberrated stable data," the GPMs, and the rest) come to be so deeply embedded and hard to comprehend. These materials are presented in much the same sketchy, rambling manner that Hubbard presented the voguish incidents of early Dianetics days; and they repeat many of the same themes. Hubbard's early works, chiefly the book *A History of Man* (1961), a collection of universal incidents first published in 1951, and fragments of Confidential incidents that have appeared in print elsewhere (Malko 1970:113; Kaufman 1972:163) permit certain generalizations and characterizations.

In *A History of Man*, each universal incident is given its name and often a nickname or two as well: for instance, "Facsimile One," a.k.a. "The Halver" and "The Coffee-Grinder." This naming and nicknaming practice has continued, though it is not used consistently. Upon examination, a named incident usually turns out to be either a repeatedly occurring sort of event or a rambling schematic cluster of events and settings to which a great variety of subjective material can be easily fitted without one's quite losing the sense that the incident in question is nevertheless a defined thing. Here is part of "Fac One" from *A History of Man:*

FACSIMILE ONE: This incident is in everyone's bank, either as a second facsimile or as an original. Only in the latter case should it be run. It is called "Facsimile One" because it is the first proven-up whole track incident which, when audited out of a long series of people, was found to eradicate such things as asthma, sinus trouble, chronic chills and a host of other ills. It has a verbal content in most cases. It is quite varied when found as an original—for in this case, it happened to the preclear in the last ten or twenty thousand years. It was originally laid down in this Galaxy about one million years ago.

The "Coffee-grinder"[1] (which might be an alternative name for it) is levelled at the preclear and a push-pull wave is played over him, first on his left side, then on his right and back and forth from side to side, laying in a bone-deep somatic [physical sensation] which cannot be run unless you recognize it as a vibration, not the solid board it seems to be. When this treatment is done, the preclear is dumped in scalding water, then immediately in ice water. Then the preclear is put in a chair and whirled around. He was quite swollen after the pummelling of the waves and was generally kept in a badly run (but quite modern) hospital for a few days. Sometimes he was given several and after the first one would report back on schedule for the next.

FAC ONE was an outright control mechanism, invented to cut down rebel raids on invader installations. It was probably designed by the Fourth Invader and used by him in its original state and "ritual" for a considerable time. It gave him a nice, non-combative, religiously insane community. THE MOST IMPORTANT PART OF FAC ONE APPERTAINS TO ITS "SUMMONS TO COURT." This was a sick quiver installed in the stomach area by the "coffee-grinder" during the first part of the incident. The coffee-grinder laid in "baps" on the pineal and other points but almost knocked out the pineal potential forever and relegated its actions to the pituitary. It knocked in every other glandular point. And these same "baps" were used against the vagus nerve to give what everyone knows as an "anxiety stomach," uncontrolled bowel action, etc., etc. The invader wanted people to report when sent for. Thus the context (WHICH MUST NEVER BE DONE UNTIL THE EMOTION AND EFFORT ARE REDUCED) when the vagus area was "bapped" concentrates on getting the preclear to report quickly when summoned and makes him terrified of arrest, of courts, of other legal hocus pocus. . . . [Hubbard 1961:60–61]

1. The double-handled winch used to hoist the sail on a sailing vessel is called a "coffee-grinder." I think Hubbard had in mind a device like this.

[191]

Core incidents tend to have certain themes in common. The most prominent recurrent theme is that of enslavement and control. The whole event is the result of a devilish plot to reduce thetans to lower levels of ability and awareness so that they may be more easily manipulated. Included in the plot are devices that protect the incident from ever being discovered. Not only is the event "heavily occluded" by the pain and unconsciousness of its content, but its approaches are "mined" and "booby-trapped" so that careless searchers will not stumble upon it by accident. One asks then how Hubbard came to discover such incidents? Well—he claimed to have stumbled upon them by accident. Another, logically more pleasing, mystique also arose in Scientology to support Hubbard's authority. From a high-level Scientologist:

> You know Ron mentions in his journal how he had gone back and recon-
> tacted that crucial point in time when—when all those things happened.
> You know. Well, you know I think Ron Hubbard is the only man alive
> today who could have done that. That's because he was the only person
> who, at that point in the whole history of the whole she-bang, was in a
> position to *see* just what was going on. He was the only person who could
> relocate the critical moments and sort out what was going on and then
> relay it to people in this lifetime. You know I was back there then when
> all that was going on. But I wasn't in a position to understand the things
> he understood. . . . I think if Ron hadn't been the person he is—by that
> I mean if he hadn't fallen at that particular place that he did on the
> Track, he would never have been able to develop Scientology or figure
> out what was necessary to do the Clearing Course and the OT Sections.

Another theme in the incidents is the use of forces of great magnitude, especially electrical and nuclear energies, as we have seen in "Fac One." A recent news account of a formerly secret incident, for instance, tells of an evil ruler having thetans crammed into volcanoes and blown up with unusually powerful H-Bombs, after which the thetans were given "implants" (*Los Angeles Times*, November 5, 1985).[2] Hubbard conceived of electronics and nuclear force as con-

2. Scientology documents made public during the course of a lawsuit against the Church formed the basis of the *Los Angeles Times* report. It should be noted that a Church official has called the account "purposely distorted" and designed "to hold the church up to ridicule and contempt." (He would not specify the nature of the distortion.) (*Washington Post*, December 1, 1985.) I cite the incident here simply to indicate general thematic similarities between exoteric and esoteric collective track incidents.

stituting the secret of engrammic control. We shall see why at a later point. Such forces must, in addition, be prefaced by deceit. In an often quoted passage from *A History of Man*, Hubbard explains: "What does it take to aberrate a thetan? Thousands and thousands of volts, thousands of amperes, poured into destructive wavelengths and thrown straight into his face. What does it take to get him into a position where he can be aberrated? Trickery, treachery, lies" (1961:53).

Lastly, in the universal incidents, we find the return of the "engrammic command" familiar from early Dianetics. The incidents usually have verbal content. These core incidents are usually referred to as "implants" because the tremendous electronic/nuclear forces in them were used to render thetans helpless so that they could be implanted with verbal messages which, like posthypnotic suggestions, come to govern future behavior. The verbal content is critical in several ways. First of all, it is part of the protection that veils the incident from discovery. The thetan is implanted with commands that tell him to go away or forget and he acts on these whenever he comes close to the secrets of the Bank. Second, the verbal messages set up enduring mental contradictions.

The available information on the Clearing Course material (outlined above) suggests that the core structures of the Bank, the GPMs, are created by the engrammic implantation of false goals that go contrary to the original purposes of the thetan, thus giving rise to the classic double-bind. The contradictory nature of the Bank's core accounts for the fact that, according to Scientology theory, this core is in a state of "continuous restimulation." After all, if impulses are contradictory, one is always being punished for violating one while following the other. The only way out of the bind, ultimately, is auditing.

If from the Scientology perspective, Scientology practice is the only way "out of" the sort of dilemmas proposed by the Scientology view of the world, from the perspective of the present work Scientology practice is the principal way "into" a belief that these dilemmas are real and the assumptions underlying their portrayal valid. My argument must now turn to illustrating how participation in Scientology makes real for Scientologists the system of ideas just outlined, or, stated otherwise, how it is that Scientologists come to inhabit, as opposed to merely think about, the world that their doctrine asserts.

[7]

Inhabiting the Scientology World

To recapitulate, Scientology's central beliefs are (1) that one is a thetan, an immortal spirit with potentially limitless powers, (2) that one has a Bank (Reactive Mind), which suppresses one's ability to be "at cause" over Matter, Energy, Space and Time (either "real" or "mental"), which exercises "force and the power of command over one's awareness and purposes" (Hubbard 1964:30), and which causes one to act on a stimulus-response basis, and (3) that auditing can eliminate the Bank and restore thetans to their original powerful state.

The people who are attracted to Scientology like the sound of these assertions, else they would not be attracted. But few newcomers "believe" them in any profound way. Scientologists express the situation accurately by saying that these beliefs simply are not "real" to most people, even to those who find them intellectually appealing. True conviction, in Scientology terms, "certainty," must await the fitting of Scientology concepts to actual experience, and this fitting takes place gradually, and unevenly, over the course of continuing participation in Scientology practices.

The concern of this chapter is to show what sorts of experiences are fitted to which concepts, and how. I hope it will become clear that despite the technocratic and often unwieldy language in which they are phrased, Scientology concepts do render a fairly close account of the unusual experiential phenomena that come to the fore under the impact of a renunciatory discipline. Because of the theory's conceptual aptness, states of consciousness that are charged with immediacy and ineffable significance come to be conceptually crystallized into structures of meaning that support the Scientology world-view, and the practitioner comes to inhabit in an immediate and convincing way the unique world that Ron Hubbard predicated: a world shot through with the demented glamour of past-life traumata, of Olympian Beings battling for whole universes as their fiefdoms, of intergalactic confederacies and mind-blighting electronic forces; a world also reducible, at a deeper level, to mental states and impulses—"postulates," "prime intentions"; a world, ultimately, of will and idea. But more than simply capturing what is unusual in the mind in terms suggestive of an unusual reality, the conceptual apparatus of Scientology carefully grounds the bizarre and nonordinary in the mundane and common, such that the most ordinary experiences are transformed into further proof of the deeper vision, and the orientations that practitioners learn to adopt in the face of the extraordinary are routinely translated back into terms of everyday life.

To illustrate this interaction between psychological process and symbolic (conceptual) form, I will concentrate on the sorts of experiences enlisted to support the view that one is a thetan or "Being," that one has a Reactive Mind, or "Bank," and that a movement is possible out of the Bank and into states of untrammeled Beingness.

Certain generalizations are necessary before I begin this exposition. First, it should be stated that there is no absolutely typical path into the Scientology world-view. While it can be argued that "more and more" of Scientology becomes real to the practitioner as he or she advances up the auditing and training hierarchy, it would be precarious to assert that any specific piece of the belief system falls into place for a given individual before any other specific piece. Each participant brings to the practice a unique temperament, life situation, and personal history, and these greatly influence what he or she will find most interesting and most "real." Some newcomers arrive with an obvious sensitivity to the high-level insights that advanced Scientologists bandy around; while others, looking back, acknowledge that on their lower levels of auditing and training they largely missed the point. About the only generalizations that hold widely are that Scientology "reality" deepens with continued exposure and that periods of sustained, intense practice generate greater bursts of understanding than does practice undertaken at a more leisurely pace.

Scientologists are quite comfortable with the fact that different people have "different realities"; even advanced practitioners may concede that there are parts of the "data" that are still unreal to them. But the assumption is that these will all one day become real. There is a rule that one does not "invalidate" the reality of another or force upon him or her one's own reality. Thus a certain amount of divergence between Scientologists as to what each believes already, is prepared to believe, or secretly considers nonsense, is allowed to percolate along under the benign cover of mutual validation. The very safety from constant self-defense which this principled toleration ensures is itself a distinctive element of the Scientology experience.

It should not be thought, however, that the practitioner is allowed to be widely off base in his or her understanding of what the data mean. Gross misinterpretation (as well as other difficulties) usually shows up in the inability to audit properly or receive auditing. When misconstrual of the data is the problem suspected, the student or pre-clear is probed for his or her understanding of the various terms and concepts that appear in the session or on the training course. He or she may be asked to demonstrate a definition of a concept with clay figures or small objects. By listening to the definition elicited or observing the "clay demo," the instructor or auditor may be able to spot the "misunderstood" and correct it by referring the student or pre-clear to the appropriate definition or bulletin. The correction does not take the form of canceling the student's prior understanding as simply "wrong" and substituting a "right" one in its place; what usually turns out to be happening is that the misunderstander is saddled with an overly specific notion of what a concept means and must be guided to a higher level of abstraction that permits alternate interpretations. "Would you consider the possibility that it means something else as well?" or "Can you give me another example?" or "Show me where in the definition (or bulletin) it says that" are common corrective approaches. In this way the student or pre-clear is gently dislodged from the "reality" in which he or she is stuck without being required to abandon it outright. As a result, a Scientologist may entertain multiple, even contradictory, "realities" regarding the data, either successively or simultaneously, and yet feel that underlying them all is a unitary consistency.

This sense of an underlying unity amid disjunctive apprehensions is a dimension of Scientology experience difficult to convey in any sequential account of the process of growing belief, so let me make some notes upon it at this point. A number of factors contribute to this sense in addition to Scientology's diplomatic way of "correcting" a person's "reality." One factor, of course, is the pressure applied in all the practices to move away from or forgo one's intellectualizing efforts and let what happens happen. The gradual dismantling of organized, goal-directed thinking that results eventually causes all matters great and small to seem shot through with ineffable, multiple significances, even when in ordinary thinking gaps or contradictions may have appeared uppermost. Under such a perspective any particular Scientology concept will seem to generate all other Scientology concepts by some intrinsic principle. At the same time, this apparent "illusion of the mind" is not out of conformity with the actual intellectual organization of Scientology concepts. As I noted earlier, Scientology overglosses experience: the same experiential material may be approached from a number of perspectives, each complementing or bringing a broader meaning to bear upon the others. It is common for auditor-trainees, as they advance up the class levels, to have all their ideas and daily experiences be absorbed into the "data" of the particular level they are studying, only to discover that these same ideas and experiences become cross-hatched with yet further meanings on the next level. There is sufficient redundancy and abstractness in each set of concepts to allow for a rich fusion and interlocking.

> Eric, an Org staffer and auditor-trainee, said that one of the nice bits that he'd picked up from one of Ron's tapes is that all ARC breaks are the result of "bypassed charge." He said that on Class 3 you hear that all ARC breaks are the result of Missed Withholds, so that at first this didn't make sense to him. On Class 4, all of a sudden Hubbard is saying that all ARC breaks are the result of "bypassed charge." But looking at it, after all, what's a Missed Withhold? Why, a form of "bypassed charge," right? So it does all make sense.
>
> Farley, a Clear, who had been sitting there with us, said that the way he'd gotten it on the Solo and Clearing Courses was that ARC breaks stem from Misunderstoods and Generality. Eric nodded, said he'd heard that too. I asked, "What do you mean, 'Generality'?" Neither answered. I asked again. Eric said, "Well, it can all get very complicated, but it's really all very simple. You'll see when you get there."

It is relevant here to refer back to Deikman's article on expanded states of awareness. He points out that while the destructuring of the thought process through mystical practice will result in influxes of vast, ineffable knowledge, the same effect is achieved by a complex "vertical organization of concepts." If one were, he suggests, to combine all the intellectual vistas opened up by the reading of Gibbon's

Decline and Fall of the Roman Empire, Tolstoy's *War and Peace,* and Henderson's *The Fitness of the Environment,* "then the *vertical* inter-relationships of all these extensive schemata might, indeed, be beyond verbal expression, beyond ordinary conceptual capacities—in other words, they would approach the ineffable" (1969:41).

Just such a "vertical organization" of concepts, when brought about suddenly in a practitioner's consciousness, is a common component of Scientology "cognitions." This is exemplified in such insights as that of the pre-clear who "cognited" that "All the world is the result of an Overt—preceded of course by an ARC break!" The ease with which a rich fusion of concepts passes into a mystical gnosis, beyond conceptual thought, is illustrated in some truly high-level "cognitions" such as the one reported in the following Scientology testimonial:

> I was reading a sci-fi book by someone or other and it contained a statement about time that was pretty real, so I correlated it with the Scientology Axioms on time and obtained a viewpoint from which I AS-IS-ED the physical universe. It was like all at once there was only me, without limitations. [From testimonials distributed by AOLA]

"Cognitions" are not confined to the end phenomena of auditing sessions. Scientologists in training or just in living are constantly "aligning data" and exulting in new insights.

To add another dimension to the complexity of Scientology "reality," there are places, as we shall see below, where immediate conviction of the realness of one aspect of Scientology belief precludes, by its very nature, an immediate conviction of the realness of another aspect. Yet even here there is a regular logic in the fluctuation from one state to the next that provides a sense of unity. Lastly, it is of considerable significance for junior Scientologists—in regard to both their handling of discrepant "realities" and their fascination with the manifold ways of "aligning the data"—that the secret materials of the Confidential Levels are, indeed, secret. The uninitiated feel sure that all ambiguities will be clarified and all discordancies reconciled on the Confidential Levels. Whether or not each Scientologist, when the time comes for the revelation, is consummately satisfied by what he or she finds on the upper levels is a variable affair. Some are, some aren't. But the Confidential Levels, especially Solo and Clear, do, in fact, pull together into a tight package most of the strands of the data previously learned and simultaneously employ auditing methods that are more austere than most in their deintellectualizing thrust. If a person is still unsatisfied after "Clearing," there are always the OT Sections to come, and following these, the new levels that are continually being released. At some point, for everyone, all the data are bound to "align."

Without discounting individual variability in the stages of dawning belief nor the multiplicity of avenues through which the same central truths may be perceived, I will try in what follows to piece together a general portrait of how experiential reality feeds into the validation of Scientology concepts by organizing the more commonly reported experiences and the more frequently encountered interpretations into the sort of hypothetical continuum of awareness that Scientologists implicitly follow in trying to communicate their beliefs to others. That is, I will treat the newcomer to Scientology as if he or she does indeed have a "low reality" on the data, and the advanced Scientologist as if he or she has a "high reality"—even though in life discrepant examples can be found—and trace out a rough course from "low" to "high" accordingly.

Being and Bank: An Initial Orientation

Initial orientation to Scientology focuses upon the fact that the neophyte is a "Being" and that he or she has a "Bank." The average newcomer to Scientology usually has a better "reality" on having a Bank than on being a thetan, or so he or she will claim. He or she falls into spells of unhappiness that seem to exceed the apparent situation, feels unable to cope, is hurt or puzzled by the sometimes arbitrary behavior of others, and may have a nameless assortment of bodily complaints, little phobias, addictions and hysterias. Scientologists explain: "This is the Bank." That seems acceptable. It equates readily enough with a person's preconceptions about the unconscious mind, neurosis, and childhood traumata; and if some deep-lying irrationality is not obvious in one's own behavior, it is certainly clear enough in the behavior of others. The idea too that auditing will cause a time-hardened amnesia to lift, letting one relive some grisly moment of the past in a vivid, Hollywood-type flashback certainly fits the common cultural conceptions of psychotherapy. Further involvement and a deeper scrutiny will reveal, however, that the Bank is a far more complex and ambiguous construct than this initial, and largely intellectual, appre-

[199]

ciation of it would suggest. I am inclined to believe that in fact neophyte Scientologists have no better "reality" on the Bank than on the concept of being a thetan. It is only that the latter is less familiar intellectually or is easily confused with rather different concepts of soul and spirit.

For an initial grasp of thetanhood, the novice is referred to Hubbard's definitions and presented with illustrations.

> You are a thetan. You are not your mind, or your body, or your name. You are You. [Kaufman 1972:34]

> Thetan: The person himself—not his body or name, the physical universe, his mind, or anything else; that which is aware of being aware; the identity that is the individual. [Hubbard 1964]

> Newcomer: "I don't see it."
> Scientologist: "All right. Get a picture of a fish. Make a picture of a fish."
> Newcomer: "Yeah."
> Scientologist: "Good, Now where is that picture?"
> Newcomer: "In my mind [head, etc.]."
> Scientologist: "Good. Who's looking at that picture?"
> Newcomer: "Me [I am, etc.]."
> Scientologist: "O.K. The 'you' you say is looking is a thetan." [From my fieldnotes]

This is the common entering wedge. The question remains in some sense so what?, but at least the newcomer has acquired certain bearings. Scientologists are not speaking of some nebulous soul stuff that comes and goes beyond the periphery of direct consciousness, nor are they asking that one get in touch with one's heart or the pit of one's stomach. Instead, one is assured that the "Being" in question is the conscious experiencing self, regardless of what that self may be consciously experiencing. Thus centered, one may begin to look with a certain amount of detached curiosity at what one is, in fact, consciously experiencing. At the same time, one is, by corollary, instructed what to look at in others: not necessarily their faces (body), nor necessarily the meanings they are trying to convey through words and gestures (mind), but simply the awareness that lies behind their physical and symbolic gesticulation.

The distinction between awareness and its phenomenal objects establishes two routes into which experience comes to be channeled throughout one's Scientology involvement. The distinction is broken only at those moments of "release," when it is transcended. In the widest sense, the still center of awareness is the Being—the "static"; while the phenomenal objects of awareness, except for a purified nonmanipulative "flow" that passes between Beings, are in the widest sense MEST, hence Bank.

Beingness

A greater appreciation of oneself-as-thetan and the nature of Bank usually begins with the first TR–0 drill: the two-hour confront. The two-hour confront doesn't seem to demand much of a person. The practitioner is asked to do literally nothing except "be there" in the presence of another. But the difficulty of doing nothing only serves to highlight how much one customarily does do instead of simply "being there." For many a novice, the drill begins with a prolonged mental squirm. Said one:

> My first two-hour confront my partner was Clarence H. I thought he was kind of cute and I couldn't confront him at all. I cracked up through the whole thing. And I remembered somebody told me once if you don't want to look at somebody but still have it look like you're looking at them, then stare between their eyes. So I did that. It was so crazy. But I had to admit that I'd never looked at anyone. I thought I had, but I hadn't.

As the squirming subsides, it is often replaced by the subsequent pitfalls of drowsiness and fantasy. Becoming drowsy is called "going anaten" (from analytical attenuation); fantasy is referred to in terms of "pictures"—one goes off "into pictures," starts "putting out pictures," or "gets stuck in pictures." "Anaten" usually manifests itself fairly visibly—eyes roll or become glazed, eyelids droop. The student is "flunked" for these manifestations. Fantasying is usually not so obvious, and beginners may not be flunked for it at all. But advanced Scientologists can easily spot it. There will be an indication in the eyes or facial tone: an overly eager gleam, a subtle haze of removal, perhaps a twinge of disdain. Depending on how demanding they choose to be, more experienced Scientologists may flunk each other for "pictures." Even without the feedback provided by flunks, most students become aware of these phenomena and begin to appreciate the extent to which ordinary consciousness is given over to them.

The appreciation extends to others as well as the self. One develops a sharpened sense of where the other's attention is, where the other as a Being is located. "Flunk for backing away," or "Flunk for leaving the room" are not uncommon corrections. After practicing the training routines one evening, I wrote:

> When "bullbaiting" another student I flunked her for following the progress of the Course Supervisor across the room, even though in fact her eyes never left mine. She burst into amazement that I should have "read her mind." Looking back on it, I think the perception could probably be reduced to subtle variables in pupil dilation, focus and muscular tension; but at the time it simply seemed as though a shadow had passed across her eyes, a shadow that corresponded to the movements of the Course Supervisor.

Many experienced Scientologists report being able to "see" the contents of another person's "pictures" or to anticipate sudden shifts in the other's consciousness. "When I'm in good shape," one told me, "I can look right through a person's head and tell you exactly what he's going to do next."

This increased keenness of perception, Scientologists point out, is not merely a matter of learning what to look for. It is a matter of being able to "confront" what one sees. The essence of good "confront" is a willingness to allow whatever is happening to happen without letting one's subjectivity become embroiled in it. To the extent that one cannot permit what one sees to go on, one will avoid perceiving it; and to the extent that one is engaged in avoiding the perception ("nonconfronting") one is not really "there." "Being there," the fundamental of TR–0, revolves around the ability to "grant Beingness" to another. "Doing nothing" oneself must be realized as the counterpart of permitting anything (subjectively, at least) from the other.

> I asked Bart, "Do you after auditing someone come away with a changed opinion of the person?" Bart said, "Yes, always." I was surprised. "I mean like after you've audited someone and heard their Overts, do you sometimes think less of them?" "No," he said, "Quite often I'll think more of them. When you're auditing a person—to me at least—that's the only time I'm really seeing that person as he is. I'm really looking at the Being. Then what I see isn't the Overt, it's the strength of the Being,

the courage level he has to face up to his life." He went on: "Overts are just conduct. If you're auditing a person and all you're looking at is conduct, that person will never change. He'll never improve if you, the auditor, are evaluating conduct. What you're looking at when you audit a p-c is an awareness. As long as you look at the awareness and ignore the conduct, the awareness will change tremendously. Then when his awareness has changed, he can use that to change his conduct."

The growing ability to assume the viewpoint that persons, including oneself, are at a bottom simply "awareness units" and, in doing so, to abstract from all surface characteristics such as automatic gestures, facial expressions, squirms, flinches—in a word, conduct—gradually alters the experience of the interpersonal environment and causes a shift in the valuation of personal qualities and types of interpersonal encounter. For instance, persons who manifest a high degree of calm, clear-eyed alertness and who are relatively free of histrionics and defensiveness strike Scientologists as especially attractive; such individuals will be thought more promising as potential converts than will be others who, no matter what their success in life or social standing, are guarded or rigid, melodramatic or distractible, ponderous or shifty-eyed or exemplify any other qualities that represent fallings away from the Scientology standard of limpid, uncluttered self-expression. Likewise, certain modes of intimacy come to be valued over other more conventional modes, even others that have heretofore been found satisfying. Effusive sympathizing, stylized flirting, or the lavishment of flattery, in effect all the overdrawn emotional patterns with which people so easily identify and experience as their own, come to seem heavyhanded to the Scientology trainee who has learned to look for and value more rarefied forms of human contact. From a junior Scientologist:

> The other day I went to call on a client. It was a middle-aged woman who ran an antique shop. She was a talkative, very nervous person. Anyway, we talked for quite a while and at one point I had just finished saying something and I looked at her and she looked back and for just like a few seconds there was total communication between us. It was totally open [making a rotating motion with his hand as if something were circulating back and forth between him and his listener]. I wasn't doing anything. She wasn't doing anything. Neither of us was putting anything out. It was just complete . . . [rotating motion]. [Pause.] Now what *seemed* to be going on was that I had just finished saying something and was

waiting for her response—but that wasn't what was going on. There were just those few seconds—do you know what I mean? I'm sure she didn't know what had happened. I'm sure she just felt "Oh, he's a nice person to talk to"—because she then proceeded to go on for another hour! And before, I wouldn't have noticed it either, it's just now I have some awareness I'll see these things.

The reality of thetanhood is reinforced not only by the highlighting of these subtle but compelling features of human communication, but by appeal as well to those phenomena classified in the literature on consciousness alteration as "extrasensory" or "transpersonal" effects. Telepathic exchanges, telekinesic happenings, seeing at a distance— all are frequently reported and at the same time ardently sought. It does not matter that the experience is often minor; a glimpse is a promise. Of all these phenomena, the most emphasized is the out-of-body state, called in Scientology "exteriorization." The significance of exteriorization is obvious: if the experiencing self is not rooted in the body, then the existence of an autonomous spiritual self and the possiblity of emancipation from the whole MEST universe "game" logically follow. Hubbard battened onto exteriorization in 1951 when he began to develop Scientology, and the extreme rigor of many of the early "imaginative exercise" processes referred to earlier derives from the fact that the direct purpose of these processes was to produce an out-of-body state.

> The goal of this procedure is OPERATING THETAN, a higher goal than earlier procedures. . . . Have preclear close his eyes and find upper corners of the room. Have him sit there, not thinking, refusing to think of anything, interested only in the corners until he is completely exteriorized without strain. [Hubbard 1965:120, 121]

The early emphasis on producing the state diminished once it was found that exteriorization did not make a Being automatically "clear"; those who could do it still acted as "aberrated" as anyone else. Still, the ability to be exterior at will "with full perceptics" is retained as one of the desiderata of Scientology practice. Now its occurrence is left somewhat more to chance, but the quieting of mind and gradual numbing of body sensations that accompany the training routines or an extended (and successful) auditing session seem to be conducive to it.

Besides its overall importance in validating the reality of a separable spiritual identity, the concept of exteriorization occupies a strategic position in another sense. It acts to mute—if not exactly to reconcile—the conflict between two orientations present in the Scientology world: a "this-worldly" manipulative orientation that I will speak of as the "magical," and a more transcendant "world-rejecting" orientation that I will speak of as the "mystical." Under a magical posture, the separate reality predicated in the belief system is sought out with a view to putting its powers to use in the achievement of material and egoistic goals. Under a mystical orientation, by contrast, true experience of the separate reality and worldliness are seen as inherently opposed to one another and the latter must be overcome if the former is to be achieved. Reflecting the inveterate psychological tension between wish-fulfillment and renunciation, the conflict between magical and mystical tendencies puts in an appearance in virtually every known religious system; Scientology is no exception. Just like other traditions (or subtraditions), Scientology can be, all things added up, charged with favoring one of these tendencies over the other—in this case, the magical. But it would be an error to overrate this emphasis, for mysticism lurks beneath the surface of Scientology's magical promises and Hubbard showed, over the years, an ability to swing first in one direction, then in the other. Just so with individual Scientologists and their understanding of what is meant by the concept of exteriorization.

Examining the sorts of occurrences glossed as "exteriorization," one finds a cluster of these that are obviously charged with magical possibilities. The most glamorous form of exteriorization, though the one least frequently reported, is that of not only feeling that one is outside of one's body but of being able to look down upon the body itself. Often momentary, this experience is said by those who have had it to be so startling that often the immediate reaction is to "slam back" into the body ("interiorize") with considerable force, after which one feels rather dazed and bewildered. Second to this in allure is the experience of being a great distance away—in another country, perhaps— with body and current circumstances totally out of awareness. Clairvoyance is interpreted as an example of this. Occurrences of hypnagogic (presleep) exteriorizations are accepted as valid, although Scientologists will not allow that dreaming has anything to do with them, nor would they try to induce exteriorization by this method.[1] The fact

---

1. Manipulation of the half-waking, half-dreaming state has traditionally been the favored pastime of occultists interested in "astral walking." The trick seems to be to

that these forms of exteriorization may be accompanied by "unreal" effects, such as bizarre changes in the environment, should not, according to Hubbard, be grounds for "invalidating" them. He explained in an early work on the subject:

> It is . . . quite startling to a preclear to discover that as soon as he is free of . . . the body (which is to say, when he has discovered he can change his viewpoint) that he is already partly out of agreement with other viewpoints, and that the MEST universe becomes slightly jumbled. He is apt to be very anxious about this, for it is in conflict with the agreements to which he is subject. He immediately may struggle very hard to regain a state of affairs whereby he can view the MEST universe as everyone else views it. Indeed, the auditor must continually be on guard to prevent the preclear from attempting to re-assume these agreements. A badly-trained auditor can always be identified by the fact that he shares the preclear's anxiety that the preclear view the environment as the environment "should be." [1965:113–14]

While there is an undeniable logic to this argument, most Scientologists with whom I talked found "realistic" exteriorizations far more interesting than unrealistic ones, and many adhered to the idea that sufficient Scientology practice would restore to a person the ability to be not only exterior at will but realistically so—this is how they interpreted the phrase "with full perceptics." The idea of such a possibility is kept alive by tales of marvelous exteriorizations that go round Scientology social circles. During the period of my research, the flames of enthusiasm were fed by a rash of success stories (testimonials) from advanced Scientologists going through the Expanded OT III Section, such as the following:

> Last night I totally left my body. I sat looking at a beautiful sunrise over Japan. My perceptions were full. It's the most fantastic freedom I've ever had. Life is very very beautiful. So is Japan at sunrise.

> I can sit at my desk and *fully* experience the reality of any place, from ocean to snow capped Sierras. Always knowing who's calling on the

---

maintain intact enough of one's ordinary reality structures such that a consciousness of self is present and the dream circumstances take on a veridical multidimensional quality. Don Juan gave Castaneda useful instructions as to how this may be done (Castaneda 1972:126–27). For an extended account of the experiences of a man who acquired this ability spontaneously, see Monroe (1971).

phone before it rings, and being able to check the progress of my cooking hamburger without walking into the kitchen. [From testimonials distributed by AOLA]

These versions of exteriorization are fraught with a magical orientation, for they clearly suggest a greatly extended arena for one's worldly games. The Classification, Gradation and Awareness Chart reinforces this suggestion by promising that the result of OT IV will be "Ability to operate freely as a thetan exterior . . . , extends the influence of the thetan to the universe of others."

However, a rather different phenomenon is in fact the one most commonly reported as an instance of exteriorization.

> Tanya explained: "It doesn't mean [necessarily] that you go a distance away, or feel you're somewhere else. It can be a feeling of being very, very large, or occupying a lot of space. You walk into a room and feel that you fill the room with your Beingness. And I've seen people who do this; you do feel that they are filling the entire room. They're not located. They can be everywhere at once. When I first went Clear, I often felt immense. I could go outdoors and feel that I occupied the entire universe.

John McMaster, the world's first Clear, in some of his taped public lectures on Scientology described the phenomenon of exteriorization as simply an "expanded state." The manipulative potential of the expanded-state form of exteriorization does not stand out as it does in the case of out-of-body movements; in fact this less dramatic form of exteriorization tends to be regarded more as a value in itself than as a launching point for adventurous magical activities.

It is apparent from comparing this last characterization of exteriorization with the preceding ones that two axes of experience are being described. Though all the phenomena in question are indicative of alterations in ordinary consciousness, the "magical" forms of exteriorization seem to feature a distinct and partially self-conscious separation of self from body, and they occur along a gradient from the realistic to the bizarre and dreamlike. They are also subject to considerable variation in affective quality. Some occurrences, such as those appearing during psychotic episodes, accidents, or near-deaths, may be distinctly unpleasant and frightening. Scientologists speak of the latter as

examples of "forced exteriorization" and, while it is considered validation of the principle, forced exteriorization is not felt to be desirable as
an experience. Death itself is, of course, a "forced exteriorization," and
any forcing of the state through drugs, shock, or threat is liable to "key-
in" the "charge" on all one's past deaths. The other axis of exteriorization is characterized by a sense of expansion, an influx of energy into the
self, and a dissolution of the boundaries imposed by defensiveness and
self-image concerns. (Indeed, any great degree of self-consciousness is
anathema to all forms of exteriorization. Scientologists speak of persons
who in ordinary parlance would be called self-conscious as "heavily
interiorized.") These exteriorizations occur along a gradient from simple states of buoyancy, or, to put it more aptly, "expansiveness," all the
way to states of oneness-with-universe. There is no question of pleasant
vs. unpleasant, since they are always pleasant; and very little question
of "realism" for, while often unusual in the scope of the feeling, the
expanded states involve no peculiar alterations of the surrounding
world. Whereas the "distinct separation" form of exteriorization is
harder to achieve and occurs only sporadically in the TR drills and
auditing, the expansive form is essentially no different from the state of
release/relief/rejuvenation that comes as part of the end phenomena of
successful auditing.

By glossing all these phenomena as "exteriorization," Scientologists
manage on the one hand to tie the experience routinely, as opposed to
sporadically, to the auditing context; and on the other hand selectively
to translate the qualities of each state into the understanding of the
other. This last leads to a number of conclusions. First, being out of
one's body, with all the implications this has for marvelous feats and
tactical maneuvers, is assimilated to the state of relief, resolution, and
energy expansion customarily brought about by auditing; ergo, auditing is the route to magical powers and abilities. Expansion one day;
teleportation the next. The fact that psychotics can leave their bodies
without benefit of auditing or that famous mediums and clairvoyants
obviously have such powers through a quirk of fate is no reason for
discarding auditing as a vehicle. Famous psychics are considered val-
idly "OT," psychotics too are considered capable of exteriorization,
but the powers of these persons, while real, are accompanied by great
suffering. Peter Hurkos, the Danish clairvoyant, suffers immensely,
one Scientologist assured me. The reason for this, he explained, is that
the unaudited OT, while a more powerful Being than most of us, still
has the Bank, and if there is any condition that makes a Being more

vulnerable than usual to the ferocity of the Bank, it is being "exterior." Unprotected by body and MEST arrangements, a thetan can be seized and ripped to shreds by the forces in the Bank. That is why, according to Scientologists, most of us never venture out, and those who do so battle against tremendous odds. But once auditing has begun to reduce the Bank, things begin to get a little safer, and after a while a Being will begin to take quick "peeks" outside. Once the Bank is eradicated entirely, one should be quite free to roam about at will. For validation of this possibility, the practitioner need only compare the happy exteriorizations that occur in the safety of the auditing environment to the rather strained and frightening ones he or she may have undergone in the past on drug trips or during moments of threat or emotional upheaval.

A second consequence of aligning expanded with distinct separation states is that Scientologists can enjoy states that in other disciplines would be considered mystical union without threat to their concept of individual thetanhood. Occupying the entire universe is different from losing one's identity in it. Indeed, the emphasis in other spiritual disciplines upon merging with the cosmos provokes scorn from Scientologists. While recognizing obvious points of similarity between Scientology states and the experiences wrought by other practices, Scientologists see the latter as unfortunately benighted as to what is really going on, benighted because motivated toward the wrong goals. Since in Scientology the un-selfed state is transmogrified into a selfed state, it is obvious that the magical/manipulative motive retains the upper hand.

As well as indicating some of the ambiguities in Scientology motivation, discussions of exteriorization among Scientologists also serve to illustrate aspects of the relationship between a cultural gloss and the elusive experiential states to which it is applied. To a certain extent the various phenomena glossed as "exteriorization" in Scientology must be considered natural or spontaneously occurring perceptual syntheses. Out-of-body states and expanded "oceanic" states have been continuously rediscovered and articulated throughout history, a fact that supports the idea that these conditions arise as a function of the way our minds are built. As I have argued above, the process of cognitive dedifferentiation lays the groundwork for the appearance of these and other nonordinary perceptions. It would follow that a specific cultural emphasis is not an absolute precondition for the experience of such states; nor yet does the absence of cultural emphasis pose an insuperable barrier to articulating the experience. During the period of my research, I was surprised at the number of non-Scientologists (and nonoccultists) who, once the subject was introduced, furnished vivid recollections of out-of-body states they had experienced; their lack of a vocabulary for the experience at the time had not caused it to escape their notice.

Still it cannot be denied that an emphatic cultural construct may act to crystallize and channel subjective perceptual conditions even to the point of bringing into being the predicted experience. I collected several accounts from Scientologists whose first vivid "reality" on exteriorization was triggered by a suitably phrased explanation on the part of another Scientologist whose authority they especially trusted.

Leo rushed up to us when the coffee-hour was breaking up and said breathlessly, "I think I understand it now! Phil gave me a reality on exteriorization." [Phil was a new Clear, just returned from the Advanced Orgs.] We asked him to explain. He said he had complained to Phil that exteriorization was an idea he just hadn't been able to get and he asked Phil to help him out. "At first he put me off, you know, 'Oh each person's reality is different, my reality on that might not be the same as yours.' I get so impatient with hearing that line! I said, 'C'mon Phil, tell me what I should be looking for.' I prodded him, you know. So he said, 'O.K. See this picture here on the wall?' I did. He said, 'From what angle are you viewing it? Where are you located?' I said, 'Right here [gesturing], behind my eyes, y'know.' He said, 'Can you conceive of how this picture would look if you were viewing it from up there in the corner next to the ceiling?' That did it! I could do it! I found I could see the picture from that angle! All you do is change your viewpoint."

Miriam claims that the first time she exteriorized was at a lecture by John McMaster, not too long after she'd gotten into Scientology. She said, "John used to deliberately exteriorize his audience." On this occasion he'd said to the audience, "Come up here with me for a moment and look down on this planet. . . ." Miriam's reaction: "For an instant I was out there—way up!"

An unusually dramatic incident of exteriorization was reported by one Scientologist who, as auditor, had witnessed it, in fact helped to trigger it, in her pre-clear. This was Tanya, the Scientologist who is quoted above explaining to me that exteriorization may feel simply like an expanded state. She chose the following account to illustrate that the expanded state and the out-of-body state were essentially the same thing:

> She said she had one case when she was auditing in L.A. who exteriorized but "didn't have a reality" on it. "We couldn't go on auditing. He'd go into session, get a free needle [right away], then from then on the needle would just rise. Finally I sent him into Review, but I don't think they ran a Review on him. They just sent him back to me and told me to find out if he was exterior. So I sat him down with the cans—and I could just tell that he was! Just from his skin. His skin looked so bright . . . and the eyes—you can often tell when a person is exterior. So I asked, 'Are you exterior?' He said, well, no he didn't think so. He felt very good but he didn't think he was exterior. And we discussed what was meant by it, but he still didn't think he was. I could tell he just didn't have a reality on it. So I said, 'Can you conceive of a person being exterior to a degree?' Squirrel [unorthodox] question—but I had to do something to make him look at it. And he went, 'Oh!' just like this [she bends over quickly, hands to chest]. At that point, see, he felt it. He suddenly exteriorized so quickly and so hard he felt he had to hold onto his body."

The foregoing examples should not be taken to indicate that anything suggested by a concept will forthwith be fulfilled in experience. The possession of a specialized vocabulary of experience serves primarily to bring into focus and render recognizable conditions bearing a similarity in form to those predicated, not to trigger such conditions. Using the concept of exteriorization and accounts of it given by others, Scientologists involve themselves in very nuanced discussions of their perceptions, discussions in which they are perfectly capable of realizing that—for instance—the suggested condition has never befallen them, or that it did not impress them when it did, or that one but not another version of the experience is most familiar to them. Miriam, quoted above, continued her observations as follows:

> She added that she had only on three or four occasions had exteriorizations she was sure of. Part of the problem she finds is that it's something that happens when you're not self-consciously expecting it. The minute you get self-conscious and think Oh boy, here I go, that ruins it.
> I asked her didn't she hear people talk about traveling to distant places while exterior. She said she'd never had any really good chats with anyone about that, but of course she'd heard it mentioned. "I do remember on one occasion—this was during an extremely traumatic sec-

ondary while I was a child, that I was standing at least three feet in front of a blackboard; I was in front of the class and the blackboard was behind me off to the side, and yet while [the teacher was humiliating her] I remember backing into the blackboard."

I: "You didn't actually touch it physically, you mean?"

M: "No. I never touched it physically, but I remember feeling myself back into it. (Pause) So I know these sorts of things happen."

I: "I've had the experience of looking at something and it seemed a million miles away, if you know that one. . . ."

M: "Yes, well for me, the most common experience of that sort is simply feeling that I'm touching the things around me, in other words, that I'm bigger than the space occupied by my body, but still my body is the focal point."

I: "Well, that's what John McMaster described [on a taped lecture] as his main thing—feeling bigger than his body."

M: "I know. But I tend to negate this as an exteriorization experience. I mean, I know that's what it's called. But when I say exteriorization, I think of that time with John Mac when it was a matter of my identity, the thing I think of as my identity or sense of identity, being outside the body. It was me, as a consciousness, up there looking down on the planet."

I: "Isn't that what most people think of when they think of exteriorization?"

M: "Well, but there are all these gradations in between. I know that most people would call this being bigger than your body 'exteriorization.' And it *is*. But to me it's not particularly unusual."

There are certain corollaries to the idea of the separability of spirit from body that must be mentioned even though they do not, for Scientologists, elicit the high fascination that surrounds the personally experienced out-of-body state. One corollary is that one may, whether oneself exterior or not, have encounters with disembodied Beings. This appears to be a notion Hubbard used in the materials of the OT III Section, where one learns of the existence of "body thetans," the little alien Beings who have attached themselves to parts of the pre-clear's body. Advanced Scientologists I knew all claimed to have been surprised by the OT III materials. One reason for this may well be that the theme of traffic with invisible spirits who are relative or absolute strangers has never been much developed in Scientology lore and is not a line of particular interest to practitioners.[2] Scientologists

2. At least it wasn't during the time of my research. Recent (1986) OT Success Stories that feature encounters with disembodied beings (*Advance* 89:14) suggest that this interest has grown in the intervening years.

do report encounters with disembodied Beings, but these are over-whelmingly encounters with friends and acquaintances who are, for whatever reason, temporarily "exterior." The favorite occasion for such happenings is just after a close friend has gone Clear. Then the new Clear will be reported to have dropped in on friends and acquaintances all over the globe. Of course, people know which of their friends is on the Clearing Course, but there is no way of knowing the exact moment (or even the exact day) when he or she will complete it, since Clearing takes varying lengths of time for different people. Some Scientologists, when "visited," go so far as to wire or telephone the other party to confirm the meeting experience. No Clear, to my knowledge, has ever been so unkind as to deny it. New Clears themselves, or advanced Scientologists just completing an important OT Section, have sometimes reported meeting a disembodied Hubbard come to welcome them or receive their gratitude. The experience of meeting disembodied Scientologists is usually recounted as one of sensing an ineffable but familiar "presence" hovering nearby—in the case of Hubbard, a "big presence."

As to the deceased, these likewise are of little interest unless they are Scientologists or close relatives or friends of Scientologists. Admittedly, the world is teeming with bodiless thetans looking around for new bodies to "pick up" or just sulking in between lives. Occasionally, a Scientologist will bump into one of these in predictable haunts: old houses, attics, cellars, near ancient ruins or burial places. These Beings are apt to give out rather unpleasant, surly, or self-pitying emanations, and no one is particularly keen on communicating with them. For all the talk about freedom from MEST bondage and the desirability of the exterior state, Scientologists do not consider it healthy to be dead. For one thing, unless a Being is Clear, death is no release, for the thetan carries its Bank around from body to body. At bodily death, it simply reports automatically by virtue of Bank programming to a "between-lives station," there receives a fresh "forgetter implant," and is either assigned a new body not of its choosing or left to make do as best it can. (One such "between-lives station" is apparently surrounded by pearly gates—there's something to these old myths.) The best advice, then, to give to a disembodied non-Scientologist if it pesters you is, "Go pick up a new body and find out about Scientology." For Scientologists, there is a worldliness to the Scientology orientation that overrides any fantasies about freedom from the wheel of births and deaths. If a Scientologist "drops the body," that is, dies, he or she is expected to go forthwith and find a new body, but with the advantage—gained through Scientology training—that now he or she knows how to choose a comfortable situation for the next lifetime and may avoid the Bank traps that usually lie in wait for the deceased. The death of a Scientologist (or the close relative of a Scientologist) is usually the occasion for friends and relatives who are expecting babies to begin wondering whether the neonate will be the deceased. The more prominent and well-liked the deceased, the greater the number of new parents who begin to bruit their suspicions about their child's real identity. These "lamaist" tendencies are not, however, an official part of Scientology "data." Hubbard made no pronouncements on the subject. (As far as I can gather, too, Scientologists practice birth control and abortion with about the same regularity as the urban middle classes from which they derive.)

All things considered, Scientologists pay far more attention to their prior existences than to their future ones, and more attention to the brief separations from the body that they or their acquaintances may have experienced in the course of Scientology training than to the ghostly realm of the deceased. This is in keeping with the idea that before any future can be worthwhile, one must first recover one's "original" abilities, abilities that have become buried under eons of accumulatd Bank.

There is more to be said on the experience of thetanhood. We are reminded by the axioms that a thetan can "postulate" and "perceive" and by ALTER-IS-ING and agreement with others can "create MEST, all things that he isn't." But this aspect of theta abilities leads directly to the Bank, and it cannot be fully appreciated until we have looked at the latter.

The Bank

As I have said, the student, even as early as the first TR drills, begins to observe the extent to which ordinary consciousness seems to be in the possession of something other than the self. This is the first step in the objectification of mental phenomena, and this objectification is the key to appreciation of the Bank as "cause." In this appreciation, one finds all sorts of mental chatter, images, and ideas rolling along as things apart and heedless of the self's consent. There is an "automaticity" to it, Scientologists point out. Exercise in the subsequent TRs brings to light the same automaticity creeping into one's interactions with others.

Another manifestation of "mind" more pointedly illustrative of Bank shows up during bull-baiting. Why is it that some bull-bait gambits (and some coaches) break the student's "confront," while others do not?

> Miriam explained to me that if a phrase, or story or gesture produces any sort of response in the student that means the student has a "button" on the subject. It restimulates (even mildly) something in the Reactive Mind. She said, "For instance I might say to you 'Fat Lips!'" I laughed. "See," she said, "that pressed a button in you." I protested, "No, I just thought it was funny." She pointed out that many people don't laugh at the phrase "Fat Lips"—she's used it before. Often it provokes no response whatsoever. Another illustration came from Lottie, who said she once sat down with a fresh student, hadn't the faintest idea what to say to the girl, so just came out with, "So you want to be an auditor!" The girl burst into tears.

This illustration of Bank, while minuscule, picks up a theme which will run through all subsequent illustrations: that of spontaneous subjective involvement, or impulse—glossed in Scientology as "charge." Charge and its transform "mass" have already been explained in connection with the E-Meter; and in fact the feedback provided by the meter serves with even greater accuracy than TR "flunks" to establish these concepts in the practitioner's mind as specific subjective phenomena. Regardless of the method of demonstration, a significant expansion of the novice's "reality" on the Bank comes about when he or she observes that Bank manifestations are not necessarily unpleasant. Mass goes for the most part unnoticed by the uninitiated, or when noticed, as in cases of lethargy or woolly-headedness, is assigned an only mildly negative value. Mass may, on occasion, make its presence felt as a sort of peaceful slovenliness, not at all disagreeable in itself. Charge, as bull-bait flunks quickly demonstrate, is as apt to be a pleasant as an unpleasant sensation. It depends upon the context. Usually, impulse or arousal that readily "grounds out" through some acceptable route will be experienced as pleasant; that which does not as neutral or unpleasant. The lesson learned in bull-baiting is that either way, it is still charge and thus still Reactive. Later one learns to consider the pleasant manifestations as "charge coming off" or "discharging." While discharge is positively valued, it nevertheless involves a component of the Bank—charge.

Thus it becomes apparent that the Bank encompasses far more than the newcomer typically imagines. Seemingly innocuous habitual responses are part of its machinery. Their origins in the Bank explain the tendency for habits ("automaticity") to degenerate easily into addiction and dependency. The seductive indulgence in erotic or egotistical daydreaming turns out likewise to "key-in" Bank—how else to account for the insidious grogginess and guilt so often associated with fantasy? As to the pleasures or expediency involved, Scientologists explain "How do you suppose we got into this trap in the first place?" The answer: pleasure or expediency.

The neophyte appreciates the dulling oppressiveness of compulsive mental workings all the more once some practice in Scientology has provoked and simultaneously outlined for him or her that special level of crisp, clear-headed alertness that Scientologists call "key-out." To many, it presents a startling contrast to their customary psychic state. This optimum state of mind is spoken of as "being completely in present time," completely "there." In this condition, habitual thought processes drop away; the immediate world is fresher, more alive. One Scientologist described the state as one of bell-like clarity; another, neatly combining in his image the idea of a thetan's individual distinctiveness, compared the desirable state to a single clear note struck on a piano. Ultimately, any departure from this state comes to be viewed as an insidious form of Bank.

Leo sat down today for coffee and said, "Boy, I want to be Clear. You know how you and Miriam were talking about when you go Clear you can go for days without thinking. I want that. It really struck me today. I went up to call on a client and he had a beautiful house up on the hill with a view overlooking Malibu Canyon. Anyway, I was waiting for him to answer the door and I noticed the view, but it didn't make much difference to me. Like wow, when I first got out here [to Los Angeles] I would've thought, 'My God, is that gorgeous and exciting and isn't it glamorous and marvelous out here.' But today I just thought, you know, 'It's nice,' but I wanted to go back to what I was thinking about. It was like there was a little cloud in between me and the view. And I really 'cognited' like now I understand the difference between what it's like when you don't have that cloud there and what it's like when you do. I realize I missed that experience. I wasn't just 'there,' right there, with the beauty in front of me. I had a 'machine' there, an 'automaticity' there saying 'Oh yes, doesn't he have a nice view.' But *I* wasn't there. And I wanted to be there and really enjoy it. I don't want this 'thinkingness' around."

While it may take some time for the dimensions of the Bank in oneself to become fully evident, awareness of its presence in others develops fairly rapidly from the start. What could be plainer, once one's attention is called to it, than the fact that in most day-to-day interactions one's interlocutor is not really "there"? He or she listens with half an ear, grunts automatic acknowledgments if acknowledging at all, snaps out standardized opinions in reaction to appropriate buzz-words, seizes every opportunity to "make self right and others wrong," and scatters the focus of the interaction with little avoidances or attention-getting maneuvers. If any of these typical Bank emanations were at one time found cute or appealing by a Scientology convert, the charm soon palls. Spoiled, as it were, by the high quality of attention he or she receives from Scientology acquaintances and relieved of the need for constant defensiveness in personal interactions, the newly aware Scientologist will often react to perceived Bank in others with impatience or even righteous contempt. Old (pre-Scientology) relationships tend to suffer as a result. "I got fed up with his Bankiness," or, "I found I didn't need to be around all that Bank all the time," are commonly heard justifications for terminating a problematic friendship or a strained marriage.

Ideally, one should learn to "handle" Bank in others, using Scientology wisdom to locate the source of an irrational reaction, and the TRs to disarm it. Often exercise of this knowledge and these skills proves sufficiently challenging that Scientologists will actually enjoy working their way through encounters that previously would have been occasions only for defeat and discouragement. The sense of confidence bred by success in such encounters may result in a certain playful detachment in interpersonal negotiations. "Wow, you did that well," exclaimed one Scientologist after an acquaintance had curtly changed the subject on him, "I'd like to see that again,"— and he reintroduced the subject. Another explained to me that he watches Banky behavior in others as one would a fine stage performance. Beings are remarkably artful in their "dramatizations" he pointed out, and as a result, the social world has become for him an endless source of entertainment.

But there is an understanding in Scientology that the Bank in others

[217]

tends to key-in the Bank in oneself, and that having to deal chronically with this sort of "restimulative" behavior can be a hazard to one's spiritual and even physical health. If it is found that the troublesome party refuses to take responsibility for his or her "case" or remains unmoved by the Scientologist's attempts to improve the relationship, especially if it is found that being around this person repeatedly causes a deterioration in one's own state of mind, then it is considered better to reduce contact or cease it altogether than to go on engaging in futile heroics.

Particularly to be avoided is the "suppressive person." This is the individual who, despite pretensions to the contrary, is simply unable to tolerate another's happiness and good fortune, another's attempts at self-betterment, another's participation in idealistic causes—such as Scientology. Acting unconsciously out of "deep implants" in the Bank, the suppressive will always find ways, often subtle ways, to upset and undermine those around him. A type of Bank activity characteristically spotted in others rather than in oneself, suppressiveness is nevertheless not an invariably obvious manifestation of Bank; it may take one a while to acquire a "reality" on it; but of course, for this reason, it is all the more dangerous.

Hubbard provides us with a detailed portrait of the suppressive, also called the "anti-social personality."

1. He or she speaks only in very broad generalities. "They say . . ." "Everybody thinks . . ." "Everyone knows . . ." and such expressions are in continual use, particularly when imparting rumor. When asked "*Who* is everybody . . ." it normally turns out to be one source and from this source the anti-social person has manufactured what he or she pretends is the whole opinion of the whole society. . . .

2. Such a person deals mainly in bad news, critical or hostile remarks, invalidation and general suppression, . . . It is notable that there is no good news or complimentary remark passed on by such a person.

3. The anti-social personality alters, to worsen, communication when he or she relays a message or news. Good news is stopped and only bad news, often embellished, is passed along. Such a person also pretends to pass on "bad news" which is in actual fact invented.

4. A characteristic, and one of the sad things about an anti-social personality, is that it does not respond to treatment or reform or psychotherapy.

5. Surrounding such a personality we find cowed or ill associates or friends who, when not driven actually insane, are yet behaving in a crippled manner in life, failing, not succeeding. . . . When treated or educated, the near associate of the anti-social personality has no stability of gain but promptly relapses or loses his advantages of knowledge, being under the suppressive influence of the other. . . . Unjustly we seldom see the anti-social personality actually in an institution. Only his "friends" and family are there.

6. The anti-social personality habitually selects the wrong target. If a tyre is flat from driving over nails, he or she curses a companion or a non-causative source of the trouble. If the radio next door is too loud, he or she kicks the cat. . . .

7. The anti-social cannot finish a cycle of action. Such become surrounded with incomplete projects.

8. Many anti-social persons will freely confess to the most alarming crimes when forced to do so, but will have no faintest sense of responsibility for them. Their actions have little or nothing to do with their own volition. Things "just happened." They have no sense of correct causation and particularly cannot feel any sense of remorse or shame therefore.

9. The anti-social personality supports only destructive groups and rages against and attacks any constructive or betterment group.

10. This type of personality approves only of destructive actions and fights against constructive or helpful actions or activities. The artist in particular is often found as a magnet for persons with anti-social personalities who see in his art something which must be destroyed and covertly, "as a friend," proceed to try.

11. Helping others is an activity which drives the anti-social personality nearly beserk. Activities, however, which destroy in the name of help are closely supported.

12. The anti-social personality has a bad sense of property and conceives that the idea that anyone owns anything is a pretense, made up to fool people. Nothing is ever really owned. [Hubbard 1968a: 10–12]

Hubbard added chillingly, "The bulk of such people exhibit no outward signs of insanity. They appear quite rational. They can be *very* convincing" (1968a:13).

Lest one be tempted to apply this concept too indiscriminately, Hubbard cautioned, a person's apparently suppressive traits should be weighed against his or her opposite, positive traits, and the diagnosis of "suppressive" considered only when the bad outweighs the good.

Furthermore if one happens to see in oneself certain suppressive traits, this indicates a capacity for self-criticism unknown to the true suppressive and renders it unlikely that one is of this personality type. (Suppressives can, however, also be groups and organizations.)

A brief digression into the policy of the Church of Scientology in regard to suppressives is necessary to make plain how this manifestation of Bank acquires a reality for individual practitioners. Hubbard considered it "important to be able to detect and isolate this personality type so as to protect society and individuals from the destructive consequences" (1968a:9). In practice what is sought is the protection not so much of the general public but of the Scientology movement and, subsidiarily, its individual members, from certain perils to which they are prey.

In the case of individual Scientologists, the typical peril attributed to the influence of a suppressive person is a chronic "relapsing" after therapeutic gains (see item 5, above). A practitioner whose ailments and symptoms clear up after auditing or training but then reappear later on, or who experiences wide swings, from positive to negative, in mood, commitment, and outlook, a pattern called "roller-coastering" in Scientology, will eventually be suspected of being "connected" to a suppressive person. It is the suppressive who, through invalidation of the individual and his or her beliefs, undercuts each gain and acts as a brake against further psychological progress. The test of whether this is or is not the situation consists of asking the troubled Scientologist, in a metered auditing procedure, "Who or what is suppressing you?" The answer indicated by the appropriate needle reads and coinciding with the pre-clear's subjective sense of its rightness is accepted as the correct answer no matter who or what is named. In this situation, however, no collective action is taken against the offending party. The Church confines itself to requiring that the troubled practitioner "handle" the situation, or, if this proves impossible, "disconnect" from the suppressive influence. It is not even concluded that the named "suppressor" is necessarily possessed of the pernicious personality syndrome Hubbard described, only that this particular pre-clear is experiencing him or her (or it) as suppressive. Understandably, however, the troubled Scientologist will, with this reinforcement from Church policy, often begin to view a person whom some sixth sense has inspired him to blame for his troubles as of this personality type whether or not the person in question possesses most (or any) of the

[220]

listed attributes. The suppressive person syndrome thus becomes a "deep structure" informing the practitioner's anxious examination of the surface characteristics of those around him.

The same principle operates when the Church of Scientology, reacting to a perceived threat to Scientology itself, officially "declares" a person or group suppressive. As a matter of policy, such declarations proceed not from personality assessment but from examination of evidence showing that the actions of a person or group have resulted (or easily could result) in a detriment to Scientology. High on the list of great suppressives in Scientology's collective vision are outside individuals and agencies in public life that have at one time or another proved damaging to Scientology. Specific politicians, journalists, medical and psychiatric professionals, judges and so on, and specific agencies and associations (for example, the AMA, the FDA, the NIMH, the NAMH, the British and Australian Parliaments) that have attempted to discredit Hubbard and his works or to erect legal or financial barriers to the spread of the Church, have been, at various points, officially declared suppressive. More ominous from the standpoint of daily life in the Scientology world are the suppressives who rise up from within the group itself. Scientologists who publicly reject or speak out against the movement, the ideas, or Hubbard, who misuse or alter Scientology "data," who are implicated in serious bureaucratic mismanagement or violations of Church policy, who embezzle funds or steal materials, who become affiliated with an already labeled suppressive person or group, or who attempt to establish competing doctrines utilizing Scientology ideas and appealing to the Scientology membership, will be—if a review of evidence by a specially appointed committee establishes their guilt—"declared."

To be "declared" in Scientology is roughly equivalent to being excommunicated and anathematized. The Scientology credentials of declared persons are taken from them, and Scientologists and Scientology establishments in good standing are forbidden any further dealings with them. Until 1968, when the policies in question were officially canceled in response to mounting public criticism, suppressives originating within the movement were treated to a barrage of official "disconnect" letters from their Scientology friends and acquaintances, and suppressive persons and groups of whatever origin were proclaimed "fair game." This meant "without right for self, possessions or position, and no Scientologist may be brought before a Committee of

Evidence or punished for any action taken against a Suppressive Person or Group during the period that person or group is 'fair game'" (Hubbard 1968a:48). The Church of Scientology has denied that this statement constituted an endorsement of illegal actions against "declared" persons and groups (Wallis 1976:144). Denials notwithstanding, Scientology had by 1968 acquired a reputation, derived from numerous allegations and circumstantial evidence, for the use of "dirty tricks" against its opponents. This reputation was in no way ameliorated in the years following; allegations of harassment, spying, and defamation of character by Scientology personnel continued to surface. Whether the majority of these can be fairly charged to Church policy is a matter of dispute (see Wallis 1976:152–53, 217–21), but the point here is that anyone within Scientology who found himself declared suppressive would consider his situation against the backdrop of these rumors and allegations. Not only feeling at risk of substantive harm at the hands of former associates, and bereft as well of the psychological and social benefits of movement participation, the "declared" Scientologist is also abundantly conscious of the fact that his or her every past and future action, indeed his or her entire character, is now subject to a malevolent reinterpretation. Did he or she seem at one point to be a "beautiful Being" who enjoyed "high levels of awareness"? Ah, yes, but these people "can be *very* convincing." Was not his or her commitment to Scientology, enthusiastic dissemination of the doctrine, or tireless performance of staff duties sufficient evidence of a desire to support "constructive action and causes"? Perhaps, but it must be remembered that covertly destroying *in the name of help* is the specialty of the suppressive person. Such people may smile and smile and yet be villains.

It seems fair to say then that Hubbard's portrait of the anti-social personality, detailed above, functions not so much as a practical guideline for the "detection and isolation" of persons whom the portrait happens to fit, but as an "ideal type," or stereotype, which psychologically galvanizes a process of detection and isolation that proceeds along rather different lines and even against persons whom the portrait does not, on the surface, fit. Though seemingly derived from outward, observable characteristics, in practice the concept more often serves as a hypothesis about hidden structures of character and mentality and as such provides a logical connection between the real, observable, setbacks that Scientology (or the individual practitioner) suffers at the hands of rational-seeming others and the thing that for Scientologists is the hidden ground of evil and suffering in the world: the Bank.[3]

One last detail of Scientology policy regarding suppressives must be mentioned as affecting Scientologists' understanding of these people. Not all declared Scientologists remain declared forever. The ban may be removed. From time to time Hubbard, in an expansive mood, issued amnesties, and during the period of an amnesty those who have been at some point in the past "declared" (as well as others who, though never officially declared, left the movement under a cloud) may petition for readmittance. If in retrospect their crimes are judged not too serious or if, as has sometimes happened, the charges against them are determined to have been false or exaggerated, they will be welcomed aboard once again. Some are required to work their way through various penalties, and it is my understanding that former staffers are seldom reinstated in their old positions; nevertheless, re-entry into the movement is possible. Even Hubbard's statement that suppressives do not respond to treatment or reform or psychotherapy has proved amenable to modification: I was told that suppressive tendencies can be vanquished by certain newly devised higher-level auditing processes. Thus it may come about that individuals who some months or years back left the Church in disgrace reappear one day among their old comrades.

If we consider that the notion of the suppressive attaches to and disattaches from persons primarily as a function of their relationships to Scientology (or an affected individual) and only secondarily and inconsistently as a function of their overall character pattern, and consider as well that one's perception of another's relationship to a group or person varies with one's own relation to that group or person,

---

3. The functional parallels between the Scientology notion of the suppressive and the notion of the witch in premodern societies will occur to the anthropological reader. But just as it is necessary to bear in mind that a paranoid person may indeed be an object of persecution, so it is necessary to bear in mind that a group with a "witchcraft" concept may indeed be the object of hostilities from internal and external sources. Opposition to Scientology (or aspects of it) has frequently erupted in its host societies and within the group itself. As Roy Wallis points out, this opposition has at times taken on an undeniably hysterical edge (1976:ch. 7)—a phenomenon supportive of the Scientology view that the suppressive is driven by irrational urges. The Church of Scientology aims its label "suppressive" for the most part at these real, if conceptually overdrawn, opponents, not at random innocents, although innocents are sometimes mistakenly charged. Where distortion enters is in the Church's overreaction to threat and its unwillingness to examine its role in provoking or exacerbating hostile reactions. Conflicts, rather than being defused, are often escalated.

we will not find it surprising that the experiential reality which shapes itself in the minds of individual Scientologists with regard to the notion of suppressive is subject to considerable variation from situation to situation and from Scientologist to Scientologist.

Obviously, the suppressive is an image of radical personal evil that can be embraced, is even, one might say, "designed" to be embraced, with paranoid intensity. Not surprisingly, this will happen primarily in situations that are conducive to paranoia anyway. It was my impression that staff Scientologists are more wont to have such intensified perceptions than lay Scientologists and, of that group, those who have them most often are people whose position requires constant alertness to and dealings with hostile or alienated parties: Ethics Officers (the organization's disciplinary wing), Sea Org personnel, the staff of the Guardian's Office. The few officials of this sort with whom I had encounters (I knew none well) could literally vibrate with outrage when the subject of suppressives came up, as it almost invariably did with them. It must be borne in mind that people willing to occupy these social and group defense positions in the organization are often more utopian in their commitment than the average Scientologist, thus less inclined to understand the difficulties that beset Scientology in any terms other than that a radical and preternatural evil is operating in the world.

Another category vulnerable to a heightened sense of the suppressive power of others are the practitioners who have got themselves into a protracted personal conflict with the Church itself, who are clinging still to their hopes but teetering on the brink of alienation. Paranoia expresses the helplessness of such persons in the face of what is indeed a serious threat to their personal meaning system. Ironically, from the viewpoint of the Church, it has typically been Hubbard, the Sea Org, or Church representatives of one sort or another who come into focus for these individuals as the source of radical evil. Ironically for these individuals, they are themselves likely targets for the label "suppressive" as their alienation begins after a while to register in their behavior, calling negative attention to them.

Among practitioners not immediately involved in these sorts of stressful situations, a more complex and distanced view of suppressives tends to prevail. Some find the idea a useful hypothesis for explaining the unpleasantness of relationships they have suffered through in the past, but inasmuch as Scientology has taught them to detach themselves from oppressive or debilitating associates their fear of psychological harm from others is accordingly lessened and with it the power of the image itself. Scientologists with long experience in the movement who have witnessed trigger-happy applications of the charge during in-group power struggles, who have seen friends or respected associates declared or been themselves nearly declared, may develop—if they remain in Scientology—a cynical humor regarding the notion of suppressives. "Oh heavens, some of my best friends are suppressive," chirped one who nonethless loved Scientology and was not about to be daunted by Church politics. Another, having heard the news that I had been asked to leave Scientology because of my connection to the NIMH (a suppressive group), greeted me upon our next meeting with a cheery, "Hi there, you old suppressive, you!" This hardy attitude does not necessarily indicate a rejection of the concept so much as a weariness with what is, in the minds of these Scientologists, the incompetent application of it.

Bank and Being Intensified

The contrast between the deep, immediate, and paranoiac appreciation of suppressive influences in the environment and the more distanced understanding of this concept that usually obtains among practitioners not caught up in stressful group situations raises an important issue with regard to the experiential realities of Being and Bank in general. This is that the states of mind supportive of these two dimensions of the Scientology world-view are by their nature incompatible. They are states between which the psyche will alternate rather than ones admitting of simultaneous appreciation. It is especially the case that the more intense the experience of the one dimension of reality, the more the experience of the other will be obliterated from consciousness and from recall.

Scientology theory recognizes, indeed emphasizes, this incompatibility. One cannot be "keyed-out" and "keyed-in" both at the same time; Bank and Being are mutually exclusive, and the more one is under the sway of the one reality the less one is accessible to its opposite. Consider for instance the Scientological understanding of psychosis. Your common-garden-variety psychosis, according to Scientology theory, is merely an extreme form of "key-in"; it is a condition in which the Being is "spun into" the Bank and "overwhelmed" by it. In fact, because the psychotic is in such close touch with the

[225]

Bank as a causative force, he or she has the greatest "reality" on the nature of it, in particular the nature of its "core"—those electronic implants.

> It may occur to the auditor that some of these [universal] incidents . . . are very reminiscent of the material which is commonly found among the insane in sanatoria. These people are quite given to chattering about fields and secret waves and telepathy and things being after them with electronic devices. . . . In a brilliant flash of insight someday those in charge of sanatoria may see that the reason the insane chatter about electronics is that electronics are peculiarly adapted to tailor-making insanity and that electronics have been used for unthinkably long times to handle and control beings. Electronics alone can make a truly slave society. [Hubbard 1961:51–52]

However, to have this deep a reality on the Bank, one must have in the larger Scientology perspective a very "low level of awareness," for by definition to be psychotic is to be completely other-determined, completely overwhelmed by the creation one has forgotten one ever created. To give the Bank this much "reality," this much "solidity," is to identify oneself as a very deteriorated thetan indeed. A Being in this condition, it is reasoned, could hardly be expected to respond to the notion that the assaults on his psyche are, at a deep level, self-authored. The very ability to have such an awareness is contingent upon a keyed-out state, a state in which it is possible to regard those things previously felt to be one's worst problems as mere figments of thetan playfulness.

It would follow from these observations that Scientology would not have its practitioners cultivate deeper appreciations of the Bank, however much this might validate the concept of it that Scientology proposes. For that matter, no psychotherapy or religion deliberately aims at casting its adherents into the state of damnation from which it promises to deliver them, and yet, paradoxically, it must have these adherents believe that the state of damnation is real.

In Scientology, it is hoped that the practitioners' greater understanding of the Bank will be achieved through the careful and selective "restimulation" of it that takes place within the safe confines of the auditing session, through the reinterpretation of past unpleasant experiences in light of Scientology theory, and through the connections that Scientology lore encourages one to make between Bank and

[226]

some of life's minor nuisances such as tension, mental dullness, or distraction. A psychotic episode, even a fairly heavy upset, is greatly to be deplored. Moreover, Scientologists are made aware that the condition of "overwhelm," that is, excessive restimulation of the Bank, renders one for the time inauditable—thus beyond the reach of Scientology help. The Bank is something that can be vanquished only if one goes after it a little bit at a time, on a "gentle gradient," as Hubbard prescribed.

Aware of these teachings and concerned as well to present themselves to the world (and to each other) as spiritually upbeat, the happy products of Scientology technology, Scientologists strive to avoid unpleasant mental states. In doing so, they rely heavily upon the device, learned early on, of objectifying mental phenomena—objectifying and, if possible, categorizing. "I seem to have a button on that subject," a Scientologist might remark, adding unconcernedly, "Something hasn't been 'flattened,'" or, "My TA is high today, I can feel it." By isolating and conceptually bracketing a problematic reaction, they often succeed in arresting its further development. Some report quite heroic successes along these lines:

[From a conversation between two advanced Scientologists]
Sammy: I had one experience that did a lot for my reality on how it is you make your own universe, d'ya know what I mean? Like, I was drugged last spring. I dunno, somebody put something in my drink. I don't know who it was, anyway, whatever the drug was it was hallucinogenic. And I got very high. Whew (shaking head), it was getting worse . . . the things I was seeing, seeing in my environment and in other people: bad. Then suddenly I thought to myself *I'm putting* it there! Everything that I was seeing I was putting there myself, it was like it didn't have to be there, y'know. Well, wham! (snap of fingers) The minute I realized that, I was *so* straight. Completely. And from then on the drug had no effect on me. Like to start with I was letting myself be the effect of the drug, and then, whip! I was cause.
Louise: (nodding vigorously) Right! Well, on a somewhat lesser scale, I'll tell you something that happened to me and Bart. [She then described the preparations she'd made for last Thanksgiving dinner when another Scientology couple was expected.] The couple I'd invited, I told them, you two are spending the night because by the time I'm through with you you won't be able to drive home. I'm gonna get you plastered. Then I mixed up these Mai Tais. . . . Bart had one to start with while I was fixing dinner. Then we both had one. So we were on number three when the [couple] showed up; then we all drank one together. And they were

[227]

strong, see. Well, all of a sudden I looked over at Bart and said, "Adelson, you're drunk!" Hah, he'd just slurred his speech, and he was looking sort of bleary-eyed. Well, he thought for a minute and then said (imitating a slight buzz), "I'm not drunk. The body is drunk." And with that we all looked around and had the same realization. *We* weren't drunk, our bodies were. And like that, sober—everyone of us. Henh, I said, "Screw it. From now on you folks fix your own drinks; I'm giving up on you."

But sometimes this sort of conceptual control of a reaction is not possible; and at any rate lower-level Scientologists are not expected to be very skilled at it. Too often a practitioner who tries outside of an auditing session to effect some resolving Scientology insight into a problem bogs down instead in obsessional thinking, called in Scientology "figure-figure." Figure-figures lead nowhere. Thus many will advise that until one can get some auditing it is best simply to "park your case," that is, refuse to think about or become involved in a troubled state of mind. Since it is expected that auditing will eventually clear everything up, the frustration of not having one's distress allayed immediately is more easily borne. Scientologists learn to forgo emotional self-indulgence.

In contrast to vivid appreciations of Bank reality, Scientology does, needless to say, encourage the cultivation of vivid and dramatic experiences of Beingness: heightened sensations of well-being, omnipotence, and intuitive knowledge. But one can predict a problem in this regard: the alterations in consciousness that make possible a heightening of pleasant states also make possible the heightening of unpleasant states. Just as one may in ordinary consciousness experience alternations between pleasant and unpleasant sensations and perceptions, so too in extraordinary states of consciousness one may experience such alternations, with the difference being that in extraordinary states these sensations are amplified.

This factor is variably recognized and exploited in different traditions. In Christian mysticism and in Zen, it is noted that increased spiritual sensitivity heightens one's vulnerability to morbid states and malevolent influences at the same time that it makes possible enlightenment and illumination. In both these traditions, great increases in spiritual awareness with their attendant risks as well as rewards are associated, as might be expected, with deepening and intensification of practice (Underhill 1967:383; Kapleau 1967:88–89, 192–204).

In contemporary Western traditions, more qualified understandings of the relationship between positive and negative expanded states of awareness have arisen. In the drug subculture of the 1960s, for instance, an assumption developed that the general thrust of an acid trip would be positive unless deviant factors in the tripper's environment turned it sour. In most Western psychotherapies it is assumed as well that the effects of practice are beneficial, with the qualification that these effects are ranged against formidable defenses within the psyche that can be expected at times to rise up against the positive trend of the discipline, making progress painful and frightening. In its own terms, Scientology reponds to both these theoretical impulses.

The major Scientological assumption is akin to that of the acid subculture: any linkage between intensified realities of "Beingness" and intensified realities of "Bank" is viewed as avoidable. Specific reasons outside of simple, correct practice will be singled out as the proximate causes of unpleasant mental states (mild or severe) that might be encountered in one's progress through auditing and training. It will be maintained, for instance, that the "keyed-in" practitioner is subject to some "restimulation" from the environment, that perhaps he is connected to a suppressive, or that he has received nonstandard auditing or training.

At the same time, some notion that a generalized increase in vulnerability to Bank accompanies expanded theta awareness circulates among advanced Scientologists. The idea is not exactly trumpeted, but it does surface in certain common observations and warnings. Two or three advanced Scientologists, eager to disabuse me of the idea that life after "Clear" is invariably perfect (a common misapprehension among junior Scientologists, and one they assumed I shared) pointed out that Clears and OTs, having enormous theta powers, are able to "mock up" Bank all over again, and to do so with unusual force. Not yet accustomed to the careful use of their new powers, new Clears and OTs may accidently turn these powers against themselves. Tanya gave an example:

> She said that self-invalidation can turn into a very dangerous weapon, and the more reality you have on your own ability to postulate the conditions around you, the more dangerous self-invalidation becomes. "You know, when I first went Clear, I scared myself. I was really scared. Because I realized how destructive I could be to *myself*. You have so much more ability to postulate, to make postulates about your life, that if

[229]

you turn these postulates against yourself you can really hurt yourself. Much more than you could before you went Clear. So I found I had to be careful with that, I had to not put out negative ideas about myself."

One will recall that the Bank is said to have arisen in the first place as a result of "postulates" by and agreements among Beings still in possession of their original powers. The "Banky" experiences of newly rehabilitated Beings can thus be interpreted as an unwitting recapitulation of this process. This is deep Scientology theory.

Another frequently voiced but less rationalized explanation for heightened manifestations of Bank is that as one gets near to the state of Clear, the Bank "beefs up," that is, it becomes stronger and more oppressive. Using a half-humorous personification, Scientologists speak of the Bank as "knowing" somehow that its existence is threatened and putting up a fight against the threat. Finally, and most straightforwardly, there is the idea that the Bank itself has levels, there are higher and lower levels of the Bank just as there are higher and lower levels of awareness. Thus as one advances through the hierarchy of auditing and training attaining higher and higher levels of awareness of oneself as a Being, one is at the same time "contacting" and eliminating higher and higher levels of the Bank. At the point of Clear, of course, one comes in touch with the highest level of the Bank, its core (the Goals-Problem-Masses).

In other words, just before the practitioner's most dramatic experience of thetanhood, he or she is likely to have vivid encounters with the Bank. As it happens, the approach to Clear in Scientology, when a heightening of both Being and Bank realities is most apt to occur, typically encompasses a stretch of intensified practice. This point requires some elaboration.

If we turn to other traditions again, it can be noted that in the mystical disciplines, and also to a degree in secular psychotherapy, it is usually recognized that upping the tempo of practice hastens or magnifies the sorts of psychological changes predicated in the tradition. If sessions spent meditating or free-associating or "encountering" are productive of personal insights and reorientations, then more numerous or more concentrated sessions can be employed to produce more frequent or dramatic versions of these transformations. It may be recognized too, as it is in Zen, that inescapable stress is an important ingredient in this magnification of the effects of practice. In Zen tradition, special seven-day "sesshins" are held during which students, under unremitting goading from their master, are pressed to try in the brief period allotted them to break through to the final enlightenment. Philip Kapleau explains:

> That an intense inner energy must be aroused for the tremendous effort of reaching enlightenment, whether it be instigated from the outside by a stick or from the inside by sheer will power, has been taught by all great masters. . . . This strategy of placing the student in a desperate situation where he is relentlessly driven from the rear and vigorously repulsed in front often builds up pressures within him that lead to that inner explosion without which true satori seldom occurs. [1967:89, 88][4]

In Scientology, the intensification of practice prior to Clearing seems to have come about in part through awareness of its virtues, in greater part through a series of tangential developments. Let me deal with the latter first.

The grades of auditing immediately leading up to and including Clear (Grades V, Va, VI, and VII [Clear]) are Confidential Levels and must be taken at the Advanced Orgs. At these establishments, the practitioner is immersed, to a much greater degree than in lower-level Scientology units, in the sense of urgency and perfectionism with which Hubbard managed to imbue the Scientology organization as a whole. The emphasis is upon "rising statistics." Staff at the AOs and Saint Hill Orgs, auditors there, and students on course are all routinely assigned a "stat"—some measure of their productivity: promotional literature mailed out, books sold, students enrolled on a course, pre-clears audited, levels of awareness attained, items of course work completed, and so on. Pressure is applied to keep each person's and each department's assigned statistic on the rise. When it drops, an Ethics penalty soon follows. While economic motives can be discerned here, the ideological rationale is that Scientology must "clear the planet fast" because mankind, lost in its aberrations, is headed for nuclear disaster.

Individual Scientologists bring to this high-pressure situation their own particular exigencies, most often a scarcity of time and money.

---

4. Castaneda's master, don Juan, cunningly threw his pupil into a series of contrived but nonetheless frightening emergencies in order to spur the latter to knowledge. Freud too observed the virtues of an externally imposed stress. "Wolf Man," his patient for some six years of laborious analysis, suddenly began to achieve deep insights and reorganizations of feeling after it was announced to him that the analysis would terminate in one year, progress or no progress.

Not a few have entered Scientology in the first place in the hope that the acquisition of Scientology skills or the reorganization of self that Scientology promises will enable them to go back into the world and attain hitherto elusive worldly goals, and they do not at first contemplate a protracted interruption of their affairs. Imbued with positive thinking, many do not make a realistic assessment of how long it will take, or—given the various digressions into which auditing often leads—how much it will cost, to achieve a certain level or complete a particular course. Many of the visitors to the Advanced Orgs are on leave from their jobs for what they can only hope will not be too long a time since during this period, unless they have some way of acquiring part-time work in the area, they must support themselves (and dependents, if any) on savings.

"Relentlessly driven from the rear," practitioners find that a variety of circumstances conspire to "vigorously repulse" them from the front. The primary hazard is a delay in one's auditing or training, and there are literally dozens of ways that this may happen. For one to be eligible for auditing at a given level, the case supervisor must review the whole procedure to determine that there are no previous steps in one's auditing that have been omitted or botched. If there are, a correction of some sort is ordered; this is often a separate auditing action with a separate price tag. Maddeningly, the standards for what is required for eligibility shift, as steps are incorporated into the auditing sequence.[5] There are other more mundane impediments to auditing that occasion delay, even without interpolated special processes. Before beginning any auditing sequence the auditor questions the pre-clear about the following factors, any of which, if found to apply, means a postponement of auditing: insufficient sleep or nourishment, pressing distractions that pull attention away from the auditing session

---

5. During the two years of my research, Hubbard inserted an entire refurbished course (Standard Dianetics), new processes on all the lower Grades, a Drug Rundown Intensive for those with a past drug history, an Exteriorization Intensive for all those who had had exteriorization experiences, and a new level near the bottom of the hierarchy called "Repair." Persons who had gone through the lower Grades and were on their way to the Confidential Levels were strongly urged, though not required, to take these steps, and if any snarl appeared in their progress through the Confidential materials, this was interpreted by the case supervisor as an indication of the need for one or another of these missing procedures, at which point the procedure *did* become a requirement. Ultimately the logjam created at the AOs by this endless interpolation got to be too much for the organization, and Hubbard declared the Confidential Levels up through OT III an area of "no interference."

(such as another appointment scheduled hard on the heels of the session), even mild physical illness such as a cold, the recent use of any intoxicant or drug (other than antibiotics): aspirin, alcohol, or tranquilizers taken within the past twenty-four hours, hallucinogens or barbiturates within the past six weeks. Since all these impediments may indicate in one way or another the presence of stress, it is easy to see how the same pressures that are driving pre-clears forward through their auditing may be simultaneously hurling obstacles into their path.

While course work does not offer quite the same opportunities for insidious self-defeat as does auditing, Scientology training courses have characteristic obstacles of their own. One is the sheer mass of data that must be assimilated. As a rule Hubbard's bulletins and tapes provide much more background than is strictly necessary for the adequate comprehension of a given level. Usually every bulletin he ever issued and every lecture he recorded on the subject of a particular level will appear in the course packet for that level. This material can span as much as twenty years of Hubbardian invention, over which time span emphases shifted even to the point of contradiction, new themes were introduced, and old ones declared inessential. Except for the minimal organization introduced into the material by the star rating of the most important bulletins, it is up to the student to sort out what it all means. While some students savor the chance to elaborate their understanding of Scientology from a multiplicity of angles, others, burdened with time concerns and hedged in by the Scientology study rule that one should never go past a misunderstood word, begin to languish under the rich diet of data. On crowded courses, students may be stuck waiting for a tape machine or for the attention of the course supervisor, who must pass them on certain concepts and exercises. Then when the time rolls around to practice auditing, all the problems listed above to which the pre-clear may fall prey are translated into problems for the student auditor. Pre-clear after pre-clear may have to be dismissed as ineligible from the start. Should the student botch the session with an eligible pre-clear, the latter is often as not routed to another auditor with more advanced qualifications for corrective auditing (to straighten out the botch). Too many "flubbed" sessions and a trainee is required to "retread" the entire course.

Even though one is relieved of the problem of finding pre-clears on the Solo Course since there the pre-clear one is preparing to audit is oneself, Scientologists describe this course as the one where the psychic crunch is most intense. Here the student is surrounded by others who, perhaps like himself, have taken temporary leave of home and job and traveled to the Advanced Orgs for the fantastic experience of going Clear. Time is precious and expectations run high. For the first time these students are getting to study and carry around Confidential materials, and the penalties for irresponsible handling are severe: one may be suspended from Scientology. The student must master endless bulletins, listen to dozens of tapes, and watch film demonstrations by Hubbard, all dealing with the grisly inner secrets of the Bank. A maze of new information comes into view, accompanied by warnings of its "highly restimulative" nature. The Bank is portrayed as a fiendish design, the outcome of a plot that has been going on for trillennia and may still be going on. Allusions are made to "invader forces" from the "old confederacy" that may be on their way to Earth once again to get us with electronic devices. Scientologists must therefore "clear the planet" fast! Clearing itself is depicted as a procedure of extreme delicacy rather like disarming a bomb. On the Solo and Clearing courses, when one is finally getting down to picking apart the core of the Bank, any clumsy bit of auditing may, one is told, spin one into the Bank for keeps.

In the mystifying Hubbardian style, these grim warnings alternate with a tongue-in-cheek joviality. The Bank may be a "tiger," but with Scientology technology there's really no problem. Hubbard has found the way. Auditing out the core of the Reactive Mind should be, if done correctly, "just a walk in the park."

Not surprisingly, many a student's deepest "reality" on Bank as an alien malevolent force creeps upon him or her during these long training regimens leading into and encompassing Clear.

> Miriam agreed [with others she mentioned] that the Solo Course is the hardest because the theory section is so long that you may have to spend a couple of months mastering it before you start auditing. That's the longest delay between theory and auditing that you run into on the Scientology levels. She said that people report all sorts of "weird things happening" while on Solo. "All sorts of strange rumblings and stirrings." Somehow the Bank knows that its very existence is under attack and it puts up a fight for its survival. "It beefs up. There's a feeling of something there, something moving and stirring."

By the same token, many a student's profoundest experience of thetanhood arises out of the same context. Ideally, one should have a superior experience of this sort, eclipsing any previous Bank sensations, while auditing on the Clearing procedures.

It must be reiterated that the grosser stresses to which practitioners are exposed on the Confidential Levels—the high-pressure atmosphere of the Advanced Orgs, the lengthy training intervals that push against participants' time and money constraints, and so on—do not seem to be part of a deliberate strategy for goading practitioners into psychological breakthroughs. These pressures arise out of tendencies built into the administration of Scientology for other reasons. I only wish to point out that a heightening of states of consciousness is one of the effects that such stresses will often have, whether instigated to this end or not. (So similarly, as earlier indicated, particularly stressful situations are usually involved when Scientologists find themselves gripped with the "reality" that suppressives are operating against them.)

It is a rather different story when we consider the auditing procedures *per se* of the Solo and Clear levels. Here one detects a deliberate intention on Hubbard's part to speed up and intensify practice. In the first place, on Solo, Clear, and thereafter, practitioners must take up solo auditing, the technique whereby one assumes alternately the role of auditor and pre-clear. Scientologists were uniform in their explanation of the purpose of solo auditing: it makes things go faster. A greater volume of psychological material can be processed during the session when the need to verbalize it in comprehensible form to another is removed. In addition, Hubbard seems to have loaded the package of Clearing procedures with unusually difficult and ambiguous exercises. To cite an example given by Kaufman, the solo auditor must contemplate, and in doing so "take the charge off," paradoxical concepts such as "creating to destroy mass," and "destroying to create mass," while simultaneously "spotting" himself as a thetan at the beginning of time. The instructions on how to spot the thetan warn against making a fuss about it. The idea is that one simply does it, "it's like pointing to something and saying THERE." (Kaufman 1972:144–46). To complicate matters further, the solo auditor is not specifically alerted to look for the familiar end phenomena of auditing while auditing the Clearing procedures (Kaufman 1972:146). Scientologists are expected to "attest" that they are Clear when they are certain that this is so, but apparently the question as to how they will know is left open. Perhaps in the end, liberation from the Bank is achieved only through a radical abandonment of preconceptions, a quantum leap beyond "fuss"; it's rather like pointing to something and saying THERE!

On the evidence of Scientology testimonials, the breakthrough into Clear is essentially a magnified version of the "key-out" experience that Scientologists have come to recognize by dint of prior auditing and training:

> It's as if an unwanted, vaguely perceived radio program had been turned off. The background chattering of the Reactive Mind has ceased to grind out its trillennia of naggings, urgings and inhibitions in my ear. And against the sudden calm, the chirping of little birds can be heard and I breathe freely and focus clearly. . . .

> It was simple. Like stepping over a stream from a muddy bank to a new green wide open field that stretches to infinity. [Testimonials distributed by the AOLA]

In sum, while progress through Scientology has its unique organization and conceptualization, this progress like that in other renunciatory disciplines involves the practitioner in bouts of intensified practice that will carry him or her more deeply into the unusual states of mind that practice always to some degree provokes. Scientologists have over the course of earlier practice learned to organize every component of experience conceptually in two broad directions, those illustrating the reality of self as Being and those illustrating the reality of an oppressive mental force, the Bank. The intensification of experience generally, occasioned by concentrated stressful practice, provides them with profounder visions of each of these realities.

From Bank to Being

The final and perhaps most critical component of Scientology reality that must fall into place for the practitioner is that these two states, Beingness and Bank, which are in immediate experience incompatible, are at a deeper level interconvertible. As I suggested earlier in the discussion of the axioms, we have here two things that are transforms of each other, as ice is a transform of water, or matter a transform of energy. Bank is Being in a particular state, a state arrived at through Being's own internal tendencies.

The interconvertibility of Being and Bank is implicit in a set of images that Hubbard repeatedly used to explain the core of the Bank: the images of electronic charge, nuclear force, "thousands of volts . . . cast into destructive wavelengths." He himself posed the question why such forces should be so "heavy on the theta line." His answer: these energies are close approximations to thetan energies, "mockeries," as he put it, of the natural forces of Beings (Hubbard 1952:20). In the electronics/nuclear force metaphor, so popular "among the insane in sanatoria," Hubbard was playing upon a characteristic image through which the contemporary psyche apprehends its own denied and alienated energies. The message he achieved through his metaphor is that the only thing that can "aberrate" a Being is, ultimately, its own disowned energy. In like fashion, the other principles of Bank transform into principles of Beingness. On higher levels of Scientology awareness, the "implants" of the Bank translate back into the desires and goals of the Being. "Stimulus-response" behavior converts back into the "playing of a game." The "they" of the universal incidents who practice enslavement and control turn out in deeper Scientology understanding to be none other than the "we" who are forever making a few "agreements" for the sake of an orderly game. In short, Bank is alienated Being. The obvious practical implication of this is that in order to eliminate the Bank and restore the Being, the alienated parts of the self must be recognized and reowned. This is the purpose of auditing.

It is in auditing, in particular in the end phenomena of auditing when insight occurs, that the interconvertibility of Bank and Being becomes real for Scientologists. It becomes real because it is at this point in an auditing sequence that a conversion of energies does indeed take place. In many respects, the "cognition" cited above, of Sammy in his drugged state, that "I was putting it [his unpleasant perceptions] there myself . . . it didn't have to be there," is the paradigmatic Scientology insight; and his sudden simultaneous reacquisition of control over his mental process is the paradigmatic result. In some little way, every "cognition" brought about through Scientology auditing expresses the principle "I'm doing it and I can stop doing it," and with this sort of insight comes invariably, to some small degree, a sense of relief.

While Scientological cognitions occur frequently and spontaneously in the life of Scientology practitioners, they are the specific goal of the auditing session and the outcome of a particular type of introspection elicited by auditing techniques. The ability of a pre-clear to arrive at relieving insights in session is intimately related to his or her ability to fall into the introspective mode required, and doing the latter entails a certain amount of learning, a familiarization with what sorts of subjectivizing and responding move the session along and what sorts are counterproductive. In order to get our hypothetical novice Scientologist to the point where Bank suddenly converts back into Being, it will help if we can see how the process leading up to insight tends to be experienced.

As explained in the chapter on Scientology beliefs, there are two guises under which auditing's rehabilitations of the Being may be accomplished. The first, incident running, takes the form of a history played backward; it involves the elaboration of fantasy scenarios that give content and visible form to the pre-clear's affective and motivational patterns. The second is the quest for implicit ideologies, sets of statements about the world and one's relation to it that also reveal affective and motivational patterns, only more abstractly. As one Scientologist explained it to me, the Bank contains "masses," by which she meant sensory images; and it contains "significances"—meanings and ideas. In Dianetic-style auditing (that is, incident running) one is looking primarily for "masses"; in the Scientological style, one is looking primarily for "significances." I will begin here with incident running since this illustrates more concretely the style of subjectivity required by the session, and the way in which a rejuvenating insight is abstracted from the session's materials.

In Standard Dianetic auditing, which is the set of contemporary procedures most given over to incident running, the pre-clear enters the session with the understanding that he or she will be asked first to list, by means of a questionnaire, complaints and ailments. These in turn will be broken down into specific sensations (emotions count as "sensations"). The auditor will interrupt this breaking-down procedure and begin incident running on the topic of whatever sensation causes, when first mentioned by a pre-clear, a "blowdown" of the meter's TA, a drop in resistance necessitating the resetting of the tone arm downward. (In the absence of a "blowdown," the auditor will, after completing the list, choose the mentioned sensation that has caused the longest needle drop.) It is understood by both auditor and pre-clear that the long drops of the meter's needle indicate the presence of charge on the item in question, charge that arises from occluded incidents in the Bank. Moreover, because mere mention of the item caused this charge to register, bits of Bank responsible for it are near the surface of consciousness. They are ready, in Scientology theory, to be "confronted." To clinch this matter, the auditor will ask whether the pre-clear is interested in running this reading item; if so, incident running can begin. (If not, the listing procedure must continue until the pre-clear finds a reading item that he *is* interested in running.)

The theory of what will happen next is plain enough. The pre-clear will "contact" locks, secondaries, or engrams—in a word, incidents— that contain the charged sensation. There will most likely be a chain of these stretching backward into the past. Sometimes the chain extends back beyond this lifetime and into previous lives. Ultimately what is sought is the Basic on the chain, theoretically the first occluded incident containing the charged sensation. When the Basic is contacted and erased, it and all subsequent links on the chain—the incidents extending forward into the present—lose their aberrative force; they will no longer "key-in" in response to stimuli in the pre-clear's environment. As a result, the charged sensation which has appeared in the pre-clear's life because of the key-in of incidents containing it will vanish.

The inexperienced pre-clear is unsure just how any of this will take place. If the traumatic incidents in the Bank are "occluded," doesn't this mean they are inaccessible to consciousness? How then does one "contact" them? How especially does one remember a past-life incident? What does it feel like when an incident erases?

All that the auditor says is "Locate an incident containing ____ [the designated sensation or emotion]." The cautious pre-clear will begin with "this lifetime" recollections. But even here preconceptions intervene. He or she may fish around for the cruelest and most devastating incident of the type specified, in the belief that this must be the one with the most charge on it. Oddly, this approach doesn't work very well. The auditing becomes labored. The problem here, explained one Scientologist, is that the pre-clear is "stuck in significance."

> Miriam said that one of the reasons people may have trouble when they're being audited on the lower grades in Scientology is that they stop and think too much about the question. The auditor, say, will ask for "a moment of loss and misemotion" and you're supposed to locate a moment of loss and misemotion. But you sit there thinking, "Well, I lost my bus ticket this morning but that's not really very important . . . and, I dunno, I lost a job back in '57 but this wasn't one of the big moments of my life . . . let's see, what's a really good juicy moment of loss and

misemotion, etc.?" She said that this is not the point at all. You start with *any* moment of loss and misemotion—whatever comes into your mind, it doesn't matter what "calibre" the moment, and you go from there.

Pre-clears sooner or later learn this first lesson in spontaneity. If the incident that "blows down the TA" is that of stubbing one's toe on the sidewalk last week as opposed to the automobile incident of last year in which one sustained multiple concussions, then the toe-stub is the incident that currently has charge on it. So may the concussions, but their charge is not yet accessible. Indeed, it may never be. A couple of years and several hundred auditing hours later, one may still not have run the auto accident to any effect. It makes no difference: one runs what runs.

On the matter of past lives, preconceptions set in again even more strongly. Spontaneous, "this lifetime" memories at least seem to have a "memory notation" on them. Will Track feel like memory? Having exhausted all this-lifetime incidents on a chain without going "release," the pre-clear realizes that there is nothing for it but to come up with some Track. Again he or she waits for the magical unveiling, and again all that the auditor says is, "Locate an earlier incident. . . ." The pre-clear must realize eventually that the secret, occluded content of the Bank and the content spontaneously generated in his or her current consciousness are one and the same.

> I had noticed the casualness with which Miriam reported Track running as opposed to Leo, who was having such difficulties. She just seems to have some images and ideas come into her mind, looks through them a little till they amplify, and gets on with it. She said that this was so. "Like the first time [her auditor] asked for 2nd Flow Engrams [Engrams one has given another], I realized it was just something I'd never thought about. So I said, 'Now wait a minute, I'm going to have to think.' Pretty soon I got a picture and a thought at the same time. The thought I left for the time being; it probably goes somewhere but it wasn't part of the chain I ran."
> I: "You mean you select some pictures or thoughts and not others?"
> M: "Oh yes. You'll get pictures from here and there and you just pick one and start with it. Or when you're running a chain you'll often get pictures from somewhere else. Well, all those pictures probably belong to other chains somewhere along the line, but you're just concentrating on one chain at a time."
> I: "You mean any picture you get in your mind probably belongs somewhere on your Track?"
> M: "Most likely."

The same principle of start-anywhere spontaneity applies to the dating of incidents. Pre-clears are asked to assign a date to an incident once it is located. This is a carry-over from the days when Hubbard was having everyone plot out their Track on "maps." At that time, before he had fully rationalized the notion of Track so that any "located" scene could fit somewhere, dating had its pitfalls. Again these had to do with the pre-clear's attempts to make sense of his productions instead of just running them. A pre-clear quoted in an early work on the subject of past lives reported: "No engram was fully run on me. I had the misfortune to have [the] heaviest needle drop on a space incident 78 trillion years ago, two trillion years further than I had ever heard existed, and this was not encouraging" (Hubbard 1968e:41). The practice of dating incidents is still retained because, according to one Scientologist, "it helps the pre-clear sort things out," but nowadays the keynote is flexibility.

> Miriam said that the important thing was that the p-c have a date that "feels right" to him. In the old days the auditor used to get dates by listing and using the meter reads as a guide; that's been abolished "because what happens is you'll get a p-c stuck with a date that he doesn't feel is right and the auditor using the E-Meter to invalidate his feeling. Now the p-c's feeling is always accepted above the meter. . . . I changed a date on myself in [her last auditing]. At first I'd said 1944. Then I didn't feel that was pinpointing it, so I said, 'Make that 1943.' So fine, we made it 1943, and it ran." Turns out you can change dates as often as you like in running a chain until you get something that "fits" with you. You can even change dates on previous things you've already run if some later incident seems to fit more aptly in that time slot. "After all," she said, "the date isn't the relevant thing. It's getting into the incident itself and running it. You can sort out dates later. It's just that it tends to help you get into an incident if you have a date to go by. I remember there's one tape where Ron says, 'A thetan is always precise.' You know, even when a thetan is creating disorder he'll do it in a very precise way. That's why in fact there always is a precise date attached to something, even if that's not the important part. You get enough auditing and pretty soon your Track begins to sort itself out and everything falls into place."

Even though, as he or she learns, the pre-clear is prevented from anticipating the "sense" of his or her productions; and even though the auditor is forbidden to offer interpretations and evaluations, the wanderings of a session do make sense and follow a discernible order. In part, the productions are rendered sensible by the constraints placed upon the pre-clear's response by the auditing question. The auditor asks for an incident containing the predetermined charged sensation, and the pre-clear must keep this sensation in the foreground of his mind when letting an incident take shape. Sometimes during the course of a Dianetic session, it may become apparent to the auditor that the pre-clear has "jumped" chains. Having, for instance, been running incidents that contained a sensation of dizziness, he or she now seems to have forgotten the dizziness and is concentrating on a pain in the back; in the new incidents furnished, this new item now occupies the foreground. In most cases, jumping chains foreshadows a failed session, since conflict between the auditor's specifications and the pre-clear's interest soon sets in. A pre-clear's wandering off the point in this fashion is usually considered a sign that the auditor's TRs are poor. For the pre-clear to be constrained by the sense of the auditing command, that command must seize his attention; this requires a focused delivery on the auditor's part.

In larger part, the sense of a session is guaranteed by the generously encompassing nature of Scientology theory. The assumptions of this theory are shared by pre-clear and auditor alike as well as being embodied in the auditing commands. The auditor sets the pre-clear the task of locating elements in his or her Bank that carry charge, and the charge registered on the E-Meter when certain subjects are mentioned indicates that this is exactly what is happening. The auditor asks the pre-clear for an *earlier* incident, and what the pre-clear responds with is presumed to be just that—an earlier incident. Inexperienced pre-clears are often amazed to learn in an auditing session what Bank is really like, or what Track is really like. "It was just a picture that came into my mind," one may say. Indeed.

The auditing session is declared a success when it leads to the end phenomena of auditing: a floating needle on the meter, a "cognition" by the pre-clear, and "good indicators" (relief, brightness, extroversion) in the pre-clear. It is most usual for these end phenomena to appear in the wake of a dramatic discharge of pre-clear tension or emotion. It will be apparent to the auditor (usually), both from the sharp drop in meter TA and from the demeanor of the pre-clear, that something in the incident he or she is running has caused a fundamental surge of feeling. Typically it is in the "cognition" that follows upon this that one can spot the reorientation that I spoke of as a conversion of Bank into Being. Something in the heavily "discharging" incident will have been recognized by the pre-clear as self-determined and self-originated. Here is an example from a Standard Dianetics session:

[Item being run: A sensation of] "suppressing myself"

[First incident] 18 May '69

Seeing myself getting a flunk for a [Standard Dianetics] session. The [Case Supervisor's] interpretation of what had happened is not correct. . . . I am faced with going through [the bulletins] three times again—as I fail to get this rectified. . . . reaction was to kick, bite, scratch til I get it put right. But when I restrained myself the mass built up. . . . By next morning I was just being other-determined. All zest gone.

[Second Incident] 1st Nov. 1968

[See] groups of people standing in . . . party. I find myself unable to reach into any of these groups so can't participate. . . . I feel if I force myself into the limelight I'll make some sort of fool of myself. So I stand around trying to look cheerful . . . and forcing myself to say something now and again—but it's a strain to do so. I'm impatient with myself for feeling this way. . . . When one chap arrived—started talking . . . with greatest assurance . . . Closed me up inside . . . I stopped trying.

[Third Incident] 8th March, 1922

. . . I'm sitting on the veranda quite unbelieving that my father can be dead. It's just not real; must be some mistake. . . . What is death? . . . Death unreal so was life—not going to accept his loss. He's around somewhere. And for years I kept dreaming he'd come back and each time dream different. I'd wake and he wasn't there.

[Fourth Incident] 1920, 4th April

I wake up and see my mother very angry with father. . . . I suppress my awareness from my mother. Never, never must know that I'm witnessing this severe scene. Not daring to move. I breathe regularly. Eyes closed, listening. . . . fear of being found out—vitalness of suppressing myself . . .

[Fifth Incident] 16 Jan, 1913

My body lying on ground below. I decide I must keep myself out of trouble. Make myself insignificant, keep in background . . . I feel I still hurt in stomach from bullet wound. Up there telling myself what a clod I was. . . . The decision to suppress myself from any possibility of getting into trouble. Result of accumulation of pains and death.

[Cognition] The great scheme was to be small, to keep out of trouble. Needle F/N, CIs. [Excerpted from a Hubbard-supervised case folder published in Hubbard 1975b:917–19]

In incident running, the complex of motive and affect that is nudged into awareness and ultimately recognized as "self" by the pre-clear is fairly easily "seen" by the outside observer as well. The recounted incidents portray it in sensory form. In the Scientology methods of auditing, the same sorts of complexes are being stimulated by the auditing commands and, as in the Dianetics style, a sequence is typically built that makes the complex more and more evident to the pre-clear. But illustrating this to an outsider is rather more difficult because the pre-clear is not compelled to elaborate his or her thoughts. Take a paired question process such as (1) Who has failed to control you? and (2) Whom have you failed to control? An auditing sequence may go as follows:

Auditor: Who has failed to control you?
Pre-clear: My parents (laugh).
Auditor: Good. Whom have you failed to control?
Pre-clear: My ex-husband (sigh).
Auditor: Fine. Who has failed to control you?
Pre-clear: Well, my ex-husband failed to control me too, y'know.

And so on. A sequence of muttered names and dimly sketched situations may make up most of the notes of the session, but these are mere allusions to the panorama of associations that has passed through the pre-clear's mind. Usually, aside from one or two of the initial responses and the cognition at the end, Scientologists cannot recount the sequence of responses they have given to a Scientology process. I myself suffered from the same difficulty in recollection.

We can attain a general idea of how these processes work, however. Here are some further Scientology processes.

1. What are you willing to talk to me about? [Pre-clear says "X."]
2. If you were talking to me about X, what exactly would you say?

1. Tell me a problem. [Pre-clear states a problem.]
2. How would you solve it?

[From a listing process]
Has an emotion been suppressed?
Has an emotion been invalidated?
Has an emotion been rejected?
[and so on through all the things that can happen to an emotion]

A process begins by isolating some discrete element of mental behavior or interpersonal dynamics: "emotion rejected," "a problem," "willing to talk," "control," "solve," and so on. The pre-clear is then repeatedly cast into situations in regard to this element: has it happened to you? do you do it? did someone else do it? how would you react to it? give an example of it. Private connotations and attitudes regarding the element are stirred and as the same situations (usually one or two) are repeated, some complex of feeling and thinking unique to the pre-clear's life and personality is dragged into view. Kaufman gives an example (reconstructed, not verbatim):

[He has just located a "problem."]
[Auditor] Thank you. *How would you solve it?*
[Kaufman] I can't solve it. I'm stuck in it. I'm helpless, that's what it is, I'm a baby a few months old and I can't do anything; it's all being done *to* me. I'm not responsible for what's happening.
[Auditor] I got that! What are your considerations on *responsibility?*
[Kaufman] The word has unpleasant connotations for me. I associate it with guilt, shame, with having to do things you really don't want to do and being blamed if you don't. [Kaufman 1972:15; his emphasis]

The experience of being "run" on these sorts of processes is often reported as a sense that the questions are repeatedly pushing one up against some mysterious, but vaguely familiar, governing impulse around which one has erected—without really knowing it—a hedge of protective barriers. As each round of questions erodes another barrier, one is dragged further away from what one thought one wanted to talk about, and closer to this uncannily familiar "old thing." The reader can imaginatively follow the thrust of some of the processes and guess where they are apt to lead. "What are you willing to talk to me about?" must inevitably push the pre-clear closer and closer to the things he is *un*willing to talk about as the stock of safe topics dwindles. "Whom have you failed to control?" paired with "Who has failed to control you?" will soon force the pre-clear into a greater scrutiny of what he personally means by and feels about "control." The service facsimile, which is chased down with a series of questions about how the pre-clear manages to "make self right," dominate others, and so on, has a notable tendency to come into play *against* the auditor while the auditor is searching for it.

Ultimately, the Scientology mode of auditing, like incident running, leads the pre-clear to a recognition of how his own "considerations" have been secretly at work shaping the world he lives in and has been, in nonrecognition of this fact, vainly protesting. The movement from Bank to Being, whether cast in the format of a history played

[245]

backward or in the style of a search for a hidden ideology of experience, begins in the Bank mode as a confrontation with the foreign, the mysterious, and the impinging. But as the pre-clear follows a designated line of "charge" inward toward an ultimate act of self-recognition, the Track incidents and all the little tenets of his private faith take on an increasing familiarity—these are, after all, the artifacts of his own desires. One Scientologist remarked, "You find as you go back up the dwindling spiral, that it's all familiar. You've been there before. You see these things along the way, and it's no surprise because somewhere inside yourself you knew them all along."

[8]

Renunciation and Reformulation

In Chapter 4, I outlined the idea that the process underway in psychotherapy and in many forms of religious observance is a renunciatory movement, whereby the desires invested in worldly objects are detached from these objects to be drawn inward and captured in symbolic representations that transfigure and, in doing so, make livable the given world. Some of the mechanisms of this symbolic "capture" have been illustrated in the foregoing chapter. Here I will turn to further, more detailed accounts of auditing sessions in order to show the process in greater detail and clarify certain theoretical ambiguities.

Renunciation

The first matter that requires clarification has to do with what is renounced. Mystics speak grandly of renouncing "the world," but it would be a mistake to conceive of what is abandoned as simply material reality or sensuous pleasure. Desire is mediated through mental structures, and in renunciation, as understood here, all that is involved is a movement away from, and dissolution of one set of structures, and the construction of and movement into a new set. It does not in fact make any difference whether the abandoned structures are realistic or not. It is as possible to renounce supernatural or "unreal" objects as it is "real" ones and through the same effort as that which conjured up the unreal objects in the first place. In psychoanalysis, the patient is being pushed into abandoning his or her neurotic symptoms which often take the form of bizarre ideas, bits of waking "dream-work," to use Freud's characterization. These are unreal objects to begin with, the products of regressive movements that have not had a successful resolution. One way of moving the patient away from the symptoms is to instigate a further regression that goes beyond the previous ones and displaces emotional interest onto a new plane. We will examine this movement of progressive abandonment in greater depth below. It is important in this matter to avoid the quibble over what is "real" and what "unreal." My point is served by saying that in the process of renunciation the degree of complexity and differentiation of mental structures is always, to some extent, reduced, and can be, if need arises, *further* reduced.

A second and related point must detain us for a moment: it is not necessary to begin the work of initiating further renunciation from any particular starting point. Recall that Freud favored having the patient free-associate to remembered dream elements. Dreams were in his opinion the royal road to the Unconscious. In the argument I am proposing here, it is the free association—that is, the mind-altering practice—that is the royal road to those constructions Freud speaks of as Unconscious. Piaget rightly observes, "Instead of a dream any news item from a paper could be taken as the starting point for 'associations.' The spontaneous assimilations of the subject would then make him give a symbolic meaning to every detail, as though he were dealing with one of his own dreams" (Piaget 1962:190). [1] It is true that a remembered dream or a neurotic idea is the product of a dedifferentation of thought; but it does not for this reason hold any superior value in the fostering of further such dedifferentiations.

This is not to say, however, that there are not certain other purposes served by holding up to contemplation an individual's personal materials, especially those that are products of free-wheeling assimila-

---

1. Piaget's remarks are supported analytically by Sebastiano Timpanaro's elegant rebuttal of Freud's doctrine of "slips." Timpanaro shows that altogether "unrevelatory" psychological processes familiar to the textual critic, such as "banalization" (the replacement of the difficult with the easy, the unfamiliar with the familiar) or omission of the semantically superfluous, can be used to account for many of the distortions and omissions cited by Freud as examples of unconscious interference. The fact that Freud caused his interlocutors to reveal their preoccupying ideas by having them free-associate to the omitted or distorted word shows only that free-association itself will sooner or later bring to the surface a preoccupying idea, not that the idea was causally linked to the missing or altered word. On those occasions when the slip is the result of interference by a competing idea, the competing idea is immediately apparent in the slip itself and it requires no free association to arrive at it (Timpanaro 1976).

tion such as dreams, fantasies, bizarre apprehensions, or private rituals. If guided renunciation is aimed at exposing and interpreting for the renouncer his or her inner self, as is the case in psychoanalysis, then such productions are of immediate relevance to this task. As for the function these personal materials serve in convincing the practitioner of the existence and personal relevance of the special realm of mind or existence that is the concern of the tradition, these materials would serve this function regardless of whether or not they are chosen as takeoff points for further practice. What is required is that they be highlighted and explained in *some* way. Calling them the royal road to the special realm is one way of doing this but not necessarily the only way.

In Scientology auditing, a concession to "personalized" starting points is sometimes made and sometimes not made. Standard Dianetic auditing (incident running) and certain listing procedures begin with the search for "reading" items on the E-Meter, a procedure which in the case of incident running is coupled with that of asking the pre-clear whether he or she is *interested* in running the item once it is found. The rationale for this is that an item with no charge on it, or one that is uninteresting to the pre-clear, simply will not run. This reasoning is discarded altogether, however, when on the Confidential Levels, for instance, the solo auditor is presented with items and incidents that are presumed to have charge on them, the testimony of the meter notwithstanding, or when, as in the case of the majority of lower grades of auditing, the session simply begins with a standard question. Obviously, neurotic symptoms, dreams, and in Scientology practice, "reading" items *are* personal to the patient or pre-clear; they will inevitably, by a longer or shorter route, connect somewhere to the motivational and affective schema that analysis or auditing brings to light. But then again so will everything else, for the very act of meditating upon or free-associating to any given thing is an act of assimilating it to the ongoing activity of the self. As a Scientologist quoted earlier explained, one can select just about anything that comes into one's head and discover that it fits somewhere on the Track.

The business of objects of and starting points for renunciation having been clarified, we turn again to what is happening in the auditing session. The focus here will be on how these happenings illustrate the process of renunciation. Scientology "reality" will continue to be of concern but less as the namer and shaper of certain experiential states

[249]

(the concern of the previous chapter) than as a thing that is itself shaped by the processes it attempts to encompass.

Once practice is undertaken and a renunciatory movement launched, one can see in the content of the subject's productions—the fantasies, ideas, images, and so on—the outlines of affective schemata that are being withdrawn from their current objects. I illustrated this briefly in Chapter 3, using a Scientology past-life incident chain. I will illustrate it again, to renew the discussion, with another such chain.

The following incident chain is somewhat messier and perhaps more typical of a difficult session. Here the drama of anthropologist versus tribe continues from the anthropologist's point of view; the chain is taken from one of my own sessions as a pre-clear. The reader must take my word for it that at the time of my own auditing experience, even though I was aware of its "symbolic" nature, I had not as yet developed the ideas regarding auditing that I am now expounding; that is, I was not fantasizing in such a way as to gratify my own opinions about Track. Neither was I particularly interested in validating Scientology reality. But great enthusiasm for the world-view is not required; all that is required is that one agree to "locate" incidents.

[I was on the Standard Dianetics Course at the Los Angeles Org and had been for many weeks. I had also been recruited as a pre-clear by Fred, an auditor-trainee on a Scientology course, who was practicing auditing the Scientology Grades. I liked him tremendously, and our first few sessions on Grade 0 had been instructive and fun. He was not only an excellent auditor but also a good informant. I told him about my research interests, but he did not seem to mind and indeed my "investigator" role had begun to slip far into the background of my mind. Then an instruction came from Hubbard that pre-clears were not to receive Scientology Grades auditing until they had completed all Dianetic auditing. Since I had had no Dianetic auditing, I had to postpone any further sessions with Fred and become a pre-clear for various fellow students on the Dianetics course. I was secretly resentful and began to wonder what the Dianetics course was worth to me in the first place. Students were instructed not to swap gossip, interpretations, or speculations while on the course because this might result in their learning the materials wrong. Thus the "anthropological returns" were practically nil. I had already read and studied the course materials to the point of boredom, but demonstrating my comprehension to the course supervisor was taking longer than I had expected. My first Dianetics auditors (fellow students) were as tense about the sessions as I was. I did not feel in these sessions that what I was doing was "running Track" but rather exposing my obvious fantasies to the inspection of people whose values would cause them to be (secretly) shocked. My role as "investigator" began to worry me again. This worry took the form of feeling that I should be looking, for comparative purposes, into other practices besides Scientology and wondering how I could do this without incurring the disapproval of the Scientology authorities.

My first Dianetics session bogged and I wound up in what was apparently an ARC break with the Dianetics Course, the course supervisor, and the whole works. I was routed into review, and the session turned into incident-running this ARC break.]

Got into an ARC break chain that went into "Track." The Track part of it went:

(1) My having joined a monastic order in the seventeenth century (England, I think) and become disillusioned with it. The ARC break was in "communication"—it was a silent order and no one would speak to me.

(2) Being imprisoned, in Roman times, for having gone to the authorities with a legitimate complaint and trusted them to fix it. The authorities wound up getting me for some wrong that I'd committed in the past that I'd had to confess to in order for them to help me with the current difficulty. They slapped me in prison without further regard to the matter I'd brought up. Again, I was cut off from talking to anyone.

(3) Stone-age times. I was living in the jungle and raising a pet lion, which grew up and ate me.

(4) Pre-Earth, "space opera" situation. I was marooned in outer space in a broken space-craft. The ARC break was with the machine itself; I'd always trusted its reliability.

At this point I began to grow discouraged with the auditing. Discouragement came to a head in the next incident.

(5) I got pictures of lying on my back in bed listening to a little bell that tinkled over my head. It turned out that I was a paralytic, and had been for most of my life, and I was lying there feeling sorry for myself. In the incident I didn't want to think about how it had happened, but I knew that it stemmed from having been "let down" by a trusted friend. Got a picture of someone lowering me over the edge of a ravine and dropping me suddenly. I fell on my spine and was paralyzed. Lying in bed, then, I had the feeling that all the past incidents of that particular lifetime were frozen in a series of "still shots," like pictures in an old family photograph album.

At this point I complained to Martin (the auditor) of feeling discouraged and not feeling I was getting anywhere. Martin broke session long enough to remark, "Could you accept the possibility that the feeling is something coming from the incident?" Quite apt in light of the incident I was running. After going through this incident again, I still wasn't satisfied and began to question the dates. By then we were back into several trillennia ago, and my feeling was that I was just making up dates to satisfy him. I said, "I just feel silly giving you dates that don't make any sense." I also pointed out that the last incident looked as though it took place in a time no more than several centuries ago rather than the time I'd given him which was four trillion years ago, or something. So Martin interrupted the session to explain to me the "cycle" theory of "Track." [Cf. pp. 188–89. I was hearing this explanation for the first time.] In effect, he said that you can't tell from the "period trappings" of an incident when it really took place, and that you shouldn't be surprised if you come up with incidents that are very much like present time. Then he added, "You've got from now to the end of eternity to figure out what all this means. For right now, are you willing to accept that this might be the sort of thing that's happening: if you feel discouraged or tired or upset that this might be a feeling coming from a past incident?" I conceded that I could play it that way, but that I didn't really have a "good reality" on the end phenomena of running chains. I felt I wasn't going to "cognite" on any of these incidents because I was more interested in looking at present time and figuring out what was going on in the present, and I wasn't exactly "seeing the light" in these incidents. He said, "That's fine. That's what you should be concerned with." He said that the very point of running out incidents is because "they are affecting the present," and the point at which you "cognite" is the point at which you see *how* they are affecting the present. He gave an analogy: suppose you were at the bottom of the ocean and you stirred around in the muck down there and released a gas bubble. The bubble would make its way up to the surface no matter how deep down you were. Well, it's the same way going back in Time. He made a little rising, spiraling motion with his finger, suggesting a bubble rising to the surface, and said that when you hit the "basic" on a chain it's like releasing that bubble. Some element of the incident will go "bloop, bloop, bloop" all the way back up through the previous incidents and into present time. So when you're running Track you don't have to take your attention totally off present time because fundamentally you're trying to see how the past and the present are related.

Then he said, "Just look back over what you've run already." He flipped through the worksheets and called the highlights from each incident, remarking, "You can see it's all on the same chain. There are similar things happening all along here." I said, "Gee, you're right." It refreshed my grip on what I was trying to work out and my interest picked up. After this little chat, I immediately ran the incident that resulted in "key-out." It was:

(6) I had agreed to let a friend do a "mental experiment" on me of some sort. In the pictures I got, it looked like a case of hypnotism. The upshot of it was that I got "stuck with some pictures" I didn't want and was very ARC broken with the friend. There was, it turned out, no way to get rid of these pictures—hence the discouragement.

Cognition: I thought, why don't I say what's been on my mind all along, viz. that to accept the idea of Dianetics is to take on a whole "Track record" that then sticks you in a long cycle of getting rid of it, whereas what I want to do is complete my Scientology auditing with Fred without getting into all this bally-hoo? This idea was not a new one, nor even, really, an unarticulated one. It was rather a case of the picture providing me with a good analogy of exactly how I felt about the situation, complete with the element of goody-goody cooperation, being taken advantage of, and of being unable to go back and "undo" what had been done. So Dianetics, to me, was a case of being persuaded that you have all of these problems that you're then persuaded you have to get rid of and then accordingly soaked for a lot of time and money. I knew all along this chain of incidents that I was making an elaborate "insinuation" about Dianetics and Scientology, i.e., it's not my bag, it's like other religions that have misled people, it's a situation that I want to get out of, it'll turn on you, betray you, make a sucker out of you. Basically, I just wanted an excuse to say all that. The incident provided it.

The needle floated and we ended session.

While this incident chain was, as I wrote in my notes, informed by an awareness that I was making a long complaint about Dianetic auditing, there seems to be some wavering, as the chain proceeds, over exactly what the complaint is. The theme of betrayal, or let-down, remains constant; but this is one of the definitions of an ARC break, and the auditor was asking for incidents containing an ARC break. The first incident reflects the complaint in terms of being surrounded by an uncommunicative group (the students on course were discouraged from discussing materials or swapping insights); the second features a vision of the authorities as persons who will not be concerned with "legitimate complaints" but only with whether their rules have been obeyed. Incidents three and four focus upon betrayal pure and simple. Then in incident five, which at the time was to me the most puzzling, there first appears the image of what later became the idea that getting "stuck with pictures" (i.e., with an unwanted cycle of auditing) was the crux of my complaint.

Incident five also portrays in an elusive way the experience of the auditing session itself. Obviously, since part of the current activity of a pre-clear consists of sitting in session with an auditor and looking at or "running out" his or her images, it would follow that portrayals of the auditing process itself (especially in cases where the process has become tedious or unpleasant for the pre-clear) are not uncommon in the productions of auditing sessions. Just how common is partially revealed by one of the "universal incidents" that Hubbard includes in *A History of Man.*

> . . . a thetan often steals the facsimiles of another thetan. . . . Thus we will find [on the Track] as a primary source of occlusion, the BOR-ROWERS. A thetan puts a retractor beam on another thetan and starts to draw out his facsimiles. The victim feels like he is going to pieces. . . . The most remarkable thing about this incident is the SLOWNESS with which facsimiles seem to run out. Each facsimile has its own time tab. No matter how rapidly they are leaving these time tabs give the ILLU-SION of a very long time. *Running up and down one's time track often gives this illusion.* [Hubbard 1961:58; my emphasis]

One implication of this kind of incident, and indeed of everything that I have been saying about the source of such fantasy constructs, is that all of the collective Track episodes that have become institutionalized as part of "theta history" in Scientology will reflect activities that are common to Scientologists generally. Marshaling the evidence to illustrate this point takes the current study too far afield, but I mention it as one logical direction for the analysis to move in.

I have also made the statement that these activity structures undergo dedifferentiation—that there occurs what could be called, in psychoanalytic terms, "regression." In any particular auditing session, the degree of dedifferentiation in the subject varies. Obviously, some abandonment of structure is necessary even to begin auditing; in incident running, it is demanded by the very rule of searching for pictorial as opposed to verbal ideation. Beyond this the most common simplifying tendency is dramatic amplification. In Track episodes, minor body ailments are translated into bullet wounds, garrotings, and electrocutions; disappointments become deaths, groups with which the pre-clear is involved become intergalactic confederacies, and present-day interpersonal tensions are played out on the famous battlefields of history.[2] Further simplification, illustrated in the following account of a session, generally leads the pre-clear into the sort of insubstantial and bizarre phenomena glossed in Scientology as "early Track," that period of thetan history before the MEST universe game had been consolidated. Some of the early Track experiences come very close to a fusion of self with cosmos.

Leo, a Grade IV, was the preclear in this session; his friend Lottie was the auditor. The subject of the auditing was Leo's constipation. They had broken down the complaint into its component sensations (called "somatics" in Scientology); they then proceeded to take each sensation and audit around it—looking for incidents in the past that contained this sensation. Here is Leo's account: "It all came down to my stomach. That turns out to be the thing that all the other somatics are linked into—the stomach somatic. Well, so we started running that, and we ran a few incomplete incidents, things that just erased, you know. Then, all of a sudden, I wasn't a body anymore. It was just me, and I was floating. Like drifting among the constellations. Although they weren't really stars. It was like 'Space Odyssey—2001'—beautiful whirling things flying past me. I was drifting in outer space and these things were going past me. It was beautiful—I didn't want it to stop! And *I* was beautiful! I was like one of those whirling things too, but I was the center of it. I was a glowing ball of fiery . . . radiance, that's the only way I can describe it. I could feel rays, energy, coming out from the center of me in every direction, and you know the center of it all was my stomach. It was like my stomach was a seed right in the center of this glowing radiance—everything was emanations from that seed. And that was where all the feeling was coming from. It wasn't pain either. The somatic was like infinite fullness, infinite richness. I felt full of this energy—so powerful—like I filled the universe. It came from the center of me, but that center was my stomach. My cognition was: 'No wonder I don't want to let go of this feeling. It was wonderful. Then [back then on the Track] I was *full*. Now, I keep eating, you know, but I don't feel satisfied, and I'll get a sour stomach, and then I'll get constipated. It's like I'm trying to recapture this magnificent feeling again in this lifetime, but it doesn't work. I just want to recapture this feeling and never let go of it.'"[3]

2. One Scientologist, a course supervisor, is reported to have ejected a student from a course when he discovered, in running some Track, that the student and he had been in a previous lifetime on opposite sides in a war. Scientology gossips relayed the tale with high amusement but agreed that this sort of response violates the spirit of what auditing is meant to do.

3. It is hard to ascertain whether a Scientologist's experience in auditing compares in

The movement away from structured mental activity has the result of generating a characteristic range of psychic "effluvia." The sensations of ineffable insight, the rejuvenating influx of energy into the self, the assimilation of self to environment, with its numerous refractions such as the illusion of telepathic exchange, disembodied travel, precognition, and so on can be understood in terms of a general experience of lessened structure. More concrete fantasy scenarios are linked to the "condensation" (mutual assimilation) of schemata, wherein stored imagery from every source (including personal history) is seized upon and reworked into portrayals of the subject's prevailing emotional postures. On the basis of these varied materials, Hubbard, like visionary leaders everywhere, put together an explanatory cosmology for which any particular autistic construct serves as evidence and into which, consequently, all the products of dedifferentiated consciousness easily flow. The concept of Track, in particular, illustrates the "regressive" direction of the renunciatory process, for at one end of the Track the pre-clear will find mundane "this lifetime" memories and at the other a virtually contentless gnosis. There is no evidence that Hubbard planned this format out of forethought as to what was needed; rather the actual construction of the theory of the Track came about through a process of trial and error during which Hubbard and his followers had to overcome the same sorts of preconceptions that often afflict new pre-clears today: literal-mindedness about dates of incidents, straining for consistency in accounts of the same time period, the idea that the Track has a finite length, and so on. Only after these considerations, which by the imposition of a structuring demand act to inhibit the free flow of spontaneous autism, were overcome did the Track emerge in its present all-encompassing form.

Given the versatility of the Track's range, Scientologists will inevitably discover, through auditing, exactly what Hubbard said will be

---

the rate of sheer acceleration to the destructuring effects of hallucinogenic drugs. Scientologists familiar with LSD varied in their reports, but the most frequent assertion was that while acid provides many of the same "high-level awarenesses" as Scientology, its effects are chaotic and unpredictable and there is the danger, in tripping, of being "overwhelmed" by the Bank. Auditing by contrast is more selective and easily controllable—the pre-clear doesn't get into anything deeper than he or she is able to handle. On the other hand the general rationale for Hubbard's instituting solo auditing on the Confidential Levels was that this method encompasses a faster flow and heavier volume of revelations and insights. Scientologists commonly speak of solo auditing as necessary because "everything is going by so fast, you'd have to slow it down to report it to the auditor."

there. Breaking this discovery process down more minutely, one can observe that it has two possible aspects. Sometimes the constructs produced by the pre-clear are plainly coming from pre-Scientology or non-Scientology sources. The images employed are not ones that are in vogue among Scientologists. They nonetheless fit Scientology reality because Scientology theory enunciates general categories of things to which a great diversity of idiosyncratic materials can be assigned. By contrast, there are typical Scientology motifs that will occasionally show up spontaneously in everyone's sessions. Space opera situations and mind-control battles with electronic forces are examples. Whatever elements of "natural symbolism" may be contained in these motifs, it is also indubitable that Scientologists become familiar with them by exposure to Hubbard's writings and other Scientologists' gossip about Track. It would therefore be easy to assert that this latter type of "discovery" is simply the product of suggestion. When we examine the material, however, this assertion boils down to meaning only that the pre-clear has borrowed his imagery from an interested as opposed to an indifferent source; in any event he must borrow it from somewhere. Any appropriation of images by activated schemata deprived of their usual context of operation is always a type of "borrowing" if one wants to put it that way; but since this appropriation consists of assimilating images and ideas to the activity of the self, it cannot fail to be personal whatever the source of the idea or image. This point is illustrated in a follow-up of Leo's "early Track" incident. Several weeks after he recounted this incident to me, he admitted he had lifted the idea for it from another Scientologist. He mused: "So— I feel a little bit like a copy cat. But that's silly. It was my incident; I was really in it, those were *my* feelings." We must return to the fact that the Scientology Track itself was, within certain broad constraints, shaped by pre-clear productions; this is true in regard to its more concrete elements—the popular motifs—as well as its more abstract ones—"incidents," "engrams," and so on. In effect, the pre-clear's "personalization" of the suggested is but the flip side of the "culturalization" of the personal that was performed by Hubbard in his elaboration of the theory of Track.

Reformulation

As stated, everything that comes to the pre-clear's mind during an auditing session can be construed as evidence in support of the Scientology world-view. Yet it is only at particular points that this evidence comes home with the sort of thrust that brings the process of renunciation temporarily to a halt and ushers in the "end phenomena" of auditing: release, cognition, extroversion. How does this take place? These critical turning points seem to break down into two steps, one wherein the merger of self with cultural format reaches an apogee of unreflective immediacy, and a following one in which reflection takes over and "makes sense" of both self and format.

In auditing, the "cognition" is typically preceded by a discharge of emotion, often sudden and sharp, and often clearly related to (one could say triggered by) a particular fantasy, memory-image, or idea. It can be said that at such points, the mental phenomena that Hubbard predicted will be "there" (Track episode, hidden postulate, or whatever) are more than just passively in view, they are, momentarily, a direct and unreflective reaction of the self. It is as if, instead of throwing up a scrambled assortment of rather distant self-portrayals, the pre-clear's structures of feeling seize upon one such portrayal and infuse it completely. At such points, a thought or image is not "reported" but instead blurted or sobbed; a scene is not merely witnessed but, for the instant, lived. The pre-clear, as in the case of Leo, may be distantly aware that he or she is running a borrowed image, but this awareness (if present) is vastly overshadowed by the sense of self-expression.

As the emotional response subsides, a sort of dispassionate reflectiveness takes over, leading to "cognition." The cognition usually embodies a two-sided appreciation of what has just transpired. On the one hand, the pre-clear is able to recognize in the materials of the session—in particular the last and most engaging bit—some deep personal configuration of feeling and thinking which has heretofore pervaded his or her daily life unconsciously. On the other hand, simultaneously with this self-recognition (and sometimes even overshadowing it) comes an insight into how the Scientology "reality" to which all the products of the session seem somehow to point can be usefully applied to the personal dilemmas that the pre-clear has just traced to their roots. Consider Leo's cognition. Leo recognized that the sour stomach of today had its source in a desire to regain, or retain, an earlier state of total satisfaction. Appearing in a vacuum, such an insight might suggest that he resign himself to the privations of the present because the gratifications of the past are bygone. Appearing within the Scientology framework, however, the insight points in quite the opposite direction. Yes, thetans have declined from their original self-sufficient state, but with the help of Scientology this downward spiral can be reversed and a thetan's original condition recaptured.

Another Scientologist reported the following final "incident" and the cognition that sprang from it.

> I saw what an absurd thing the whole [Track] incident had been. It was during a war, and I realized the whole absurdity of war. I was on the one side, see. And I'd been captured, or rather, let myself be captured, and executed—along with several others—by the firing squad. But the night before I was shot, the leader of the other side came to visit me in my cell. We had a long discussion and it turned out that we both had the same ideals, the same feelings about things. We were in agreement! What were we fighting about? It was absurd. Here I and thousands of people were dying because the two sides were in a big MISUNDERSTOOD about each other's purposes. I saw what war was all about. What non-sense war was. A complete waste of thousands of lives. And all wars are like that.

In Scientology, a "misunderstood" can be spotted and straightened out—just as the auditor spots the pre-clear's misunderstoods on the auditing commands or the course supervisor the student's misunderstoods on the course materials. So—it follows logically that Scientology could eliminate war. Along the same lines, yet another Scientologist reported the following cognition: "All the world is the result of an Overt, preceded by an ARC break." This means, in rough translation, "All the world is the result of a crime, preceded by an upset (or disappointment)." The implication of such an insight might be dreary indeed, were it not for the fact that Scientology training provides one with an "exact technology" for handling such things as overts and ARC breaks; ergo, Scientology can handle the world.

In this way, the relinquishment of a current emotional problem which begins with its expression in emotional discharge and crystal-lizes in the act of self-recognition is, through the implications of the cosmological system to which this self-recognition is fitted, converted at one stroke into a reinvestment.

Taking a broader view of the pre-clear's progress into Scientology, we can see that several factors interact to produce a sort of conversion-ary spiral. These are, first of all, the hope-engendering promises that

[259]

Scientology holds out to the newcomer. These in themselves are sufficient to induce many a potential convert to give the practice a try. The
enforced frustration of the practice then furnishes experiential evidence that Scientology's view of the world is correct, thus further
facilitating the relinquishment of old investments that is the thrust of
the practice. At the point of "cognition," this conversionary spiral
momentarily culminates, for while the self-referential aspect of the
insight nails down a relinquishment of some prior attachment, the
Scientology-referential dimension of the insight, by confirming the
special relevance of Scientology's promise to the individual's personal
problems, nails down a reinvestment of affect in Scientology itself.

Scientologists, and converts to any tradition, may experience any
number of these relinquishments and reinvestments over the course
of their participation in the practice. These moments may vary widely
in intensity and in the ease with which they are triggered. Neither
Scientology's model of conversion, that it occurs bit by bit along a
"gentle gradient," nor the model popular in Christian traditions, that
conversion is a single blinding flash on the road to Damascus, is really
adequate to the empirical variability of the process. I would maintain,
however, that whether most of the work of conversion is accomplished
in one dramatic leap, in a succession of minor hops, or in some mixture of the two, and whether all of these moments occur directly in the
midst of practice or unexpectedly in some tangential context, the basic
ingredients of conversion are as I have described them in regard to the
successful auditing session. In the successful session, we see the dynamics of conversion in microcosm.

What I have described so far I have situated in only one major phase
of the development of belief—the initial, youthful phase. As the bud-
ding convert is first exposed to the new belief system and begins his or
her first experiments with practice, the process of renunciation tends
to take as its target the practitioner's problematic attachments to the
"old" reality he or she has heretofore inhabited. With each little wave
of renunciation, some complex of emotional energy is withdrawn from
this old reality and transferred to the new. Typically this new reality is
relatively untested, hence easier to feel hopeful about. Typically too it
is structurally softer and more ambiguous than the old, and for this
reason less susceptible to the world's contradictions. Even so, we
must remember that "other-worldly" or "supernatural" orders, no
matter how well shielded these are from the conflicts and contradictions of the mundane realm, are still invariably more-or-less elaborate

detours back into the world. The locus of worldly action may shift, but there will nevertheless be some points of intersection between this world and the "other." A man who, failing in business, quits it to join an order of monastic agriculturalists may fail at farming also. The millennium may fail to arrive when prophesied. Or, most commonly, the vision is betrayed by the failure of its human adherents to behave as the redeemed should. In short, while he escapes frustration at one level, there is no guarantee that the religious convert will not reencounter it at the next. What happens then?

The Freudian answer to this question—that illusion is in the end therapeutically valueless because it only shifts neurotic demand to a new focus—raises a second question. This has to do with the similarity of psychoanalytic and religious renunciation. Freud and all subsequent psychoanalysts have argued that psychoanalysis is not creating "converts" but doing just the opposite: disensnaring the patient from the web of illusion and forcing him to face reality. If we are to argue that psychoanalysis itself is utilizing the process of renunciation, how do we reconcile this psychoanalytic claim with the foregoing portrait of renunciation?

The following chapter will attempt to come to grips with these two questions: (1) what happens when the new vision itself proves frustrating? and (2) is what happens any different in secular psychotherapy than in religion?

[9]

The Future of an Illusion

The conversionary spiral dissected in the last chapter has its exact parallel in psychoanalysis, for it constitutes one phase of what is called "transference." If we examine Freud's description of the early or positive phase of transference, it will be seen to differ very little from religious conversion, and it has an almost point-to-point correspondence with the behavior that Hubbard seized upon to characterize the "smoothly running," or, in Scientology slang, "flying" pre-clear.

Freud: . . .

> The patient understands the suggestions offered to him, concentrates upon the tasks appointed by the treatment, the material needed—his recollections and associations—is abundantly available; he astonishes the analyst by the sureness and accuracy of his interpretations, and the latter has only to observe with satisfaction how readily and willingly a sick man will accept all the new psychological ideas that are so hotly contested by the healthy in the world outside. [1958a:447]

Hubbard:

1. Pc cheerful or getting more cheerful.
2. Pc cogniting.
3. Fundamental rightnesses of pc asserting themselves.
4. Pc giving things to auditor briefly and accurately.
5. Pc finding things rapidly.
6. Meter reading properly. . . .
12. Pc running easily and if pc encounters somatics they are discharging. . . .

21. Pc not much troubled with present time problems and they are easily handled when they occur.

22. Pc stays certain of the auditing solution.

23. Pc happy and satisfied with auditor regardless of what auditor is doing. . . .

25. Pc looking better by reason of auditing.

26. Pc feeling more energetic. . . .

28. Pc wanting more auditing.

29. Pc confident and getting more confident. . . .

31. Auditor easily seeing how it was or is on pc's case by reason of pc's explanations.

32. Pc's ability to itsa [say what "it is" that's on his mind] and confront improving. . . .

36. Pc on time for session and willing and ready to be audited but without anxiety about it.

37. Pc's trouble in life progressively lessening. . . .

39. Pc getting more interested in data and technology of Dianetics and Scientology. [1975b:228–29][1]

Freud's description of the positive transferee's adulation of the analyst to outsiders should not be lost on the relatives and friends of newly converted Scientologists:

> The patient at home is never tired of praising the analyst and attributing new virtues to him. "He has quite lost his head over you; he puts implicit trust in you; everything you say is like a revelation to him," say the relatives. Here and there one among this chorus having sharper eyes will say: "It is positively boring the way he never speaks of anything but you: he quotes you all the time." [1958:447]

Moreover, this positive new attachment can be seen in psychoanalysis, as in religious situations, to energize and facilitate the effort toward renunciation that the practice demands. Says Freud, "let us realize at once that the transference exists in the patient from the beginning of the treatment, and is for a time the strongest impetus in the work" (1958:450). The writings of the mystics are particularly revealing of how transference-love reinforces the renunciatory struggle which in turn reinforces the transference, for here the object of devotion is of an entirely spiritual nature and interaction between

1. Hubbard's list has been shortened here to eliminate redundancy and items concerned with E-Meter behavior.

lover and beloved a completely intrapsychic one. St. John of the Cross writes: "In order to overcome all our desires . . . and to renounce all those things, our love and inclination for which are wont so to influence the will . . . we require a more ardent fire and a nobler love—that of the Bridegroom. Finding her delight and strength in Him, the soul gains the vigor and confidence which enable her easily to abandon all other affections" (Underhill 1967:203). As Evelyn Underhill expresses it, after the first convincing experience of God's love, "a never to be ended give-and-take is set up between the individual and the Absolute" (197). In Madame Guyon's words:

> I endured . . . long periods of privation, toward the end almost continual: but still I had from time to time inflowings of Thy Divinity so deep and intimate, so vivid and so penetrating, that it was easy for me to judge that Thou wast but hidden from me and not lost. . . . Every time that Thou didst return with more goodness and strength, Thou didst return also with greater splendour; so that in a few hours Thou didst rebuild all the ruins of my unfaithfulness and didst make good to me with profusion all my loss. [Underhill 1967:384]

It is a common belief, especially in the psychoanalytic community, that psychoanalysis shows its distinctiveness from religion and from other forms of suggestive therapy most decisively over this matter of transference (Fenichel 1945:559–61, 571). Religion attempts to keep the transference attachment alive, propping up the illusion with chicanery if necessary, because the apparent transformation of the believer's personality, under which old deleterious ways are dropped and new styles of behavior adopted, is dependent for its endurance upon continued faith in the new illusion that has taken the place of prior attachments. If the illusion should fall to the ground, a lapsing convert will immediately revert to his former ways and a temporarily cured neurotic resume his neurosis, the conversion or cure having been only superficial. Psychoanalysis, by contrast, eventually turns upon the transference itself, and subjects it to the same illusion-stripping interpretations that have earlier been directed toward the symptoms. The transference is treated as a "new edition" of the symptoms, and it too must be broken down before libidinal energy can be freed to seek realistic outlets. It is important for the maintenance of this claim that psychoanalysis see its practice as inherently illusion-destroying, and not, as I seem to be suggesting, inherently illusion-creating.

I think there is a way that we can see around this objection and continue to maintain that the practice of psychoanalysis (and other depth therapies) and the practice of religion work along one and the same dynamic. What is insufficiently appreciated is that a process that creates illusion may also destroy it, yet the process of renunciation described here does exactly that. The new arises from the wreckage of the old. Once accomplished, the new itself may become grist for the renunciatory mill. In the most fully systematized renunciatory traditions, the rhetoric and intentions of religion conform exactly to those of psychoanalysis. In Zen, for instance, the worlds of attachment—whether by our standards "real," or supernatural—are all considered illusion: *makyo*. Kapleau points out: "Other religions and sects place great store by experiences which involve visions of God or hearing heavenly voices, performing miracles, receiving divine messages, or becoming purified through various rites. . . . In varying degree these practices induce a feeling of well-being, yet from the Zen point of view all are morbid states devoid of true religious significance and hence only makyo" (1967:40). When the goal of the practice is recognized as some condition beyond illusion, then the initial conversionary sweep of renunciation is followed by secondary and tertiary sweeps that progressively transform each level of belief into a yet more rarified one until there remains, in Ruysbroeck's words, only "an imageless and bare understanding."

What is of particular interest here is that this trend toward further renunciatory sweeps may arise even when religious or therapeutic leadership has exercised no particular forethought as to its necessity, and even when there is no recognition that it is happening. Attempts to maintain a transference dependency and attempts to eradicate such a dependency tend to converge upon the same point: further practice, hence further renunciation. The reason for this is to be found in certain perils to which belief is prey. Let me illustrate these perils by excerpting from the various traditions discussed here—psychoanalysis, mysticism, and Scientology—accounts of characteristic things that go wrong. In all these accounts we will see certain commonalities. The chief of these are that disciplined practice collapses and the supportive illusion which hitherto sustained it takes on a frustrating, burdensome, or even hostile coloration.

In psychoanalysis, the better-known meaning of the term "transference" applies actually to a later transformation of the positive conversionary spiral described above. The "fair weather" of the positive phase, Freud declares, "cannot last forever. There comes a day when it clouds over." The attachment to the analyst which has hovered helpfully in the background of the treatment for some time suddenly becomes focused and manipulatory.

> No matter how amenable [the patient] has been up till then, she now suddenly loses all understanding of and interest in the treatment, and will not hear or speak of anything but her love, the return of which she demands; she has either given up her symptoms or else she ignores them; she even declares herself well. A complete transformation ensues in the scene—it is as though some make-believe had been interrupted by a real emergency, just as when the cry of fire is raised in a theatre. [Freud 1959:160]

This transformation typically ensues, according to Freud, just as the symptoms which have brought the patient into analysis are on the verge of vanishing. The impression that the new "love" is a replacement for these symptoms is inescapable: "in place of the patient's original illness appears the artificially induced acquired transference, the transference-disorder; in place of a variety of unreal objects of his libido appears one object, also 'phantastic' of the person of the physician" (1958:462). Freud also saw as the immediate trigger for the change the analyst's demand for some deeper effort at self-discovery on the part of the patient.

In the mystical traditions, the fair weather of early practice clouds over as well. The gratifying states in which the mystic has luxuriated become less dependable and give way to periods of "spiritual aridity" during which God withdraws from the devotee. "Mystics call such oscillations the 'Game of Love' in which God plays, as it were, 'hide and seek' with the questing soul" (Underhill 1967:383). For a while, more scrupulous practice and more thoroughgoing efforts at self-denial succeed in bringing the divinity back, but a point is reached at which practice collapses entirely and the negative state of consciousness settles in unbudgeably. The mystic then enters a prolonged period of suffering termed "the dark night of the soul."

> When they [the mystics] are in it everything seems to "go wrong" with them. They are tormented by evil thoughts and abrupt temptations, lose grasp not only of their spiritual but also of their worldly affairs. . . . The health of those passing through this phase often suffers, they become

[266]

"odd" and their friends forsake them; their intellectual life is at a low ebb. [Underhill 1967:384–85]

The "Dark Night of the Soul," once fully established, is seldom lit by visions or made homely by voices. It is of the essence of its miseries that the once-possessed power of orison or contemplation now seems wholly lost. [381]

Worldly structures, previously abandoned, flood back chaotically.

As regards the will, there is a sort of moral dereliction: the self cannot control its inclinations and thoughts. In the general psychic turmoil, all the unpurified parts of man's inheritance, the lower impulses and unworthy ideas which have long been imprisoned below the threshold, force their way into the field of consciousness. "Every vice was reawakened in me," says Angela of Foligno . . . St. Catherine of Siena, in the interval between her period of joyous illumination and her "spiritual marriage," was tormented by visions of fiends, who filled her cell and "with obscene words and gestures invited her to lust." [392]

But to give up on divine revelations and "restructure" back into the old world of available gratifications proves no easier for the mystic than it does for the ordinary lover forsaken by his or her love. The renouncer winds up, in the words of St. Teresa, "crucified between heaven and hell." In these higher negative states, just as in the lower, rebellious impulses may surface. Freud makes note of this in regard to the negative phase of transference; in medieval Christianity, demoniacal possession, to which monastic personnel seemed unusually prone, was a convenient interpretation for those states of mind during which formerly devout persons were seized with blasphemous impulses (see Osterreich 1966).

In the career of Scientologists, we find patterns of renunciatory backlash that resemble both negative transference in psychoanalysis and the disorderly collapse of the mystics. In his writings on "repair" and "review" auditing, Hubbard provides us with quite a detailed portrait of the renunciatory "failure." Paralleling his list of good indicators just cited in regard to the "flying" pre-clear is a list of bad indicators that signal to the auditor that the pre-clear is "in trouble on his case."

1. Pc not wanting to be audited.
2. Pc protesting auditing.

3. Pc looking worse after auditing.
4. Pc not able to locate incidents easily. . . .
6. Pc less certain.
7. Pc not doing well in life. . . .
9. Pc in ethics trouble after auditing [i.e., with the disciplinary wing of the Church of Scientology]. . . .
11. Pc wandering all over track. . . .
13. Pc demanding unusual solutions. . . .
16. Pc trying to self-audit in or out of session. . . .
19. Pc using, or continuing to use, other treatments. . . .
23. No TA action on running incidents.
24. Pc not cogniting.
25. Pc dispersed [unable to concentrate, mentally scattered].
26. Pc trying to explain condition to auditor or others. . . .
28. Pc not available for sessions. . . .
30. Pc attention on auditor. . . .
32. Pc overwhelmed. . . .
37. Pc sick between sessions. [Hubbard 1975b:227–28][2]

The majority of Scientologists suffer at least mild backswings of this sort sooner or later in their careers, and the reports of many, especially those engaged in extensive cycles or high-pressure training courses such as the Solo Course, reveal the same oscillation-with-increasing-intensity pattern remarked upon by Underhill. Scientology even has a word for this: "roller-coasting." Ex-Scientologist Robert Kaufman's description of his own progress through Scientology provides an informative illustration.

Kaufman's decline from his initial happy conversion to Scientology began while he was on the Solo Course at Saint Hill Manor, one of the Advanced Organizations in Great Britain. The first signs of a backswing were spasms of doubt and scrupulosity:

> One . . . unhappy-looking man in his early forties . . . perpetually wore on his sweater the slip *I am on Power Processes. Please Do Not Ask Me Questions, Audit Me, or Discuss My Case with Me.* . . . The sign, which he had to wear day and night, made me jumpy. . . . Occasionally my heart would leap as I realized I'd said the wrong thing. At breakfast I had asked, "Would you like more coffee?" Surely this question was innocuous and yet the sign forbade questions. [Kaufman 1972:107–8]

2. Hubbard's list is shortened here to eliminate redundancy.

Characteristically, Kaufman resorted to increased rigor to overcome any niggling weakness. He explains:

> I was being taught to crack down. It was one more burden lifted not to have to be rebellious anymore—rather, to be obedient. . . . An almost imperceptible change was occurring in me: I no longer supposed I was using Scientology for my own purposes. I liked the feeling; it was a clean one. My old ways had been grandiose—impure. [101]

> I knuckled down harder than ever on the [solo audit] checksheet, never going anywhere on weekends; not to London to visit my friends, or to Brighton for a look at the ocean. I got no exercise, not even walking; my legs felt weak. The manorhouse grounds and their surrounding area represented something I wouldn't allow myself to *have* as yet, identified, in my submerged world of fantasy, with the core of the bank, which was to remain sacrosanct until the day of Solo Audit. [114]

Further strict practice eventually paid off with an unprecedented "high" following a training checkout with a fellow student:

> When we were finished, we could sense our own freedom and certainty, a well-being approaching ecstasy, at finally having mastered the precious data. We got up, briefcases in hand, and set out down the path over the luscious meadows. I had never been this way in my life; my body was a via [device] which I was operating, in control, making it step along in any manner that appealed to me, shedding my glasses to marvel at the tiny blue and lavender flowers near our feet with eyes that seemed to get sharper with each step. . . . I knew then that THIS WAS IT. The words sang through my being: God, to be clear, is just this . . . all the time! [116]

Before he reached the solo audit, however, Kaufman's problems set in again with renewed sharpness. Creeping doubt spread to the materials of the Solo Course—did he remember them correctly, had he studied the proper bulletins sufficiently? The final trigger to collapse was a rebuke from his course supervisor for using "highly restimulative" words in the labels of a clay demo portraying the core of the Bank. A tiny matter but sufficient to crystallize the swing from Beingness to Bank. Renunciation suddenly took on the colorings of privation.

[269]

That afternoon, I took sick. . . . I felt flushed and feverish, and by six o'clock my sole desire was to pile into bed.

I awoke the next morning and couldn't get back to sleep. A malevolent force kept me awake mulling over in my mind the coming Solo audit. I lay shivering under the covers, thinking of all the ways I was dramatizing. Some of the words ended in *ness*. It could be *Unhappiness*. I had been stuck out in Sussex for weeks, with perhaps several more months of study to follow, away from city streets and old friends, subjected to considerable discomfort and rigid discipline which left me no time to myself. For this period of my stay, I had denied myself what I thought of as "living" as a test of my determination. Now, thinking about it in the early morning hours, it struck me that life had become quite forlorn. As light began to brighten up the room, and the first birds of morning shrieked in the tree-tops, a vibration shot through my body like a charge of electric voltage: it was fear. I lay huddled around the shock, revulsed by the feel of the sheets against my legs. I was aware of the sharp, antiseptic smell of English coal-tar soap on the window-sill above my head, and the shrill buzzing of an electric-razor converter under the bed. . . . sound and smell which keyed-in primitive terror from the bank. [119]

Again characteristically, the backswing was accompanied by an inability to follow the discipline of the practice. The solo audit materials warn the student, Kaufman tells us, not to mull over the solo audit procedure before the time comes to do it. Students who catch themselves thinking of "dramatizations," are supposed to say, "THAT'S IT!" and go back to whatever else they were doing (112). Kaufman reports: "I spent each morning from three o'clock lying awake in a state of terror. . . . My broodings on dramatizations became far-fetched. . . . I tried to stop this madness with the training command, 'That's it!' and must have repeated the words dozens of times in the course of each hour" (123). His oscillations continued, much to his chagrin, even after he had attained Clear—the point at which he had been given to believe all Bank would cease. He later experienced states of extreme disgust with auditing and finally, on the OT III section, rebelled by wildly disobeying the auditing instructions. Stalled in his auditing progress and routed onto a training course, Kaufman lasted only another few weeks before fleeing the Org and returning to New York. But departure was no relief:

I had expected to make a quick recovery from my Scientology experience: in reality the slow decline begun at St. Hill was still in effect. I inhabited two worlds simultaneously, and though the beloved [New York] world seemed the same as always, there was something different about me. . . . I used to pray that I could be as I'd been before, full of weaknesses and hopes, never knowing what I was doing . . . stumbling about, planning, whoring, wasting time. I observed with clarity the awful things my brain was doing, and compared it with the way it had worked before. . . . I couldn't bring it back and I missed my beloved old brain. [214, 224]

Underhill considers the failure of renunciation to be simply a function of fatigue. Relentless self-denial places a formidable strain on the psychic apparatus and eventually this effort along with its pleasurable fruits—the illuminated states of consciousness—flags and gives way to a disorder of impulses and a heightened sense of the deprivation that is renunciation's other face. Freud's interpretation of negative transference is that the transference has moved "into the service of resistance," meaning that the psychic forces which oppose the revelation of the patient's unconscious libidinal attachments have seized upon feelings for the analyst and are using these to create a diversion.

Scientology explanations for the pre-clear's troubles cover both these bases plus a further one. In regard to the first, fatigue, there is the Scientology concept of "over-run." To over-run a pre-clear on a process means to continue auditing beyond the end phenomena of auditing. Instead of being left with a happy "cognition" and temporary relief from further introspection on the subject of the process, the pre-clear is "pushed further into the Bank," and the result is a disorderly mess and often an irritable or disillusioned pre-clear. Kaufman reports that over-running is a fairly common "goof" on the upper levels where pre-clears are solo-auditing themselves: he attributes this fact to Hubbard's not having specified the end phenomena for some of the Confidential Levels (Kaufman 1972:212–13).[3] The condition that Underhill calls fatigue may also be glossed in Scientology as "overwhelm." An overwhelmed pre-clear is simply one who has been "spun into the Bank" for whatever reason (auditing mistakes, severe personal problems, etc.) and who is as a result temporarily inauditable. Very, very light auditing actions and "assists" can sometimes be used in these cases; apart from those, the pre-clear is advised to rest and recuperate in a relaxing environment.

3. Three of my informants mentioned in passing that they had over-run one or more of the Confidential Levels.

[271]

Another explanation of collapse in Scientology theory is that the pre-clear is being audited "over withholds"—he or she is consciously or unconsciously trying to keep something from the auditor. Here Freud is echoed. The signs of this, besides a failed session, are that the pre-clear "natters" (criticizes Scientology or the auditor) or becomes overly focused on the auditor. The sorts of withholds commonly suspected (and found) are negative attitudes toward Scientology or a past history of having done something against Scientology.

The final large category of matters that can cause a collapse of practice and of faith are in fact things that act as disconfirmations of the Scientology vision and thus as sources of doubt: auditors who fail to audit as the pre-clear thinks they should; gains which the pre-clear expected Scientology to give him or her but which failed to materialize; outsiders ridiculing, debunking, or bruiting scandals about Scientology; other Scientologists misbehaving, getting "in trouble on their cases," or conducting themselves in an un-Scientological manner; authoritarian or unjust behavior on the part of the Church authorities or tales of such behavior; policies coming down from above that delay the pre-clear's progress, demand more money, or indirectly invalidate the levels which he or she has attained; the pre-clear's failure to impress friends or family with Scientology or his or her new skills. According to Scientologists, the areas just listed come to light again and again in "review" auditing sessions. It is not surprising. These are things which chip away at the protective armor of the faith. They suggest that Scientology may not be, after all, a safe haven for the hopes. Roller-coastering, the pronounced oscillation between keyed-out and keyed-in states, is specifically linked to the pre-clear's association with a suppressive person or group. In Scientology theory, the pre-clear's "gains" are undercut by the suppressive's invalidation, and these invalidating persons or groups must be shunned if the pre-clear is to maintain his gains.

While these three causes of renunciatory failure—fatigue, resistance, and doubt—appear heterogeneous, there is a way in which they all amount to the same thing. The edifice of faith is held aloft by a column of effort, the renouncer's effort at relinquishing prior attachments. Beyond the first and easy stages wherein relinquishment covers primarily attachments that were highly problematic already, this effort becomes increasingly a strain. Soon a precarious balance exists between the inducement to continue—that is, the attractiveness of the illusion—and the amount of energy available for continuing. At this point various things can intervene to upset the balance. The sorts of things that most commonly do so are determined in part by the nature of the illusion. The Christian mystics studied by Underhill provide us with something of a limit case. First, their tradition apparently imposes no limitations on the amount of time per day spent in renunciatory practice and thus no brake on psycho-physiological exhaustion. Second, the object of their transference-love is entirely "otherworldly"; it does not act independently of the believer's intrapsychic state. The collapse of Christian mystical practice and the concomitant disappearance of God may thus be an almost perfect function of loss of energy. Periods of "spiritual aridity" become more and more frequent until finally there is nothing left but desolation and disorder.

When the transference-object (or objects) is one that has a greater intersection with the world outside the renouncer's head, as is the case when these objects involve people, an organization, or a set of predictions about how ordinary reality will behave, then renunciatory lapse may be triggered prior to complete exhaustion. This may take place in two ways. First, such objects suggest the possibility of obtaining gratification through a direct manipulation of the world, a possibility that becomes more tempting as the interior search becomes more difficult. Rather than manifesting themselves in interior images, the emotional schemata begin to function as they have been accustomed to function: in the world directly. In Freud's terms, "recollection" is transformed into "repetition." The other "snare" occasioned by more worldly objects and articles of faith is that these may violate the expectations that the believer has vested in them, thus decreasing their attractiveness and the believer's motivation to continue practice. When this occurs, not only may energy be directed away from practice and into attempts to manipulate the situation directly—in acts of protest or rebellion, for instance—but spontaneous uncontrolled regressions, in this case aimed at the objects of the faith, may arise as competitors to the disciplined and guided regressions of the practice. We detect this factor in Kaufman's inability to cease his terrified broodings. Asked during one of his many sessions with a review auditor, if anything or anyone was "suppressing" him, he found himself answering, with relief, "Scientology, specifically Ron." This response surprised him, but the auditor explained afterward, "It frequently happens that Ron is the SP [suppressive person]" (Kaufman 1972:213). It frequently happens, in other words, that what was once part of the cure, comes to constitute part of the symptom.

The hopeful illusions obtained through renunciation are, it would

[273]

seem, inherently fragile. But there are two major ways, observable historically, in which the problems posed by this fragility are overcome. The first and most familiar is the waning of reliance upon visionary experience as a source of support for the belief system. Concerning the fate of new religious doctrines, William James remarks:

> . . . if [the] doctrine prove contagious enough to spread to any others, it becomes a definite and labeled heresy. But if it then still proves contagious enough to triumph over persecution, it becomes itself an orthodoxy; and when a religion has become an orthodoxy, its day of inwardness is over: the spring is dry, the faithful live at second hand exclusively and stone the prophets in their turn. [1967:269]

At this mature stage, illusion is cut loose from its depth psychological roots and passes into the realm of unreflected-upon dogma. Rather than a simple "triumph" over persecution, more often a process of accommodation between sect and surrounding society takes place which leads to the taming of the sect's original zealous ambitions and, concomittantly, a greater acceptance on the part of the host society. Both sides of this process act to reduce the need for renunciatory effort on the part of believers. Social acceptance is itself a source of religious authority and one that tends to replace rather than add to the authority obtained through apodictic experience. At the same time, the taming of a movement's original visionary program—to usher in the millennium, to "clear the planet" or whatever—amounts to a partial abandonment of the earlier and more fervid hopes, and a diminished vision of this sort requires less pent-up energy for its sustenance.

For some belief systems, however, this passage to comfortable dogmatism may prove impossible. In order for it to take place, the belief system must, first, enjoin a clear program for action in the world and not simply for conversion to the belief: second, this program must be, if only through strategic modifications, ultimately successful, that is generative of wider and wider social acceptance. When such a program is lacking or is actively ruled out by the tenets of the faith, or when it is present but ineffective, then a system's only recourse against the eventual loss of its following is to counter their inevitable lapses of faith with demands for renewed and deeper renunciation. Moreover, even those religions that have enjoyed the widest social success and the greatest dogmatic acceptance must depend, for continued vitality, upon a leadership whose faith is of a more "inspired" and intimate sort—the more so when social change threatens to overturn traditional dogmas. Thus rising up in the institutional heart of traditionalism is the same problem of belief sustainment encountered among the more marginal sects. And the response here will be, and has been, the same. The mystical traditions of the great world religions testify to this solution, for in these renunciation is most thoroughly systematized and its effects most radically understood. In all these traditions, further and deeper renunciation is rationalized on the grounds that the believer's initial faith is naive, faltering, and imperfect—a state of belief that must, on principle, give way before more thorough self-purgations if a "perfect faith" is to be obtained. Lapses of practice and upsurges of doubt are clear evidence of the believer's imperfect condition, and thus a clear signal that further acts of renunciation are necessary.

Psychoanalysis took the same direction through a related route. Not "belief" ostensibly, but symptom remission, was the condition Freud sought to stabilize. Furthermore, there was never any question of a program for worldly action to be undertaken by the psychoanalytic client; change in his or her internal state was the solitary goal of psychoanalytic treatment from the outset. After having comprehended the obstacle to this goal occasioned by the tranference, Freud, like the mystics, required that this corrupt condition of faith, transference onto the physician, become the target of all subsequent renunciation. "Repetition," in the form of resistive transference, had to be converted back into "recollection."

What is the ultimate result of this continual re-renunciation, the swallowing up of illusion in the process that originally engendered it? Again, the mystical traditions provide the clearest answer. On the cognitive side, each new stage or level of the mystical voyage produces an experiential understanding of the world that is more ineffable and contentless than the one before, and thus, more protected from the world's invalidation. The mystics cited by Underhill who achieve these rarefied heights look back upon their prior apprehensions of the divine as the products of a gross and unrefined consciousness which mistook symbol for reality, and illusion for truth. On the emotional side, with each advance, the hopes vested in the lesser illusion must be abandoned, and abandonment ultimately extends even to the hope for continuation of the ecstasies, releases, and raptures that enlivened earlier practice. Indeed, the dark night of the soul does not lift until the mystic has embraced it, and thus embraced frustration, as his lot.

> Thus, when St. Catherine of Siena was tormented by hideous visions of sin, she was being led by her deeper self to the heroic acceptance of this subtle form of torture, almost unendurable to her chaste and delicate mind. When these trials had brought her to the point at which she ceased to resist them, but exclaimed, "I have chosen suffering for my consolation," their business was done. They ceased. [Underhill 1967:398]

> His [Suso's] torments and miseries, his fears for the future, continued to grow until they at last came to their term in a sort of mental crisis. . . . After thus suffering . . . his brain was exhausted, and at last he became calmer, and sitting down he came to himself: and turning to God, and abandoning himself to His Will, he said, "If it cannot be otherwise, *fiat voluntas tua.*" The act of submission was at once followed by an ecstasy and vision, in which the approaching end of his troubles was announced to him. [411–12]

The flight from a frustrating world ends when it has come full circle and the fact of frustration—at last—accepted. Once this final surrender was accomplished, Underhill's mystics were to be found reentering the world (usually as religious trainers or administrators) without the aid of further rigorous practice. In this respect they were not unlike the ideal psychoanalysand who, after finally overcoming the "new neurosis" of the transference, emerges from the therapy an accepting realist. The future of illusions, even religious ones, is ultimately extinction.

From a cynical point of view, it seems as if the renouncer might just as well skip the entire climb up the spiritual ladder since the top so closely resembles the bottom, yet those who have made the climb successfully argue that it is the only "way." Far from the lower levels of the belief system being discredited by the higher conclusions, they are in a way reinforced, for however gross and inaccurate these lesser conceptions, they occupy the position of keys or gates through which the seeker must pass to reenter the Real. If we consider that the bottom-most level of the hierarchy is simply the given world itself and that this level reappears at the top, transfigured through renunciatory eyes into a school in which the lessons of the cosmos are taught, it is apparent why "world-rejecting" religious traditions are so paradoxically complacent toward the status quo.

Scientology's case is more complex, for Scientology policy envisions both of the two principal directions that illusion may take: rarefication through continued renunciation, and the establishment of an unquestioned orthodoxy. On the one hand, the idea is accepted on principle that, following the model of both psychoanalysis and mysticism, auditing should continue until the pre-clear achieves a well-nigh perfect mental health and is pushed to exalted levels of awareness. Thus, when the pre-clear fails to make headway in auditing and training, the general remedy for this is to locate, through review auditing, the source of the difficulty, handle it, and return the pre-clear to the main auditing (or training) route. In the *Book of Case Remedies*, a collection of tips on how to handle stalled cases, Hubbard states wryly, ". . . the basic problem of making clears and O.T.'s is not really getting pre-clears to have auditing. That's easy really. It's getting preclears to KEEP ON getting auditing" (Hubbard 1968c:7). If we look over all the things that Hubbard suggested can stall a pre-clear's progress, we find in many of them an indirect articulation of the idea that the pre-clear may be suffering from an imperfect, faltering faith. He or she may have "hidden standards" for Scientology, a goal that he or she expected Scientology to fulfill that has not been fulfilled, an ARC break (disillusionment, upset) with Scientology or some of its personnel, or perhaps, most fundamentally, a "misunderstood." As all these sorts of problems are located in review auditing and the pre-clear's "considerations" about them "pulled," his or her "repetition" is gradually converted back into "recollection."

On the other hand, Hubbard mixed the continued renunciation solution, which pushes the pre-clear in the direction of transcending his illusions about Scientology, with an almost equal number of tactics aimed at shoring the illusion up. The pre-clear may be audited out of an ARC break occasioned by a clumsy auditor, but at the same time clumsy auditors are redrilled and training elaborated further so as to produce perfect auditors in the future. The pre-clear is audited over his or her anxieties about negative reports on Scientology in the press; and at the same time, a stiff libel suit is brought against the journalist responsible for them. The pre-clear must overcome his or her impatience to have Scientology imbue its followers with magical abilities; at the same time, a fresh batch of "success stories" is periodically released testifying to the obtainability of these powers. In this sense, even with its pronounced mystical tendencies, Scientology moves in the direction of a utopian or "transformative" religious movement— that is, one in which an attempt is made to alter the world to fit the illusion rather than to abandon all illusions about the world.

The utopian world-building actions are rationalized in part as efforts to "create a safe environment" for Scientology. Attacks against the enemies of Scientology are justified on this ground. There is also the theme that Scientology technology is not itself complete. Therefore it is necessary to tinker constantly with the auditing and training hierarchy, streamlining and perfecting it, and to come up with new and more effective ways to administer the dispensation of data and technology. The reasoning in either case is that Scientology's basic goal— to "clear the planet," that is, create a world society of utterly sane, nonreactive people—is attainable: it's just a matter of getting the technology perfected and effectively dispensed.

In terms of the usual drift of religious movements toward social accommodation, social acceptance, and dogmatism, the Scientology movement, at the time I was acquainted with it, appeared still relatively immature. Its utopian vision was still relatively undimmed, its spiritual claims still more or less incredible to outsiders, its relationship to the surrounding society still conflictful. Nevertheless there had been during the 1960s and early 1970s a widening of public acquiescence to the idea that Scientology is a religious sect that is here to stay, and along with this, an acceptance on the part of the sect itself that its basic assertions are "religious" in nature and thus on a rather different plane from inexorable fact. This attitude constitutes somewhat of a cooling of its initial claims. All in all, I had to judge Scientology's vision as slightly, but only slightly, altered, by the dimming effects of sect maturation.

Inasmuch as Scientology continues to hold out a utopian promise and to suffer from the animosity of the surrounding society, its renunciatory thrust must continue strong, for upon rigorous practice depends its believers' ability to maintain an inner certainty of the truth of their beliefs. By the same token, of course, those who find themselves incapable of the more heroic acts of renunciation that their system demands will fall by the wayside. To put it another way, the extremity of Scientology's claims makes its membership ever vulnerable to doubt; the nonacceptance, even hostility, of the surrounding society reinforces this doubt. A believer may, accordingly, capitulate to his or her doubts, or, relying upon practice, transcend them through further renunciatory activity. Finally, there is the third alternative, at this point only incipient among the membership, to adopt an unreflective, conformist, acceptance of the beliefs.

In the careers of individual Scientologists, some mixture of all three of these tendencies is usually apparent. That many fall by the wayside seems undeniable, judging from the small percentage of Clears and OTs relative to the numbers initially attracted. Not all these departers are disillusioned, to be sure; some have never really converted, others have lacked the time or money for further participation. But definitive repudiators of Scientology exist, and often, if they are higher-level people, the noise of their departure will be heard round the Scientology world. Robert Kaufman is an example, William Burroughs another, John McMaster, the best known-figure in Scientology other than Hubbard, yet another. Many of these people never return. Some by their defamations make themselves anathema to the organization to the point that they will never be readmitted. Yet others, after a year or two or even after a decade, drift back in. At that point they begin to fade into a class of seasoned old-timers who are the true "transcenders" of the movement. These are people who, after battling their way through a succession of disappointments with the movement and with Hubbard, have no further illusions about either, but are nevertheless sincerely dedicated to the principle of spiritual enlightenment and to Scientology's "technology." As a spiritual "way," Scientology, they feel, has no equal. Typically these more seasoned souls have gone through earlier phases of intense involvement with the group, either during their progress through the Confidential Levels, or as gungho franchisers or Org staffers, or all of these. They reach a point, however, where their participation becomes more modest and more controlled. The people of this type that I knew stayed within a circle of like-minded Scientology friends and often affiliated themselves to a local Mission where less pressure was brought on them to support the utopian crusade and where more flexible and informal arrangements existed for doing for others and for each other what they felt Scientology does best: auditing. Dipping into the Advanced Orgs occasionally for a new level or additional training, they held themselves aloof from excessive expectations.

Louise and Bart [who had sold their franchise after a financially damaging tangle with the Scientology higher-ups] explained that they'd pretty much decided to stay out of the mainstream of Scientology after all.

[279]

Louise said, "You know all our natter (criticisms, complaints)—well, we found out we agreed with it!" They no longer thought of it as just "bankiness" on their part. "We were so interiorized into Scientology," she explained, "that we couldn't see what we were doing, or what was being done to us. Now that I get some distance, I can see all the games conditions I'd gotten into with the people in it—with Ron. I look back on some of this and laugh." They argued that all of the problems lie with the Organization, not the "tech," not the ideas.

Bart had decided, after some hesitation, to go back to the AO for a training course that was owed him. He opined that the solution for handling the ups and downs of Scientology and the ups and downs of life generally was "the ability to connect and disconnect at will."

This outer circle of sophisticated lay and field (Mission-affiliated) Scientologists often serves to cushion the fall of more bitterly disillusioned converts who return home from the Advanced Orgs "in trouble on their case."

I asked Ruth [part-owner of a franchise] about the scene at the Advanced Orgs in Los Angeles. She said, "Oh—I don't know. We send some of our people out there and—we have to be careful. They can come back so ARC broken. We had one boy, a young guy, go over, and he was a beauty. He'd had all the wins he could get here and he was a Grade IV, so we finally sent him out for his Power (Grades V and Va), and he came back so ARC broken we didn't see him for a year. He did not set foot in our Center for a whole year afterwards. It wasn't us he was mad at, he was ARC broken with Scientology. Something went wrong out there. Of course he did show up eventually and we gave him a clean-up [review] session. We'll do that if it's one of our own people. . . . He's fine now; he's going ahead.[4]

A smaller percentage of Scientologists succeed in keeping their involvement relatively under control all the way along, in slowing down, as it were, the process of renunciation so that its bite is never too deep. Miriam, a young computer programmer, slowly but surely worked her way up the auditing ladder to the highest available OT

---

4. Kaufman, whose miseries were detailed earlier, was given hours of free review auditing by the franchisers who had first introduced him to Scientology. They were not reluctant to criticize the Organization, to reveal their own past crises to him, and to assure him that his tribulations were common among high-level Scientologists. He was not won back, but he seems to have used the auditing as a way to make sense of and thus ease the pain of his deconversion (see Kaufman 1972:227–58).

Levels with only one short period of involvement on the staff of an Org (not an Advanced Org) and without ever becoming an auditor (other than to learn solo auditing). Never seriously disillusioned with or critical of Scientology, she nevertheless refused to throw her all behind the cause.

> She said, "The people who're on staff and in the Orgs and busy being auditors say they're there because they've 'cognited' that that's the way to 'clear the planet'—why, be an auditor, go on staff! Then there are all sorts of fringe people like me, and the trouble with us [according to them] is we just haven't 'cognited' yet." She chortled.

While she looked forward to each new auditing level with obvious relish, she was more apt to find solutions to personal problems not in the auditing sessions but in a matter-of-fact, practical approach facilitated by Scientology lore about how to handle one's interpersonal environment. Auditing, which she saw as a route to subtle awarenesses, was just the icing on the cake. Her attitude is revealed in the following exchange.

> I complained to Miriam that although I know Scientology tells you to take responsibility for what's going on around you, suppose what's messing you up is your anger over other people's refusal to do their part. She answered that a Scientologist won't necessarily go around *always* taking responsibility just because it's the thing to do—it's a matter of choice. "But I figure, well it's my universe and I'm the person who has to live in it. And if something comes along and makes a mess of it, I'm the one whose stuck with that mess so I figure it's up to me to straighten it out. That's just the way I am. I like my little universe to be neat and tidy."

It is possible that Miriam's calm internalization of Scientology discipline and her freedom from excessive magical hopes have to do, in part, with the fact that she is a second-generation Scientologist, brought into Scientology by a converted (and still involved) parent. Thus an element of traditionalism, small but emotionally important, informs her faith.

Conclusions

I began this inquiry with a question current in cultural anthropology: how do ritual, magical, and religious activities work to
bring about certain characteristic subjective changes in those who
participate in them? It is now possible to return to this question and
examine previous answers more carefully in light of what has been
argued here. I think it will be seen that previous answers and the one
I am proposing here do not contradict, but in many respects, "talk
past" each other, and that this is to some degree a function of the
historical condition of the ritual or religious activity being examined.

The sorts of religious actions most frequently observed by anthropologists are communal ritual performances in which dramatic
displays (masked imitations, clowning, narrative enactments) and the
unveiling and manipulation of symbolic paraphernalia hold center-
stage. Specialists versed in ritual lore direct the activities and often
assume the central dramatic roles. The rotation of performance re-
sponsibilities and collective dancing and singing may, over the course
of the rite, guarantee at least temporary active participation by just
about everyone, but at any point in time a large number of those
present may be merely spectators. The average nonspecialist, when
asked how he or she understood the ritual may prove vague, inarticulate, or puzzled by the question. Certainly he or she does not deliver
up a spiritual diary of the kind that we associate with religious visionaries of the Western tradition. When it comes to explaining how the
ritual accomplished its presumed psychological effects (or is geared to
do so, whether or not it succeeds in every case), the anthropologist is
not awash in the native's subjective data but is dominated rather by

the image of a spectacle with spectators. Insofar as ritual participation is spectatorship, the anthropologist reasons, it should be possible to extrapolate what went on in people's heads from what went on in the show, and to argue that the subjective outcome of a ritual is comparable to that of listening to a piece of music, witnessing a dramatic performance, or hearing a persuasive argument. And indeed, it can often be shown convincingly that the ritual's drama—its symbolic unfolding—is, once all the meanings are understood, organized so as to elicit certain concerns and lead to certain conclusions. Emotional discharges on the part of participant-spectators during the course of the ritual—expressions of anger, fear, exuberance, and so on—can be seen as reactions to some part of the message. When considering evidence of more bizarre subjective changes taking place in the participants, trance or possession states, for instance, contemporary anthropology has moved away from the ethnocentric psychiatrism of an earlier school that saw these displays as examples of "contained psychosis," and toward arguments that tend to "culturalize" the behavior in one way or another. Trance and possession states, for instance, may be seen as highly conventionalized expressions of certain widespread beliefs, such as the belief that souls can escape the body (trance) or that spirits can possess it (possession) (Lewis 1971). In another example, Geertz interprets Javanese mystical contemplation as a ritualized act that "rehearses" the upper-caste Javanese in the controlled equanimity that their cultural value system enjoins, while the self-mortification of the Plains Indian vision-seekers rehearses Plains Indians in the "passionate willfulness" emphasized in their warrior culture (Geertz 1972:94–95). Mind-altering techniques, that is, the practices that lead to trance, possession, quietude, or vision, are also susceptible to being swept under the theoretical carpet of conventionalized expression. There is, of course, justification for this inasmuch as such techniques are seldom viewed by the practitioners as purely instrumental in their function; rather they will be seen as the logical extension of significant social relationships or of cosmological theories. A night-long harassment of New Guinea initiates, for example, may be viewed as an exercise of the elder generation's authority over the younger (an extension of social relationships); the self-torture of the American Indian vision-seeker as an extension of his cosmological theory, which maintains that one must appear pitiable in the eyes of the supernaturals before they will deign to offer their magical assistance. These social and cultural explanations are correct as far as

[283]

they go; but when anthropological interpretation pursues these themes alone, all religious actions come to be swallowed up in stylized expressive form and, as such, can play back upon the psyche only as evocative drama. While no anthropologist would go so far as to claim that when people eat "the flesh of the gods" in the form of hallucinogenic mushrooms, it is only the symbolic value of the mushroom that gets them high, such a statement would be an appropriate parody of the position I am criticizing.

Of course there has been recognition among cultural anthropologists that a number of types of religious activity serve to "heighten suggestibility" in the participants. But conceding a factor such as heightened suggestibility is not the same as explaining it, nor has this concession had much influence on the dominant portrait of religious action as spectacle and evocation as the fount of psychological transformation.

What I have tried to explain in this book is the psychological process categorized as "heightened suggestibility" and to show in detail its organic relationship both to the development of faith and to the resolution of the life dilemmas that religion characteristically addresses. This explanation if applied broadly does not deny the evocative power of religious symbolism but it cuts up the pie of "efficacy" in a way that reduces the role of evocation and places greater emphasis upon the interpretive function of the symbolism in handling the unusual experiential world called into being through practice. It peels back whatever expressive overlay may mask the infracultural effect of practice and allows us better to see "suggestibility" not simply as an increased passivity of the mind toward received truth, but as the active production of personal truths to which the received categories are fitted.

Nevertheless it is legitimate to ask how broadly we should apply this second view. Obviously, in psychotherapeutic and mystical traditions, practice is foregrounded and the material to which the received categories are applied moves far beyond the realm of daily experience. In the average communal ritual performance, the production of unusual states of mind through special practice may be only minimal, haphazard, or confined to a minority of the participants. Moreover, behavior associated with altered states of consciousness may indeed pass over into conventionalized expressions that are valued for their dramatic effect but indicate little about the performer's inner state. It is quite possible then that in some rituals psychological reorientation has more to do with the organization of symbolically evoked sentiments whereas in others the symbolization of practice-evoked sentiments plays the more prominent part. It cannot be assumed in advance which of these two processes will be of greater importance. James Fernandez, who investigated the private experience of Fang ritual participants, was surprised to learn that there was little agreement among them as to what the symbolism of their ritual meant and a lack of awareness on the part of some that it meant anything at all, even though ritual experts could give elaborate exegeses. The average participant looked only for the experience of "one-heartedness" with his fellows that the night-long ritual dance was supposed to, and in fact did, provide. The ritual happened to be part of a new reformative cult that still recruited through personal conversion (Fernandez 1965). To go to the opposite extreme, there have been historical periods during which Zen training, ordinarily the most rationalized of renunciatory regimes, has consisted merely of the mastering of standardized answers to the koans, devoid of interior revelation (Kapleau 1967:49, 51). In the end, for us to know in any particular case what is going on in the mind of the religious participant, we must give up extrapolations and ask.

References Cited

Advance. 1972–75. (Official Publication of the Advanced Organizations.) Issues 13–37. Los Angeles: Church of Scientology of California.

The Auditor 1971–75 (The Monthly Journal of Scientology). Los Angeles: Church of Scientology of California.

Bakan, David. 1958. *Sigmund Freud and the Jewish Mystical Tradition*. Princeton: D. Van Nostrand.

Barnes, Mary, and J. Berke. 1971. *Two Accounts of a Journey through Madness*. New York: Ballantine.

Berger, Peter. 1965. Towards a Sociological Understanding of Psychoanalysis. *Social Research* (Spring 1965):26–41.

Breuer, Joseph, and Sigmund Freud. 1964. *Studies in Hysteria*. Boston: Beacon.

Brown, J. A. C. 1963. *Techniques of Persuasion from Propaganda to Brainwashing*. United Kingdom: Penguin.

Burch, N. R., and T. H. Griener. 1960. A Bioelectric Scale of Human Alertness: Concurrent Recordings of the EEG and GSR. *Psychiatric Research Reports* 12:183–92.

Canary, R. H. 1977. Science Fiction as Fictive History. In *Many Futures, Many Worlds*, ed. T. D. Clareson. Kent, Ohio: Kent State University Press.

Castaneda, Carlos. 1968. *The Teachings of Don Juan: A Yaqui Way of Knowledge*. New York: Ballantine.

———. 1972. *Journey to Ixtlan*. New York: Simon & Schuster.

Conway, Florence, and James Siegelman. 1979. *Snapping: America's Epidemic of Sudden Personality Change*. New York: Delta.

Darrow, C. W. 1964. The Rationale for Treating the Change in Galvanic Skin Response as a Change in Conductance. *Psychophysiology* 1:31–37.

Deikman, Arthur. 1969. Deautomatization and the Mystic Experience. In *Altered States of Consciousness*, ed. Charles C. Tart. New York: John Wiley.

Devereux, George. 1956. Normal and Abnormal: The Key Problem of Psychiatric

References

Anthropology. In *Some Uses of Anthropology: Theoretical and Applied*, ed. J. B. Casagrande and T. Gladwin. Seattle: Anthropology Society of Washington.

Dohrmann, H. T. 1958. *California Cult: The Story of Mankind United*. Boston: Beacon.

Durkheim, Emile. 1961. *The Elementary Forms of the Religious Life*. New York: Collier.

Fenichel, Otto. 1945. *The Psychoanalytic Theory of Neurosis*. New York: W. W. Norton.

Fernandez, James. 1965. Symbolic Consensus in a Fang Reformative Cult. *American Anthropologist* 67:902–25.

Fingarette, Herbert. 1963. *The Self in Transformation*. New York: Harper.

Flavell, John. 1963. *The Developmental Psychology of Jean Piaget*. New York: D. Van Nostrand.

Forbes, T. W. 1964. Problems in the Measurement of Electrodermal Phenomena. *Psychophysiology* 1:26–30.

Foster, B. 1975. The Recapitulation of Development during Regression: A Case Report. In *Psychotherapy of Schizophrenia*, ed. J. G. Grunderson and L. R. Mosher. New York: Jason Aronson.

Foster, Sir John. 1971. *Enquiry into the Practice and Effects of Scientology*. London: Her Majesty's Stationary Office.

Freud, Sigmund. 1950. *Totem and Taboo*. Trans. James Strachey. New York: Norton.

1958. *A General Introduction to Psychoanalysis*. Trans. Joan Riviere. New York: Permabooks.

1959. *Observations on Transference Love*. In Standard Edition of the Complete Psychological Works 12:157–71. Trans. and ed. James Strachey. London: Hogarth Press.

1960. *Group Psychology and the Analysis of the Ego*. Trans. James Strachey. New York: Bantam.

1963. From the History of an Infantile Neurosis (1918). In *Three Case Histories*, ed. Philip Rieff. New York: Collier.

1964. *Introductory Lectures in Psychoanalysis* (1916–1917). In Standard Edition of the Complete Psychological Works 16. London: Hogarth Press.

Furst, Peter. 1972. *The Flesh of the Gods*. New York: Praeger.

Gardner, Martin. 1957. *Fads and Fallacies in the Name of Science*. New York: Dover.

Geertz, Clifford. 1972. Religion as a Cultural System. In *The Interpretation of Cultures*. New York: Basic.

Goffman, Erving. 1961. *Encounters*. Indianapolis: Bobbs-Merrill.

Hebb, D. O. 1955. Drives and the CNS (Central Nervous System). *Psychological Review* 62:243–54.

Hopkins, J. M. 1969. Scientology: Religion or Racket?. *Christianity Today* 6:110.

Hubbard, L. Ron. 1949. *Triton*. Los Angeles: Fantasy Publishing Co.

1950. *Dianetics: The Modern Science of Mental Health*. New York: Paperback Library.

1952. *Scientology 8–80*. East Grinstead, England: Publications World Wide.

1956. *The Fundamentals of Thought.* East Grinstead, England: Publications World Wide.

1958. Axiom Booklet. East Grinstead, England: Publications World Wide.

1961. *A History of Man.* East Grinstead, England: Publications World Wide.

1964. *Scientology Abridged Dictionary.* East Grinstead, England: Publications World Wide.

1965. *Scientology 8-8008.* London: Grant Publication Co.

1966. *Dianetics: The Evolution of a Science.* London: F. E. Bording, Ltd.

1967a. Advanced Procedures and Axioms. East Grinstead, England: Publications World Wide.

1967b. *The Book Introducing the E-Meter.* East Grinstead, England: Publications World Wide.

1967c. *E-Meter Essentials.* Phoenix: Hubbard College of Scientology.

1967d. *Slaves of Sleep.* New York: Lancer Books.

1968a. *Introduction to Scientology Ethics.* East Grinstead, England: Publications World Wide.

1968b. *Fear and the Ultimate Adventure.* Berkeley: Medallion.

1968c. *The Book of Case Remedies.* East Grinstead, England: Publications World Wide.

1968d. *The Phoenix Lectures.* East Grinstead, England: Publications World Wide.

1968e. *Have You Lived before This Life?* East Grinstead, England: Publications World Wide.

1970a. *Death's Deputy.* Hollywood: Leisure Books.

1970b. *Final Blackout.* Hollywood: Leisure Books.

1970c. *Ole Doc Methuselah.* Austin, Tex.: Theta Press.

1975a. *Dianetics and Scientology Technical Dictionary.* Los Angeles: Church of Scientology of California (Kingsport Press).

1975b. *Dianetics Today.* Los Angeles: Church of Scientology of California (Kingsport Press).

Hubbard, L. Ron, and Mary Sue Hubbard. 1968. *The Book of E-Meter Drills.* East Grinstead, England: Publications World Wide.

James, William. 1967. *The Varieties of Religious Experience.* New York: Collier.

Jung, Carl. 1973. *The Portable Jung,* ed. Joseph Campbell. New York: Viking.

Kapleau, Philip. 1967. *The Three Pillars of Zen.* Boston: Beacon.

Kaufman, Robert. 1972. *Inside Scientology.* London: Olympia.

Koestler, Arthur. 1964. *The Act of Creation.* New York: Dell.

Kris, Ernst. 1964. *Psychoanalytic Explorations in Art.* New York: Schocken.

Lacan, Jacques. 1968. *The Language of the Self.* Trans. with notes by Anthony Wilden. Baltimore: The Johns Hopkins University Press.

Laing, R. D. 1972. Metanoia: Some Experiences at Kingsley Hall, London. In *Going Crazy: The Radical Therapy of R. D. Laing and Others.* New York: Bantam.

Langness, L. L. 1965. Hysterical Psychosis in the New Guinea Highlands: A Bena Bena Example. *Psychiatry* 28:259–77.

Laplanche, J., and J.-B. Pontalis. 1973. *The Language of Psychoanalysis.* Trans. Donald Nicholson-Smith. New York: W. W. Norton.

[289]

References

Lévi-Strauss, Claude. 1963. The Effectiveness of Symbols. In *Structural Anthropology*. Trans. Claire Jacobson and Grundfest Schoepf. New York: Basic.

Lewis, I. M. 1971. *Ecstatic Religions*. Harmondsworth, England: Penguin.

Lifton, Robert J. 1961. *Thought Reform and the Psychology of Totalism*. New York: Norton.

Malko, George. 1970. *Scientology: The Now Religion*. New York: Delacorte.

Marks, John. 1979. *Search for the Manchurian Candidate: The CIA and Mind Control*. New York: New York Times Books.

Masters, R. E. L., and J. Houston. 1966. *The Varieties of Psychedelic Experience*. New York: Delta.

Monroe, R. 1971. *Journeys out of the Body*. New York: Doubleday.

Moskowitz, Sam. 1966. *Seekers of Tomorrow: Masters of Science Fiction*. New York: World.

Munn, Nancy, 1970. The Transformation of Subjects into Objects in Walbiri and Pitjantjatjara Myth. In *Australian Aboriginal Religion*, ed. R. M. Berndt. Nedlands, Aus.: University of Western Australia Press.

1973. *Walbiri Iconography*. Ithaca: Cornell University Press.

Naranjo, Claudio, and Robert Ornstein. 1973. *On the Psychology of Meditation*. New York: Viking.

Oesterreich, T. K. 1966. *Possession: Demoniacal and Other*. New York: University Books.

Ortner, Sherry B. 1978. *Sherpas through Their Rituals*. New York: Cambridge University Press.

Piaget, Jean. 1962. *Play, Dreams and Imitation in Childhood*. Trans. F. M. Hodgson. New York: W. W. Norton.

1963. *The Origins of Intelligence in Children*. Trans. Margaret Cook. New York: W. W. Norton.

1965. *The Moral Judgment of the Child*. Trans. Marjorie Cabain. New York: Free Press.

Prince, R., and C. Savage. 1966. Mystical States and the Concept of Regression. *Psychedelic Review* 8:59–75.

Rappaport, Roy. 1971. Ritual, Sanctity, and Cybernetics. *American Anthropologist* 73:59–75.

Ricoeur, Paul. 1972. *Freud and Philosophy*. New Haven: Yale University Press.

Sargant, William. 1957. *Battle for the Mind*. Baltimore: Penguin.

Scholem, Gerschom. 1965. *On the Kabbalah and Its Symbolism*. New York: Schocken.

Scientology. 1968. (The Field Staff Member Magazine) (1). Los Angeles: Church of Scientology of California.

The Scientology Classification, Gradation and Awareness Chart. Los Angeles: Church of Scientology of California.

Shor, Ronald. 1969. Hypnosis and the Concept of Reality-Orientation. In *Altered States of Consciousness*, ed. Charles C. Tart. New York: John Wiley.

Szasz, Thomas. 1971. *The Manufacture of Madness*. New York: Delta.

Timpanaro, Sebastiano. 1976. *The Freudian Slip: Psychoanalysis and Textual Criticism*. New York: Schocken.

[290]

Turner, Victor. 1969. *The Ritual Process*. Chicago: Aldine.

Underhill, Evelyn. 1967. *Mysticism*. New York: Meridian.

Van Vogt, A. E. 1964. The Reflections of A. E. Van Vogt. Compiled under the Auspices of the U.C.L.A. Oral History Project. Unpublished MS.

Wallace, A. F. C. 1966. *Religion: An Anthropological Approach*. New York: Random House.

Wallis, Roy. 1976. *The Road to Total Freedom: A Sociological Analysis of Scientology*. New York: Columbia University Press.

Watts, Alan. 1961. *Psychotherapy East and West*. New York: Ballantine.

Weber, Max. 1958. The Social Psychology of the World Religions. In *From Max Weber*, ed. H. H. Gerth and C. Wright Mills. New York: Galaxy.

Whitehead, Harriet. 1974. Reasonably Fantastic: Some Perspectives on Scientology, Science Fiction and Occultism. In *Religious Movements in Contemporary America*, ed. I. Zaretsky and M. Leone. Princeton: Princeton University Press.

Wilson, Brian. 1970. *Religious Sects*. New York: World University Press.

Winter, Joseph A. 1951. *A Doctor Looks at Dianetics*. New York: Julian Press.

Wuthnow, Robert. 1976. The New Religions in Social Context. In *The New Religious Consciousness*, ed. C. Y. Glock and R. N. Bellah. Berkeley: University of California Press.

Wymer, T. L. 1977. Perception and Value in Science Fiction. In *Many Futures, Many Worlds*, ed. T. D. Clareson. Kent, Ohio: Kent State University Press.

Index

Abreaction therapy, 45, 51, 83
Advanced Orgs (AOs), 35–36, 132
Altered states of consciousness, 22, 105–114; cultural anthropology and, 102–105; dreams and, 102–103; drug-induced, 25; the ego and, 110–111; mental structure and, 107–108; mystic disciplines and, 106, 113; psychological explanations of, 104; revelation and, 101–102; structural dedifferentiation and, 107–109; trances and, 102
Analytical Mind, subject of, 59
Analytical Psychology. *See* Jung, Carl
Anaten, defintion of, 201
Anti-social personalities, 218–223
ARC (affinity/reality/communication), 33, 181
ARC breaks, 155–156, 181
Archetypes of the Collective Unconscious, Jung and, 80, 81–82
Auditing, Dianetic, 21, 45, 62–63, 133, 162, 171; incident chain in, 243
Auditing, Scientology, 21, 127–135, 171–172; Clear and, 128, 131; "cognitions" in, 153, 237, 258–260; delays in, 232–233; E-Meter and,128; end phenomena of, 153, 159, 165, 258; format of, 127–128; imaginative exercises and, 163–166; incident chain in, 90–92, 250–254, 255; incident running and, 161–163; intensives and, 132; levels of, 130–132; listing actions and, 159–161; paired question processes and, 163; processes in, 158–167; purpose of, 237; Recall Release process and, 133; review, 272, 277; solo, 128, 131, 235; successful, 242. *See also* E-Meter

Auditor: review, 132, role of the Dianetic, 21, 63; role of the Scientology, 127
Auditors, use of TRs for training of, 127, 128, 129, 135–136; bull-baiting, 136–137; good, 140–141; TR–0 (confront), 136, 140; TR–1, 137–138, TR–2, 138; TR–3, 138; TR–4, 139
Automaticity, 138, 214 215
"Axioms of Scientology, The," 170; Axiom 1, 173; Axiom 3, 186; Axiom 10, 174, 178; Axiom 11, 173; Axioms 12, 173–174, Axiom 23, 181; Axioms 26 and 27, 174; Axiom 39, 174, 184; Axiom 42, 174; Axiom 51, 178

Bank, the: awareness of, in others, 217–218; Being and, 199–201, 236–246; elimination of, 131; levels of, 230; meaning of, 59, 170; mental phenomena and, 175–176; objectifying, 227–228; psychotics and, 225–226; restimulation and, 226–227; spontaneous subjective phenomena and, 215; suppressiveness and, 218–225; unpleasant mental states and, 229–230. *See also* Reactive Mind.
Battle for the Mind, 23
Being: Bank and, 199–201, 236–246; unpleasant mental states and, 229–230. *See also* Thetans
Beingness, 168, 169, 201–214; communicating and, 203–204; exteriorization and, 204–214; increased perception of 201–203; two-hour confront and, 201
Birth traumas, 52, 81
Book Introducing the E-Meter, The, 154
Book of Case Remedies, 277
Brainwashing, 23–24, 57

[293]

Library of Congress Cataloging-in-Publication Data

Whitehead, Harriet.
 Renunciation and reformulation.

 (Anthropology of contemporary issues)
 Bibliography: p.
 Includes index.
 1. Scientology. 2. Conversion. I. Title. II. Series.
BP605.S2W47 1987   299′.936   86-16211
ISBN 0-8014-1849-6 (alk. paper)